P9-CNE-424

HURON COUNTY LIBRARY

3 6492 00430793 7

Date Due

BRUJan94		APR 1 8 2002
MAR 04 '94	AUG 2 ? 2???	
DEC 08 '94		

Printed in U.S.A.

3633

940
.5421
Stu

STURSBERG, P.

THE SOUND OF WAR.

He

THE SOUND OF WAR

Also by Peter Stursberg

Roland Michener, the Last Viceroy

The Golden Hope

Gordon Shrum

EXTRA! When the Papers Had the Only News

Lester Pearson and the American Dilemma

Lester Pearson and the Dream of Unity

Diefenbaker, Leadership Gained, 1956–62

Diefenbaker, Leadership Lost, 1962–67

Mister Broadcasting

Those Were the Days

Agreement in Principle

Journey into Victory

PETER STURSBERG

The Sound of War

Memoirs of a
CBC Correspondent

UNIVERSITY OF TORONTO PRESS
Toronto Buffalo London

3633

JAN 2 0 1994

© University of Toronto Press Incorporated 1993
Toronto Buffalo London
Printed in Canada

ISBN 0-8020-2992-2

Printed on acid-free paper

Canadian Cataloguing in Publication Data

Stursberg, Peter, 1915–
    The sound of war

    Includes bibliographical references and index.
    ISBN 0-8020-2992-2

    1. World War, 1939–1945 – Campaigns – Western.
    2. Canada. Canadian Army – History – World War,
    1939–1945. 3. World War, 1939–1945 – Press
    coverage – Canada. I. Title.

    D743.S88 1993   940.54'21   C93-093689-2

The illustrations in this book are courtesy of the author with the following
exceptions: CBC: Benoit Lafleur; Art Holmes and George Drew; Canadian
War Museum: General McNaughton; *The Hitler Line* (12796); NAC: Mc-
Naughton and Allied leaders (C 64027); Sicilian battlefield (PA 116846);
interview with Jack Charles (G 66627); Stursberg, Holmes, and Bridgeman
(C 137556); liberation at last (PA 133323); Dutch girls (PA 130067); Gedechneskirche (PA 188923).

For the fallen,
who would never tell their story

Contents

Preface

R adio had a tremendous and lasting impact in the Second
World War, and half a century later I can still remember
five news broadcasts, the exact time and place that I heard them,
and the effect they had. The first was the doleful declaration of
war by Prime Minister Neville Chamberlain, which sounded like
a sentence of death, which in fact it proved to be for a couple of
those at the post-dance party in Victoria, BC. The second was the
Japanese attack on Pearl Harbor and the frenetic reaction in the
United States that Sunday morning as we sat listening in my
Vancouver apartment. The third was the announcement of the
Allied invasion of Sicily, and, *mirabile dictu*, we heard it in the
process of landing on Pachino Peninsula. The fourth was the news
of D-Day, the Normandy invasion, that came crackling out of a U.S.
army half-track, parked on a sunny Roman street. And the last
was the victory proclamation on VE Day, which was a bit of an
anti-climax for those of us covering the wild celebrations that had
been going on for days in liberated Holland.

The Second World War was the first war to be covered by the
electronic news medium of broadcasting; it was a new kind of
journalism, much more personal and involving, taking one by
means of invisible air waves over vast distances to the very scene
of the action, the battleground itself. I have started each chapter

with a radio bulletin, which does not so much summarize its contents as put them in reference to the progress of the war. Sometimes, when developments warranted it, I have included a bulletin within the text. Those that I remember, the five above, are given with the exact time when they were heard, while the others have merely the date and place.

For most of the surviving veterans, especially for those who went overseas, the Second World War was their finest time. They remember it as a period of great excitement and adventure, of escape from domestic ties, of self-indulgence and camaraderie. It is a flame burning brightly in the twilight of their lives, and it was when they were young. They have forgotten, or closed their minds, to all the death and destruction, the long stretches of mind-numbing boredom and the sudden moments of morale-destroying terror. I realize how selective memory can be, and while it may have had some influence in the composing of these memoirs, I did not have to rely on recollection.

There was a wealth of reference material: books, among them the official war histories, G.W.L. Nicholson's *The Canadian in Italy*, C.P. Stacey's *The Victory Campaign*, and my war correspondent's book, *Journey into Victory*, as well as A.E. Powley's work on our CBC Overseas Unit, *Broadcast from the Front* (see bibliography). I wrote the first articles on the Canadians in action for *Maclean's* magazine, and there were the hundreds of CBC war reports, including my own, which are in the National Archives in Ottawa and available for research (see list of war recordings). Most revealing were my own papers, however, also lodged in the National Archives, the letters that I wrote home, the notes and bits of a diary that I had forgotten about, the memos and telegrams, much of which contained information that I did not or could not put into my broadcasts because of censorship. Also, there were the surviving war correspondents and PR officers, as well as other old friends and colleagues; I got in touch with many of them.

I was fortunate to have had several telephone conversations with Art Holmes before his sudden death in 1991. I had a long chat with Yvon Beaulne at his home outside Gatineau Park in

Hull, Quebec. I interviewed Marjorie Morton about her husband, Paul Morton, and spoke to C.W. 'Bill' Gilchrist, Doug How, and the *Toronto Star's* David MacDonald about this tragic case and received documentation from them. Others from the war whom I talked to include Royd Beamish, Ken Bell, Bill Boss, Gerald Clark, Jock Carroll, Jack Donoghue, Eric Downton, Ron Gadsby, Mark Holmes, Gordon Hutton, Charles Lynch, Alec McDonald, Doug McFarlane, Lloyd Moore, Jack Peach, Wallace Reyburn, Gordon Root, Bill Stewart, Maurice Western, W.A. 'Bill' Wilson, and, from the early days of the CBC National News Service, Roger Baulu, David 'Stan' Catton, Lawrence Duffy, Les Jackson, Pat Keatley, and Hugh Palmer.

The passage of time has brought the war into focus. As reporters, we tended to look at it through rose-coloured glasses, owing, in part, to the prevalent patriotic fervour, and, in part, to censorship, which allowed no criticism of the war effort. This was total war, and there was total censorship. There was no way of evading it – one could leave the fighting for the rear, for London, or even for Canada, and the same censorship would apply. If one somehow evaded it, or broke an embargo, the penalties were severe: dis-accreditation, disgrace, and even imprisonment.

It took years of research and analysis, untrammelled by war-time restrictions, to come up with the answers to questions that puzzled us when we were covering the daily action at the front, such as: Why did the Germans fight the way they did? Why didn't they give up, as the Italians did, when all was so obviously lost? Who was responsible for breaking up the Canadian army? Were the Canadian generals so bad and the British generals so good? How did the Anzio Beachhead almost become a Gallipoli? Who gave the order to destroy that great monument of Christianity, the Benedictine monastery of Monte Cassino? Was Ottawa's conscription crisis really necessary? What was wrong with the Allied leadership? The European war should have been over in 1944; why did it go on so much longer?

In writing this book, I was greatly aided by Sylvie Robitaille and Peter Robertson of the National Archives in Ottawa, who had copies made of selected CBC war reports, including my own, and found some of the photographs that I wanted as illustrations – all of which are from the Archives, the Canadian War Museum, or my own collection. I had the cooperation and assistance of Simon Fraser University in Burnaby, BC, particularly of the staff of its archives, where most of my recorded interviews are lodged. I would like to thank Dan Glenney and Fred Gaffen of the Canadian War Museum for their advice, and also George Powell, who revived the old Canadian War Correspondents' Association and put me in touch with many former colleagues and friends. I appreciated the way that the West Vancouver Public Library's reference department answered all my queries so expeditiously.

These memoirs, in their present form, are due to the keen interest that Gerald Hallowell, the editor at the University of Toronto Press, had in them from the beginning and his persistence in bringing them to publication. It was a pleasure to work with Catherine Frost on the editing of the book. Once again, I wish to express my gratitude to Betty Jane Corson, who was my counsellor, agent, and friend, and to my wife, Jessamy, a stickler for syntax, who showed great patience and support.

Peter Stursberg
West Vancouver, BC
November 1992

THE SOUND OF WAR

Prologue

In the summer of 1938 I was in Czechoslovakia and attended the tenth Slet, the Congress of Sokols (gymnasts): 250,000 people in the mighty Masaryk Stadium watched 10,000 young men and women do calisthenics to music on a field five times the size of a football field. It was a tremendous spectacle that rivalled the great rallies and parades of the Communists and Fascists. Along the steep road up Strahov Plateau to the stadium, the anti-aircraft guns were stripped of their coverings, their long barrels searching the sky, their crews on the alert. The crowds cheered them. 'We are ready,' said my guide, Mr Kaufmann; he apologized for his German name. The British newspapers had been running stories and pictures of the Czech defences along the Sudeten border; there were concrete fortifications every few hundred yards and steel-helmeted troops standing guard.

Then, why didn't the Czechs fight? They had the best-equipped army in Europe and one of its greatest armament industries in the Skoda works. When I visited Pilsen, I saw the outside of this huge war machine, a high wall surrounding acres of noisy buildings belching smoke. Even if they were betrayed by their friends, the British and the French, the Czechs could have fought, and who knows what would have happened if they had? But they didn't, and Hitler got Skoda without firing a shot.

That did not mean that I was not as relieved as anyone else at Munich. I remember that London seemed greyer than usual that day, and then suddenly the newsboys began crying out, 'Peace in our time,' and the sun broke through clouds and cast a pale light on the city, and the dark, sombre crowds became joyful and excited. There was laughter again on the streets of London.

On the days before, the unemployed had been put to work digging trenches in the parks. It was pathetic, this scrabbling around, and at night too, under floodlights – the grass would be ruined. They were piling sandbags by the ground-floor windows in Whitehall and unlimbering anti- aircraft guns around Westminster Abbey and the Houses of Parliament. Then, the government began shovelling out gas masks to anyone and everyone, including even visitors like myself, and that really scared the bejesus out of the British.

I had just been accepted as an Empire Press Union exchange reporter on the *Daily Herald*, the Labour party's newspaper. I exchanged with Basil Dean, a tall, bespectacled youth, a junior reporter who was acting as a researcher and leg man for Hannen Swaffer, the featured columnist on the newspaper. Through him I met Swaffer, a remarkable popular journalist, dubbed the 'Pope of Fleet Street'; he looked like an Edwardian actor, with his long white hair, high collar, and flowing cravat; there was always a cigarette dangling from his tobacco-stained lips, even when he talked. He was a left-wing socialist and also, since the death of Sir Oliver Lodge, the leading spiritualist in Britain.

Just before Basil left, Swaff did us the signal honour of inviting us to lunch at the Savoy Hotel. He had a special table on one side of the dining-room, where he held court. It was at the height of the Munich crisis; some ministries had been moved out of London, the Home Office to Wormwood Scrubs prison, 'the right p-p-place for it,' Swaff declared, to the amusement of the diners. A businessman came over and said that the odds were on war; his bookmaker was giving 'two to one for.' Some prominent politicians were at the Savoy. 'What are you going to do if there is a war, Swaff?' one of them asked. 'Just what I d-d-did in the l-l-last war,' the great journalist said. 'N-n-nothing.'

Basil Dean went to the Hamilton *Spectator*; he stayed in Canada and, when he died in 1968, was publisher of the *Edmonton Journal*. I was on the *Daily Herald* for nine months, returning home in the summer of 1939. That was not the way the Empire (now Commonwealth) Press Union's exchange program was supposed to work, but it was difficult to persuade newspapers on either side of the Atlantic to provide three-month training courses. I broke the rules by coming over before an exchange had been arranged; I went on a tour of Europe, but my presence and the fact that I kept pounding on the EPU's door helped to produce results.

It was a great thrill to be working for the *Daily Herald*, which had a circulation of 2 million a day and was published in two centres, London and Manchester, at the same time. This was in sharp contrast to the *Victoria Daily Times*, which boasted – and we did – 10,000 copies. Yet the rickety old *Times* had a special place in my heart; it was the first paper I worked for, and it rescued me from the awful nothingness of the Great Depression, the depression that had cut short my time at McGill University. In those days, I was the only reporter on the *Times* who had even been to university.

One night, just after I joined the *Daily Herald*, I climbed the side of a ship to tell the British Legion men aboard that their trip was off. There was to be no plebiscite in Czechoslovakia. The recruitment of these veterans was one of the dirtiest deceptions of the whole Munich mess. It was part of the 'Runciman mission to Czechoslovakia,' which was an elaborate cover to prepare British public opinion for the sell-out of the Sudetenland to Hitler. Lord Runciman never had believed in a plebiscite, and said so, but Prime Minister Chamberlain had to have something to cover up the dismemberment and ultimate destruction of a democracy.

So the old soldiers were taken on to police a plebiscite that would never be held, and their 'embarkation' in two liners was given maximum publicity. The deception could not be maintained for long, and finally the government had to announce there would be no vote. When I climbed aboard and went from cabin to cabin spreading the news, the veterans grumbled and cursed, but they must have smelled a rat, since their ships had been anchored off

Southend pier for days. I wrote my story and telephoned it from the lighthouse at the end of the pier, thereby earning my first byline on the *Daily Herald*.

The Spanish civil war was sputtering to a close. It had been a great testing ground for the Fascists and to a lesser extent for the Communists. The 'ante-room to Armageddon,' someone called it. The British and French had never looked more pathetic and were only too anxious to put the whole sorry issue behind them; on 28 February 1939, some weeks before Madrid fell, they recognized the Franco government. On a warm spring day, I was sent to Newhaven to meet the Spanish Loyalist refugees who, as a result of Labour party pressure, had been given temporary asylum in Great Britain. They were mostly senior officers, including General Leopoldo Menendez, who headed the bulk of the Spanish Republican forces at the end of the war. They were dressed in rather shabby civilian clothes and looked like any other foreign visitors who had just stepped ashore, not the heroic defenders of democracy.

One of General Menendez's corps commanders, Colonel Gustavo Duran, a fair-haired Catalan, spoke English. As the boat-train sped through the green and pleasant English countryside, Colonel Duran talked about the chaos of the last few days. While making his way to the coast, he had been caught by the Fascists but escaped. He had seen Valencia in Franco's hands, however, and he said there were Moors everywhere, on guard at every building and taking the place of police in the streets. It was ironic that the Moors should have reconquered Spain for the Fascists. The Spanish Loyalist refugees, from General Menendez down, had no idea what they would do. Most were professional soldiers, but Colonel Duran had been a musical composer in Madrid before the civil war. He wondered if there was any chance of his going to Canada.

I found the editors of the *Daily Herald* to be singularly uninterested in Canada. 'We n-n-never have anything about Canada in this paper because n-n-nothing ever happens there,' the news editor, L.M. McBride, said; he had the same elitist stammer as Hannen Swaffer. When it was announced that King George and Queen Elizabeth were going to Canada, however – it was the first visit of a reigning monarch to the dominion and was, in a way, a royal recruiting mission – I was asked to do an editorial-page article on Canada. No, no, Tom Darlow, the features editor, said, not about the places they would visit; the movies would do that much better than I could. 'Do me a piece,' he ordered, 'about half a dozen prominent Canadians the King and Queen will meet.'

The trouble was that I did not know who these worthies were or anything about them. My total experience in journalism was a few years in Victoria, which was really off the Canadian map. Nevertheless, I was not going to pass up the opportunity to write an article on the editorial page of the *Daily Herald*, even if the subject was beyond me. But where could I get the information? I racked my brains and then recalled that there was a famous Canadian journalist in London, J.B. 'Hamish' McGeachy, the correspondent of the *Winnipeg Free Press*.

After a lot of telephoning around, I got hold of him, and we met in The Falstaff, a pub on Fleet Street. When I apologized for picking his brains in this blatant manner, Hamish, who looked like a pirate, a Captain Hook with a Scots accent somewhat muffled by cigarettes and whisky, said that he was delighted to be of service and that he hadn't much to do in London. It was all too easy for him, and he rattled off the names of six leading Canadians with a few juicy details about each, while I scribbled notes. In fact, he almost dictated my editorial-page piece.

It is interesting to recall who the six were. Prime Minister Mackenzie King headed the list; the others were Premier Maurice Duplessis of Quebec; Premier Mitch Hepburn of Ontario; Bible Bill Aberhart, the prophet of Social Credit and premier of Alberta; Dr Allan Roy Dafoe, the country doctor who delievered the Dionne quintuplets; and Dr Lyle Telford, the socialist mayor of Vancouver and the only one I knew anything about. That editorial-page piece, although hardly my work, was the greatest triumph of my young life. It was well received, and I did two more articles, entitled 'The Indians' and 'The Great North,' which conformed with the popular British view of Canada as a land of wide-open spaces, Mounties, and moose.

In March 1939 Hitler took over the whole of Czechoslovakia, without any apparent opposition. Even the most dedicated pacifists now gave up hope; war seemed inevitable. Chamberlain had been humiliated. There was a desperate scurrying around to find some way to stop the Nazis, and in April the British and French guaranteed Polish independence. 'It'll be the supreme b-b-bloody irony,' Hannen Swaffer said, 'to go to war over Poland, an out-and-out d-d-dictatorship, when we wouldn't fight for a democracy like Czechoslovakia, and in f-f-fact were instrumental in destroying it. And m-m-mark my word, there's g-g-going to be no getting out of this treaty.'

On the summer day that I left the *Daily Herald* to return home, there was a gas warfare drill in front of the boat-train platform at Waterloo Station in London. Several men in yellow overalls with goggle-eyed black gas masks used an apparatus like a small tank car to spray chemicals on an area that was supposed to have been contaminated by mustard gas. The demonstration served to frighten the American tourists, who chattered about the likelihood of war and how glad they were to be going back to God's country.

1

News Comes to the CBC

Victoria, BC, Sunday, 3 September 1939, 2 a.m.:
Britain declares war on Germany.

P rime Minister Chamberlain's pronouncement was no clarion
call to arms but the mournful epitaph of a defeated man, and
it had a sobering effect on the late-night revellers in Victoria,
British Columbia. Some of us had gone to a friend's house after the
Saturday night dance at the Empress Hotel to continue partying
and to wait up for the broadcast that the newspapers had foretold
in headlines:

ALLIES DECLARATION OF WAR IMMINENT
BRITAIN, FRANCE ISSUE FINAL ULTIMATUM

We were tuned in to a dance band at some hotel when the
networks switched to London; vast distances vanished and we were
at Number 10 Downing Street, inside the cabinet room, listening
to the prime minister say what a bitter blow this was, that all his
efforts at peace had failed. His tone was lugubrious, but his voice
was clear and there was no static, a tribute to the modern magic

of radio transmission that was to change the way the Second World War was reported.

That afternoon, several of the fellows, myself among them, who had heard Chamberlain's chilling utterance went for a walk in Beacon Hill Park. It was a bright and beautiful day in Victoria, and by all accounts the sun was shining in London and throughout the British Isles when the air raid sirens sounded, as if taking their cue from the BBC broadcast of the declaration of war. But then wars often begin in good weather. August 1914 was the finest August in years, and those warm golden days were remembered as a dream of times long gone, especially by the soldiers stuck in the cold slime of the winter trenches. However, the reverse is not always true. The First World War ended on a cold November morning, at the eleventh hour of the eleventh day of the eleventh month, although the Second World War came to a halt in Europe on 8 May 1945, a fair enough spring day, as I recall. VJ Day on 15 August was a hot summer day but an anticlimax for most of us.

My friends and I walked in the park by the sea, and we looked out across the Straits of Juan de Fuca at the snow-capped Olympic Mountains. The scenery was just as picture perfect as ever. The sky had not fallen after that ominous announcement. Yet we knew that an era had ended, that everything would change, perhaps not immediately but inevitably. There might not be many more Saturday night dances at the Empress Hotel as we had known them, with everyone in evening dress, the bottles of booze within easy reach under the tables, and the whole fling costing little more than five bucks. A dreadful prospect. It was an end all right, but also a beginning. I had just returned from London where I had been an Empire Press Union exchange reporter on the *Daily Herald* and was leaving the next day for Vancouver and a job on the *Province*.

Although the war was on everyone's mind, no one talked much about it, if I remember rightly. No one wondered aloud whether London was being bombed, or spoke of the impregnable defences of the Maginot Line, or asked how in the world the British and the French expected to save Poland from the Nazi Blitzkrieg. Instead, the comments were personal. What were we going to do in the war? Nothing. That was the reply, to put it in one word. Or to put it another way: Hell, no, we won't go! There was a fierce and angry unanimity. We were not joining up, we were not going to fight for King and Country. We were not going to be suckers, we would not be taken in like the poor old sweats of the First World War whom we had known, the veterans grumbling over their beers in the Canadian Legion halls.

The attitude of young people I knew at the beginning of the Second World War was very different from that of youth of a quarter of a century before. Then patriotism ran wild; now there was abounding cynicism. Then bands played and flags flew and crowds cheered, but in making my way to Beacon Hill Park, I saw nothing to enliven the dull Sunday emptiness of the streets of Victoria.

We were, I realized, a privileged group: it was said in the thirties that there were only two classes, the employed and the unemployed. We were the employed, and although in retrospect our pay seemed ridiculously low, we were well off. The unemployed were at the bottom, and the lowest of all were those in the relief camps. When I was a cub reporter on the *Victoria Daily Times* I visited one of these camps, an assembly of tar-paper shacks on the edge of the forest; it was at Jordan River on the west coast of Vancouver Island, which was then far away from any habitation; and the whole purpose of the relief camps – they were really concentration camps – was to get the single unemployed off the streets and as far away from the cities as possible. At Jordan River the unemployed were supposed to be working on the gravel road, and they received the prison pay of 20 cents a day.

The attitude of the unemployed to the war was different in the sense that they wanted to join up, not for any patriotic reasons but because it was a job. For some, it was the first and last job they ever had. There was a dilemma for the more radical unemployed, since the Communists were denouncing the war as an 'imperialist war' because of the Hitler-Stalin Non-Aggression Pact. In fact, Communists and Communist sympathizers were turned down at the recruiting stations, and veterans of the Mackenzie Papineau Battalion in the Spanish civil war found their services were not wanted until 1941, when the Germans attacked the Soviet Union and the Russians came on side.

It was probably apocryphal, but we newspapermen delighted in a story that made the rounds at the beginning of the war. A pressman on his coffee break was accosted by a dowager lady recruiter wielding a white feather. 'Young man,' this formidable Daughter of the British Empire cried out, 'why aren't you in the army defending democracy!' The pressman, who was shocked by this assault, nevertheless had a way of striking back. When the great Hoe presses were running at full speed in the underground cavern where he worked, the noise was such that the only means of communication was by sign language. So the pressman pointed to his head, rolled his eyes, waved his arms, and made motions with his hands; he put on such a performance that this patriotic virago retreated, muttering, 'I'm so sorry, I'm so sorry, I didn't know.' As soon as he was a block down the street, the pressman cupped his hands and shouted, 'Now, let that be a lesson to you: don't speak before you're spoken to.'

This pacifism, this avoidance of the war, or whatever you call it did not last long with me. I was beginning to feel that I was missing out on the greatest adventure of all time. That did not mean that I had reversed roles and was now wrapping myself in the flag, which then was the Union Jack or the good old Canadian ensign, and was going to join up. Nothing as stupid as that. However, I did want to go overseas and take part; I wanted to be a war correspondent. And the way things were going, it looked as though I might miss out.

Vancouver, 17 June 1940:
Marshal Pétain sues for peace. The Battle of France has been lost.

The Nazi Blitzkrieg was sweeping everything before it. All this cock-and-bull about elastic defences and and falling back on prepared positions covered a pell-mell retreat and a catastrophic defeat. Hitler had conquered France in an incredibly short time, and Jimmy Coleman, the sports columnist, and other wiseacres on the news desk of the *Province* were betting that England would fall and that it would be all over in three or four weeks, by mid-July 1940 at the latest. What would happen to Canada? Oh, the United States would look after us.

I went to see the editor, 'Biff' McTavish, a large, round man. Biff said very little and had a disconcerting habit of staring out the window at the cenotaph down below in Victory Square instead of looking at the person who was talking to him. I could not tell whether he was shy, which was hard to believe, or whether this was a deliberate act on his part to put off any confrontation and thereby make no commitment and offend no one. As to my becoming a war correspondent, he offered no encouragement, although I got the impression that this was not in his jurisdiction. So I called on the publisher.

M.E. Nichols was very different: craggy, white haired, he was the boss and looked the part. As publisher of the *Province*, he was a most important executive of the Southam chain, since the *Province* was its biggest paper and its biggest money-maker. The *Province*'s circulation then was more than 100,000 and the largest west of Toronto, and we reporters walked tall because of this preeminence. It was the establishment paper, and the *Vancouver Sun* was a distant second, not in the same class. Mr Nichols – and that was the way we addressed him, there was no 'Biff' about *him* – Mr Nichols came straight to the point. They had a war correspondent, Alan Bill, who was from the *Calgary Herald*, and Mr Nichols let on that it suited the Southams to give their Calgary paper a break at this time. There wasn't any likelihood of Alan Bill's retiring, and the publisher wondered whether he was worth all the money it was costing to keep him in London. But in any case, he said, I wasn't senior enough to have any hope of succeeding him.

So I began to look around. In the fall of 1940 I heard that the Canadian Broadcasting Corporation was about to set up a national news service and was recruiting staff; I applied and in due course was taken on as a news editor at CBR, the Vancouver station of the CBC. It was a big move to quit the long-established field of print journalism for the largely untested realm, at least in Canada, of radio news, made bigger because of the way we newspapermen tended to look down on broadcasting. However, my qualms were overcome by a monetary incentive, or the cash nexus, as my Marxist friends would say. The starting salary at the CBC was to be $45 a week, which was considerably more than the $32.50 I was making on the *Province*.

A few years earlier – I believe it was 1937 – there had been astonishment in the newsroom of the *Victoria Daily Times* when Bill Herbert, a zealous and abrasive young reporter on the morning paper, the *Colonist*, asserted that he had joined the CBC as an announcer. Good God! He must be crazy! Broadcasting seemed such an ephemeral business, depending on the air waves, compared with the solid down-to-earth reality of the daily newspaper with its great Hoe presses and those remarkable machines that made lines of type out of molten metal. Bill said that he would be doing the 'news bulletins.' But the only radio news that we knew of was regularly and systematically pirated from the papers. It was a completely unethical procedure, a case of clip and read, with no credit or source being given.

Just before, I had been shown around the local Victoria radio station – the owner or operator was after publicity. The station was above a shoe store; there was a small, shabby office and a combined studio and control room full of a clutter of electronic equipment and stacks of records; behind the microphone hung a blanket, and that was the announce booth, I was told. I was not impressed. But the owner or operator was full of enthusiasm and confidence; he was proud of his new equipment, especially the latest-model turntable, and was certain that the future belonged to radio.

Of course, the CBC was different: it was not a single station but a coast-to-coast network like the NBC or CBS; it was a government agency modelled on the British Broadcasting Corporation, however, and it carried the BBC news. (In fact, some people thought it was part of the BBC.) The clipped English accent of the BBC news reader was not appreciated by the younger generation of Victorians, at least those whom I knew, despite the fact that some of them had distinct English accents of their own.

Yet the CBC was little different from the small local stations as far as news was concerned. It might have been more ethical in that it labelled the source as Canadian Press (CP), the cooperative agency of the Canadian daily newspapers; CP delivered, usually by bicycle, three or four news summaries a day, especially written so they could be read, to the corporation's stations in Toronto and other key regional centres such as Vancouver. Thus, in the end, the CBC was getting its news from the papers, as the local stations did, and CP made certain that radio never scooped its proprietors, the newspapers. In fact, news could be delayed for as much as twenty-four hours, since most major newspapers at that time came out in the afternoon.

The arrangement whereby CP produced the CBC newscasts was a comfortable one both for the corporation and for the agency's principal, the CDNA, the Canadian Daily Newspaper Association. It meant that the latter maintained control of the news, and the newspaper publishers considered a monopoly of the news to be their God-given constitutional right, and had stood Canute-like against the swelling demands of the broadcasters for any kind of a news service. They justified their action by asserting that radio wanted news as a vehicle for advertising, which would somehow defile the news; they brushed aside the rebuttal that the news in their newspapers was sandwiched between advertising. Actually, the publishers were afraid of this new medium, which was growing at such a pace and posed a threat to their advertising revenue.

If you can't beat them, join them. Some of the larger newspapers, including the *Province*, had established their own radio stations and were broadcasting news, thus breaking the press monopoly. As might be expected, this action led to dissension and heated arguments among the directors of the Canadian Press. The *Province's* station, which had the call letters CKCD, was in the main building, just a short walk from the news room. Earl Kelly, who had the rather lowly position of night editor, was given the job of broadcasting the news and almost immediately became famous as 'Mr Good Evening.' He was Australian, a tall, soldierly figure with a deep, rich voice and clear diction, and he used to end his newscast by wishing his listeners 'on land, in the air, on the water, in the mines, in the woods, in the lighthouses, and especially ... a restful evening, good night.' His special wishes varied from night to night, and one June night he delighted his audience by wishing his regular list of listeners, 'and especially June brides, a restful evening, good night.'

There has been nothing like Earl Kelly's newscast before or since in terms of its hold on the public, according to Stu Keate, who at the time was a sports reporter on the *Province* and who later became publisher of the *Victoria Daily Times* and, before he retired, of the *Vancouver Sun*. 'I am told that in those days,' Stu said, 'if you walked down the main street, say, of Kelowna or Trail or Nelson at nine o'clock at night [in the summer] that voice would be coming at you from every open window.'

Since the CDNA refused to allow CP to sell its news service, it could not very well charge the CBC for the newscasts. The publishers, who were a tight-fisted bunch, made the most of this unwonted generosity by declaring that it was their contribution to keeping news pure and unsullied and to preserving national unity. For its part, the CBC, which was always strapped for cash, was only too pleased to get its news service free. Furthermore, as Dan McArthur said, the corporation was glad to let Canadian Press have the responsibility for the news, since it stood in fear and trembling of being labelled a government propaganda agency – there had been some blunt hints to that effect in newspaper editorials.

Daniel Carman McArthur, the newly appointed chief news editor of the CBC, came from a family with a literary-journalistic background. His godfather was the Canadian poet Bliss Carman, who had been a great friend of his father, Peter McArthur, a well-known turn-of-the- century editor and essayist. In fact, Dan selected and edited two collections of his father's essays and letters; the first book, *Around Home*, was published in 1925, the year after Peter McArthur's death, and the second, *Friendly Acres*, in 1927. D.C. McArthur, as he signed himself, was a relatively young man, just over forty; he was of medium height with a swatch of curly black hair turning grey and a round tranquil face of sallow complexion. He showed a shy hesitancy on first meeting the new applicant – me – in his room in the Hotel Vancouver, but he soon warmed up and seemed to be genuinely interested in my career and aspirations.

It was his job to set up the National News Service, and Dan spoke quietly and earnestly in explaining why the CBC had to take this step. For some years, the American networks, the NBC Blue and Red and CBS, if not Mutual, had had full-scale news services and were reporting the war from overseas: Ed Murrow was in London describing the Blitz and William Shirer was in Berlin speaking on the enemy's plans and deployment. I had heard some of these broadcasts and said that I hoped that CBC would be doing the same and that I would be involved; Dan nodded his head but did not reply.

As a matter of fact, the American networks had been broadcasting from overseas for a couple of years or more before the war, and I said that I remembered listening to the Canadian journalist Pierre van Passen reporting from the Pyrenees on the Spanish civil war. It was hardly an eyewitness account, because he was nowhere near the fighting, although this fact was not admitted at the time – who in North America knew where the Pyrenees were? nevertheless it was a thrill to listen to someone who was actually there; it made you feel much closer to events in Europe than reading about them in the papers. That was the appeal of radio: its immediacy and the way it made you feel involved.

Of course these American reports were being heard in Canada, McArthur said. Radio knew no borders. All you had to do was to tune in to the United States station, the only limitation being distance and the time of day (at night the reception was much clearer). It was different in Montreal, Toronto, or Vancouver, since the major stations in those cities were affiliates of the NBC networks or CBS and carried their war reports – in fact they made a feature of them. There was growing concern in Ottawa among Canadian nationalists, who had been proponents of public broadcasting and were the strongest supporters of CBC, about the way that Canadians were getting so much of their information from American sources, which were, after all, neutral. It would be more than a year before the United States became involved. While Dan did not say so, it was generally assumed that the dominion government had been urging the corporation to do more about publicizing the Canadian war effort than the second-hand CP reports it was airing. All that he said was that CBC had come to the conclusion that it would have to have its own news service.

Dan noted from my résumé that I had been an Empire Press Union Exchange reporter on the *Daily Herald* in London, and we talked about the difference in writing for the popular papers of Fleet Street and the metropolitan dailies in Canada. The British went in for a more personal style of reporting, and since space was limited – the London papers were much smaller than ours, about a third of the size of the Toronto or Vancouver papers – did much more subediting and rewriting. Copy had to be kept short and terse. McArthur thought that my work on the *Daily Herald* would be a good preparation for the briefer, more conversational style of the radio newscast.

The chief news editor had had limited experience of journalism in Toronto, and his main claim to fame was verses that he and a friend, Jack Charlesworth, had written in the winter of 1933–4 about the way the *Toronto Star* built its huge circulation. The newspaper went in for features such as the love letters of Charles Dickens, Dickens's 'Life of Christ,' the letters or diary of Edith Cavell, and a series of gruesome, corpse-strewn battlefield pictures of the Great War, which were spread over the first page of the second section; much of the rest of the paper was taken up with plugging these features. The verses, entitled 'Ad Astra,' struck a popular chord and became an underground sensation; someone (not the authors) had them printed, and hundreds of copies were distributed and have since become collectors' items. Here are the first verse and the chorus (sung to the tune of 'Bonnie Dundee'):

To Hindmarsh and Knowles, Mr Atkinson spoke:
If we don't sell more papers the Star will go broke.
I've three super-salesmen who say they can sell,

They're Jesus and Dickens and Edith Cavell.

Chorus
Come fill up our columns with sobstuff and sex,
Shed tears by the gallons and slush by the pecks.
Let the presses revolve like the mill-tails of Hell
For Jesus and Dickens and Edith Cavell.

Since Dan had to spend the weekend in Vancouver, I took him fishing that Sunday. I drove him in my yellow 1937 Ford convertible with its rumble seat, of which I was very proud, across the four-year-old Lions' Gate toll bridge to Horseshoe Bay, then a small resort at the very end of the road, the North Shore's Marine Drive. Beyond was an untracked wilderness. We hired a boat and I rowed him out into the shimmering splendour of Howe Sound with Bowen Island and the other islands rising green and forested from the sea and with the Coast Range mountains as a magnificent backdrop. I think I would have remembered if we had caught a salmon, but that was the beginning of a friendship which lasted till Dan's death in Ottawa in 1967; in fact, I made the presentation to him at his retirement party, which was in 1962, in the National Press Club.

The CBC National News Service was scheduled to start with the beginning of the new year, 1 January 1941. There were just four of us in the Vancouver station: the senior editor, Jim Crandall, whose father had been one of the founders of British United Press; two news editors: Dick Elson, the younger brother of Bob Elson, the news editor of the *Province* and I; and a copy boy, Lawrence Duffy, a dreamy young fellow who wrote poetry.

I actually joined the staff in December 1940 and spent the month learning how to write a newscast. That meant going to the Canadian Press's office at five o'clock in the morning to begin work on the eight o'clock news bulletin. Perhaps it was the darkness of the early winter morning, but the Dominion Bank building on Hastings Street, across the road from the *Province,* where the Vancouver bureau of CP had its office, seemed a dreary place, its dimly lit tiled hallway as depressing as a public lavatory. There was really little to learn, and I felt it was a waste of sleeping time. However, Sam Ross, the bureau chief, was a delightful fellow. He was my mentor, my chief instructor on the art of writing for radio; some four years later we were to reverse roles when I, as a veteran war correspondent, was to show Sam, who was going overseas for the first time, the way around the European war zone.

Any beginning is exciting, and the National News Service got off to a good start; we felt that our newscasts contained more information than the old CP bulletins. There was no chance of having the embarrassment of an upside-down logo as happened at the beginning of CBC television. I exulted in my new career, and when I ran into Bob Elson and some others from the *Province* at a sporting event that spring, I was foolish enough to say that I felt like a rat quitting a sinking ship. (Bob, who was a martinet of a news editor and was to have a brilliant career in New York with Time Inc., had the habit of chewing paper as an antidote to tension. One day when he was putting the final edition to bed, he got excited about something or other and ate up the copy paper with the main headline written on it; there followed a hue and cry because the paper could not go to press without a headline.) As might be expected, Bob was not going to let me get away with this bombast; he averred that I might be a rat, but print was rising not sinking.

However, my euphoria soon faded. The National News Service was a delusion: we had no reporters, only editors, and we produced the newscasts by rewriting agency copy, just as the Canadian Press editors had done, only we had the benefit of not only the worldwide service of the Associated Press with which CP was affiliated but also the United Press or British United Press as it was called in Canada. It was no fun, and the news room was on the mezzanine floor of the Hotel Vancouver, a dull and dingy place compared with the news room of the *Province* and far from the studios of CBR, which were on the ground floor of the hotel and had their own entrance on Hornby Street.

The only thing that kept me from quitting was that I was allowed to do some broadcasting. The new news editors were given voice tests, and I was surprised at how different I sounded in the play-back from the way I heard myself and how slowly I spoke, as if I were explaining some abstruse point to half-wits; I was, of course, reading, but I had written the text; I learned quickly that you had to 'get the words off the paper,' that you had to give more to the microphone than you would do in conversation with another person.

Radio, as I discovered in later years, was a more demanding medium than television. You could take it more easily on TV, you didn't have to worry so much about fluffs or stumbles because they were compensated for by your appearance on the screen. As long as you looked at the camera and did not appear shifty-eyed or unshaven like Nixon, you could get away with some pretty sloppy reporting. (By the way, those who heard Nixon on radio figured he had won hands down over Kennedy, but those who saw and heard him on TV knew he had lost.)

On the radio there was nothing but the voice, and as a neophyte, I concentrated on my enunciation. I reported on the Pacific coast defences, which consisted of some very large but very old guns, and I described flying with the RCAF on patrols along the rugged British Columbia coast. I remember on one occasion running into a hurricane; the old Stranraer flying boat was making no headway, the islands and the coast below were standing still. The pilot turned tail and came down at Bella Coola, where the RCAF had a couple of rafts; we spent an uncomfortable night on one of the rafts. These were features, not news, and I was given fully fifteen minutes to tell my stories. I even put on a weekly interview show with a title (hardly original) of 'In Town Tonight.'

There was an interesting social life at CBR; it was very different from what I had known on the newspapers. The radio station had a small staff and everyone mixed; I met actors and performers and producers, including Andrew Allan, who was putting on 'Baker's Dozen,' the forerunner of the acclaimed 'Stage' series of CBC radio plays. He developed what was really a repertory company with the best of the young Vancouver actors and actresses: John Drainie, Claire Murray, Bernard Braden, Barbara Kelly, John Bethune, Bill Buckingham, Alan Young, just to mention a few. And to write the 'Baker's Dozen,' he found a teenaged playwright, Fletcher Markle, who modelled himself after his hero, Orson Welles. (By the time I met Fletcher he was twenty years old.) John Drainie was to marry Claire Murray, and Bernard Braden Barbara Kelly, but were all single when I knew them. They were probably the most talented group of performers in Canada at the time, and almost all of them were to follow their guru, Andrew Allan, to Toronto when he moved there in 1944.

Bill Buckingham stayed behind to run 'Theatre under the Stars' in Vancouver, and Alan Young, who had his own comedy show on the CBC called 'Stag Party,' produced by Andrew Allan, went to Hollywood, where he became a star on American television. John Drainie won many awards; he came to be regarded as the premier Canadian actor and was much revered at the time of his death. Bernard Braden, a versatile performer, was reputed to be earning more than the program director in Toronto, which aroused some resentment at the top of the CBC bureaucracy; when he heard of this reaction and that his pay might be cut, he moved his whole family to greener pastures in London, where he became a leading actor – I saw him playing opposite Vivien Leigh in *A Streetcar Named Desire* – and had a long-running and enormously popular BBC program entitled 'Breakfast with Braden.' Fletcher Markle moved to the United States after the war but returned to Canada in 1963 and eventually became head of CBC TV Drama.

Among the announcers was Jack Peach, an amusing and ingenious fellow, who worked with Andrew Allan on sound effects, jumping around slamming doors, crackling paper, simulating horse's hooves; he put on quite an act. Almost all programs were done 'live' in those days; there was little ad-libbing and even interviews were scripted, both questions and answers. Jack also did some writing, but everyone could try his or her hand at different jobs – there were no restrictions, no unions. John Bethune wrote the occasional play for 'Baker's Dozen.' Bill Herbert, the brash young reporter from the *Colonist*, was the chief announcer at CBR and read the newscasts that we had prepared; he also did 'special events' and was to succeed me as the CBC war correspondent on the Italian front in October 1944. Other announcers I knew were Hugh Palmer and Stan Catton, who became a music producer, and also Ray MacNess; Ray was older than most of us and had served as a wireless operator with the rum runners in the old bootlegging days.

Looking back, it is extraordinary to recall how young most of us at CBR were. John Avison, the conductor of the CBC orchestra, the main orchestra in Vancouver, was in his mid-twenties. We felt that Avison would never get anywhere as a maestro with his name – he should change it to Avisonovich – but he disagreed. Andrew Allan, at thirty-five, was almost a father figure. Youthfulness led to some high jinks at parties; many years after, Stan Catton, who in his later public relations–advertising days was known as David Catton, was to recall a party where, he asserted, I had had a boxing match with Pat Keatley, who was with the *Province* but was to join CBR. Georgina Murray, daughter of the famous Lillooet homespun philosopher and journalist, Ma Murray, was in charge of public relations.

The technicians who used to put us on the air were all part of the CBR 'family.' They included Clayton Wilson, who took up flying at a late age and at eighty-three was the oldest Canadian with a pilot's licence, Jimmy Gilmore, who proved to be the exception to the rule that no one in the corporation could rise from the bottom to the top. Gilmore became vice-president of the CBC and was acting president in 1968 before an outsider from the federal bureaucracy, George Davidson, was appointed president. Ken Caple looked after the school broadcasts; he was to succed Ira Dilworth as regional director of the CBC and was chancellor of Simon Fraser University in the seventies. Professor Dilworth was the regional director when I joined CBR as a news editor. He had been a highly respected educator and it was difficult for him to get used to the informality of radio, which was so different from the decorum of teaching; he tried his best to be informal but still addressed us by our surnames, even at office parties.

Dan McArthur encouraged me in my broadcasting; he sent me one of the first books on radio news, a semi-fictionalized account of an on-air reporter, entitled *Carry On Garrison*, written by an American network news editor. Dan also suggested that I should let Toronto headquarters know that I wanted to be a war correspondent. He must have been taking part then in the discussions on restructuring the CBC Overseas Unit in London and making the news service responsible for its main function of reporting the war.

Bob Bowman was CBC's first war correspondent; he started the Overseas Unit when he accompanied the 1st Canadian Division to England in December 1939; this experienced broadcaster had made his name with his knowledgeable 'live' descriptions of the visit of the king and queen' in 1939. He had the title of supervisor of actuality, or outside broadcasts, in the CBC, and these broadcasts, which covered events such as the royal visit, the Canadian National Exhibition, and so on, continued to be a separate department after the news service was formed. Bob covered the 'phoney war,' the evacuation of Dunkirk, and the London Blitz, but after reporting on the Dieppe raid, he returned to Canada for a lecture tour. His old friend Gladstone Murray had been forced out of his job as general manager, and Bob could not get on with his replacement, James Thomson, a clergyman who had been president of the University of Saskatchewan; he submitted his resignation and left broadcasting. Bowman was but the first example of how the CBC could treat its best performers; it was as if the bureaucrats who ran the corporation resented the celebrities they created.

So I wrote to Ernest Bushnell, the program director, and he replied saying that he had put me on the list. I wrote again and he assured me that I was being considered; I asked the regional director, Ira Dilworth, to put in a word for me, and he received the same assurance.

Vancouver, Sunday, 7 December 1941, 10 a.m.:
Surprise attack on Pearl Harbor. Japanese planes destroy U.S. Pacific fleet. Thousands of casualties.

We sat around the apartment that my brother and I shared above the garage of the boarding house at 1201 Pendrill Street, a few friends and ourselves listening to the alarmist reports about the carnage at Pearl Harbor and the frenetic reaction in Washington. It was incredible, absolutely unbelievable, and we shook our heads as the radio blared out the latest horrifying details. 'The goddam Japs!' someone exclaimed, 'How did they do it?' He sounded awestruck; and in the annals of warfare it was an extraordinary achievement. This aura of invincibility was increased when, three days later, on 10 December, Japanese bombers sank the pride of the British navy, the battleships *Prince of Wales* and *Repulse*, off the coast of Malaya.

Not much really was said when we were listening to the radio that Sunday morning, however, and no one remarked that the attack on Pearl Harbor was one of those great turning points of history and that, at the very least, it meant that the war had become a real world war. I felt that I should have been out reporting, interviewing the military and the civil defence about what they were going to do about the new enemy, but I lay back in the broken-down old lounge chair because I knew that we at the CBC could do no first-hand reporting; we could only rewrite the agency bulletins, and the editor on duty was quite capable of doing that.

There was a general panic-stricken response to the attack on Pearl Harbor and the destruction of the U.S. Pacific fleet, partly because of the way that British Columbians had patronized the Japanese as underlings, as good shopkeepers, fishermen, and servants; now they appeared to be supermen. Japanese submarines were reported off Vancouver Island, one actually shelled the lighthouse at Estevan Point, and Japanese planes were said to have been seen making reconnaissance flights or on bombing missions – who knew? It was like the sightings of Cadborosaurus, Vancouver Island's sea monster. There were all kinds of people who swore they had seen it, and even photographs. Most of the Japanese planes turned out to be Canadian aircraft. Yet the alarms continued amid the fear of invasion.

A test blackout was ordered for Vancouver, and since there had been no preparation and there were no proper curtains in any building, it simply meant turning off the lights. The result was chaos and pandemonium. Traffic came to a crashing halt in the darkness of the unlit streets. I remember trying to drive home that night with only my parking lights on. It was a hair-raising experience. The blackout proved impractical, but the civil defence zealots insisted on a brownout, requiring lights to be dimmed in homes and offices and streets to be in darkness. This demand was given up, however, because of the mounting number of accidents and nary a whisper of an air attack by those apparently ubiquitous enemy planes.

The evacuation of Japanese-Canadians from the coast to camps in the interior of the province was a direct result of the mass hysteria. Nothing less would have satisfied the populace at the time, and the Japanese were in danger of vigilantes and lynch mobs. I heard of reports that a Japanese submarine had landed spies at the mouth of the Fraser River near Steveston and that they had mingled with the Japanese fishermen there and were organizing a 'Fifth Column.' These reports were false, but the authorities did very little to stop this insidious rumour mongering and allay the fears of the citizens. In addition, the Christmas Day 1941 surrender of Canadian troops to the Japanese in Hong Kong only added to the hysteria. Some 2,000 men in a couple of ill-trained regiments, Quebec's Royal Rifles of Canada and the Winnipeg Grenadiers, had been sent on the hopeless mission of aiding in the defence of an indefensible British colony; they had been there for only a few weeks before they were slaughtered and overwhelmed. It was a humiliating disaster.

The evacuation of the Japanese went ahead quietly and without any incident, or none that came to our attention. At the CBC, we could include in the newscasts only what the agencies reported, which was not much more than the government's announcement that 'for reasons of national security, all Japanese Canadians have had to be moved into the interior of the country.'

Of course, we had a reputation in British Columbia for being 'racists,' for being anti-Oriental, although I doubt if we were any worse than Canadians in any other part of the country; the fact was that there were more East Indians, Chinese, and Japanese on the Pacific coast than anywhere else. I was friendly with a shaved Sikh, who was a merchant in Vancouver (I don't recall his name), and a second-generation Chinese-Canadian, Wilf Seto, who was a student at the University of British Columbia. Before the war, the racism was directed more at the East Indians and the Chinese than at the Japanese, who were generally more prosperous. It was the attack on Pearl Harbor that reversed the situation, and the Chinese and the East Indians, but particularly the Chinese, took advantage by buying up the Japanese stores and fishing boats at fire-sale, or war-sale, prices.

Wilf Seto had taken officer training with the UBC contingent of the COTC under its formidable commanding officer, Colonel Gordon Shrum. (After retiring as a physics professor, Shrum became head of BC Hydro; he had Simon Fraser University built in record time and was its first chancellor.) Arthur Erickson, the famous architect, and Robert Bonner, who was to become a prominent lawyer and politician, were also in the university's OTC and remembered Colonel Shrum as a 'fearsome figure' and strict disciplinarian, who demanded and got unquestioning obedience. 'He used to strike terror in all of us,' Erickson said. When Wilf Seto was called up, he was asked which regiment he would like to join, and he told me that he said 'any Scottish regiment.' The last time I saw him was in Italy, where he was a captain with the Seaforth Highlanders.

The appeal of the Scottish regiments was such that I started off an early feature on recruiting in the *Province* by writing: 'Yampolsky, Quovadis, Costello, and Zorn, they are all good Scots in the Seaforth Highlanders of Canada.' It was the only first line of any of my stories that I remembered: 'Yampolsky, Quovadis, Costello and Zorn' – and Wilf Seto. (It was almost fifty years later, in August 1992, that I heard of Wilf Seto again. I met a fellow West Vancouverite, Hugh Garling, who told met that he had got to know Wilf Seto very well during the war. He had taken an officers training course with the Seaforth subaltern, and they had gone overseas together. It was Hugh who had dubbed him, in good-hearted jest, 'Hamish McSeto.' After the war, Garling was associated with Seto in an export-import business in Vancouver. The nickname, or *nom de guerre*, 'Hamish McSeto,' stuck, and Hugh Garling said that the late Senator J.W. de B. Farris mentioned it in speaking to veterans as an example of racial harmony in the Canadian armed forces. Wilf Seto died in Vancouver in 1960; he was forty-six years old.)

Finally, the draft caught up with me; the manila envelope with the summons from His Majesty's Government, which was long expected, was delivered one summer day in 1942. Now, I had to act. I doubt if I could have got an exemption and I did not really want one, because I was anxious to go overseas and I was giving up hope of ever becoming a war correspondent. I heard that the navy's officer selection board was expected in Vancouver shortly. So I went to *HMCS Discovery*, the brick 'boat' on a spit of land off Stanley Park. When I saw the commanding officer, whom I knew slightly, he was gracious enough to say that I was 'definitely of officer timber.' They would sign me up as an ordinary seaman and this would get me out of the clutches of the army. Now, just a minute. Did this mean dressing up like a sailor and turning out for parades? No, no, he assured me, no wearing bell-bottomed trousers, no parades, no drill, nothing at all. They would just hold me until the board arrived. That was towards the end of July, 23 July 1942 to be specific.

But weeks went by, and months went by, and the board did not arrive. The war went on, and although there was news of the Allies advancing or at least holding their own, the Japanese still seemed to be encroaching.

2

Recording the Alcan

Vancouver, 3 November 1942:
Japanese face annihilation in the Aleutians. Massed bombing
of Kiska.

I n retrospect, this radio news bulletin was somewhat premature.
Months went by before the Japanese could be driven out of the
Aleutians, and only after a bloody battle for Attu. Still, the report
helped to assuage the fears of people in the Pacific northwest. It
was pointed out that Kiska and Attu were not somewhere in the
Arctic but on a latitude south of Prince Rupert and that the
islands of the Aleutians were stepping-stones to North America.
That was why a highway was being driven through the northern
wilderness of Canada to Alaska by the United States army. At the
beginning of November I was assigned to cover the completion of
this military road and the opening ceremony in the Yukon. Since
the navy board had not arrived, there was nothing to stop me from
going.

I was to join a CBC team that was headed by Frank Willis, the
director of feature broadcasts, Toronto, and included Roger Baulu,
the chief announcer of the French network, Montreal, and Clifford

Speer, an engineer, also from Toronto. Frank Willis was a legendary figure in radio because of his coverage of the Moose River Mine disaster of April 1936; it was he who broadcast over the only telephone line from this remote area in Nova Scotia where three men were buried in a mine cave-in; he did so almost continuously for four days. 'So great was the tension,' E. Austin Weir wrote, 'that all fifty-eight stations in Canada and some 650 in the United States carried these broadcasts.' It was a remarkable feat of endurance and Frank made history, since it was the beginning of the recognition of radio as an instant purveyor of news.

My plane left Vancouver and skirted the peaks of the Rockies – with oxygen masks on hand but not used – and landed at dusk in a Christmas scene of snow falling on warmly lit houses. The others joined me at the Calgary airport and we flew on to Edmonton, where we were put up in the plush comfort of the old Macdonald Hotel, to await our subarctic equipment and the military travel orders.

It was my biggest assignment, an introduction to becoming a war correspondent, and I was to meet uniformed American war correspondents in Whitehorse. I also learned a lot about the extraordinary hierarchical set-up of the Canadian Broadcasting Corporation, which was probably typical of the country at the time. Although I was the junior member of the team, and from Vancouver, an outpost of the CBC, and the other members were from headquarters, it was I who had to take charge when Frank Willis became incapacitated. Roger Baulu refused to take responsibility; this was an English show, he said, and, in any case, he was from Montreal and knew nothing about the arrangements. It was not a matter of his being under contract; he was on staff, as I was. Baulu left the CBC later to become a star in private broadcasting and a household name in Montreal. Clifford Speer was an engineer, and operating engineers were not expected to take charge. Towards the end of the war he joined the CBC overseas Unit and tragically was killed in a traffic accident in London on VE Day.

So I had to check with the military authorities and find out about our flight plans, the time of our departure for Fort St John and the journey up the highway. I also reminded them of the bulky disc-recording equipment that we were taking with us to record the opening ceremonies at Lake Kluane in the Yukon. I had to sign for the so-called subarctic equipment which arrived in a large cardboard box on the day before we were scheduled to leave. When we opened the box, we found a letter from the RCAF director of equipment and supplies; it said that it would be appreciated if we would let them know about the 'progressive sensations of cold at various parts of the anatomy' that we felt with this clothing. We laughed, but we were to be guinea pigs. I only wish I had kept the letter.

The box contained blanket parkas that became a cold weight in -30°F temperature; the sort of gauntlets that flyers or cowboys wear, which induced frostbite; and fur-lined air force boots, fine for sitting still, but when you walked, your feet sweated and then froze. There were no sleeping-bags, and we were supposed to sleep in tents at the American army camps up the road. I remember the look of astonishment on the face of the lieutenant who had been delegated to look after us at the first camp we reached when we told him that we had no sleeping-bags. The U.S. armed forces knew little about living and working in the north, as we were to discover, but the Canadian military knew even less.

Instead of blanket parkas, we should have been supplied with padded parkas or anoraks, proper fur mitts, and certainly not heavy air force boots; we should have taken a lead from the way the Indians dressed and put on two or three pairs of woollen stockings and over them mukluks or long moccasins. It was obvious that the military knew nothing about the 'true north, strong and free' and were incapable of living or working or 'standing on guard' there. After the war, the situation was not much better, although there was an attempt to come to grips with the Arctic, and, as a result of exercises above the sixtieth parallel, some thermal underwear was developed. But the Canadian armed forces had no enthusiasm for these grim manoeuvres in the crackling cold; they much preferred to conduct their war games in the sunny south. The navy used to show the flag in the Caribbean regularly, but hardly ever, if ever, around Greenland.

The Canadians were not alone in this ignorance of the north. Although the Americans had the good sense to provide double duck-down sleeping-bags for the 11,000 troops, mostly southerners and blacks, building the highway, they could not start their motors in the really cold weather. So they kept a couple of trucks running all night and used them to drag start the rest of their vehicles, hauling some of them, with their tires frozen square for miles down the snow-covered road. Nor could they service equipment in the subarctic winter. If a tractor or bulldozer broke down, it was simply pushed over to the side, and the highway was littered with abandoned machinery. It was conspicuous waste, but if the U.S. army had been held up for repairs, or attempts at repairs, it would never have been able to drive the road through in eight months. Eight months. Before the war I wrote a piece about the construction of a highway to Alaska, based on reports in the B.C. Archives, and the expert opinion then was that, if the highway could be built, it would take at least ten years.

After the war came the Cold War, and the United States built the DEW Line, the Distant Early Warning Line, across the Canadian Arctic. I visited the station near Pangnirtung in the late fifties and found that the Canadians and Americans who were manning the radar equipment lived and worked in modules, which was what their unearthly dwellings were called. It was as if they were living on the moon. The modules were kept so warm that the men wore T-shirts. As far as I know, they seldom went out to brave the arctic air.

Amazingly, the Norwegians, a northern people, were just as ignorant as the Canadians about the north. I was in Oslo shortly after VE Day and attended a press conference given by an officer who had just returned with King Haakon and the Norwegian government-in-exile. The reason for the press conference was that this officer had been sent up to the subarctic Kirkenes Front to make contact with the Red Army; he did not have much to say about the military situation and seemed satisfied that the Soviets would pose no threat, but he was astonished at the way the Russians dressed and fought up there. All they wore, he said, were fur jackets and pants inside out with the fur next to the skin; the white overcoats were for camouflage purposes; no boots, but two or three pairs of thick socks with the outer pair greased. They slept in these garments and wore them day and night for a week to ten days. And, he added, when they changed, they got cleaned up in mobile baths and laundries that were kept as close to the front as the artillery.

It was just another sign that, generally speaking, westerners shun the 'true north' or the real north, even though as Canadians and Scandinavians and Americans they live closest to the pole and even include parts of it in their territory. But who can blame them? Who would choose to live in the metal-snapping deep freeze if they could live elsewhere? Look at all the Canadians who escape from their snow-bound homes to Florida or California. Blame it on affluence, which has made westerners too soft to cope with their subarctic lands.

But back to the building of the Alcan (Alaska-Canada International) Highway as it was called then. We flew to Fort St John, and after a night in this frontier town at the only hotel, a grey clapboard structure with no flush toilets, we started up the road in an unheated, heavy-utility personnel carrier, a sort-of army station-wagon, with a heated van for the recording equipment. We had a conducting officer with us who was supposed to be our guide, but he misjudged the distance to the first U.S. camp with the result that we arrived late at night.

As I said, the American officer was horrified to learn that we had no sleeping-bags; he provided us with blankets, but despite the fact that I had nine blankets, four below me on the cot and five on top, and kept my clothes on, including the parka, I was suffering from those 'progressive sensations of cold' that the RCAF would have dearly liked to hear about. Before being frozen stiff, I got up and left the frigid black hole of the tent; Roger Baulu, who shared the tent with me, followed suit. We looked around the cold moonlit encampment and saw the warm light of a Nissen hut on a snow-covered rise just above the lines of tents.

We stumbled along the hard-packed snow paths between the tents towards that shining eldorado of the Nissen hut. And glory be, there was blessed warmth and light. The two big buck privates, who were black and who were the only inhabitants of this empty building, seemed surprised to see us but made no objection to our bunking down on the wooden floor. I did not get much sleep, since the soldiers kept chopping logs and throwing them into the pot-bellied stove in the middle of the hut until it glowed red hot. Finally I got up, and then I saw the large black boxes containing our recording equipment on the other side of the stove. There they stood, inanimate but warm, and it slowly dawned on me that this electronic equipment was probably the reason why the GIs kept the stove going all night.

The CBC, in making arrangements for the Alcan trip, had informed the United States army that the recording equipment we would be taking with us (to cover the opening ceremonies at Lake Kluane) needed a temperature of 65°F to operate. The military issued orders to this effect, that the equipment had to be kept at 65°F, and the orders were carried out to the letter, which accounted for the Nissen hut's being kept warm all night and for the heated truck, while we shivered in the unheated tents and personnel carrier. It was ludicrous, an example of the stifling bureaucracy of the United States army or any other nation's military establishment, for that matter.

It was incredible that such a ponderous, hidebound organization could get anything done, let alone build the Alcan Highway and complete the tote road in record time. Yet there was a certain competence in the great unwieldy masses of the armed forces, and despite pitfalls and SNAFUs (Situation Normal: All Fucked Up) everywhere, they did accomplish much of what they set out to do, as long as the orders were simple and direct. The war was a great impetus; it was their raison d'être, of course, and yet it had to be their kind of war, which was really total war. There were no complications then, no caveats, no conditions. They were hopeless when it came to guerrilla wars, where the enemy melted away and was not clearly identified. I covered the Greek civil war, which followed the Second World War, and saw the paralysis of the military when faced with Communist guerrillas. The regular Greek army did not know how to attack the partisans and settled down into fortified encampments, leaving the countryside in the hands of the insurgents. The civil war ended only when Tito broke with Stalin and the Communist guerrillas no longer had a green frontier and an ally in their rear.

The orders for the Alcan Highway were to get it done as quickly as possible to forestall a Japanese invasion. It was a military operation, and the U.S. army deployed nine regiments for the task, seven of which were newly organized engineer–general service regiments, but two were regular combat units. Such were the exigencies of the times that all the troops arrived in the northern wilderness with battle equipment, prepared to fight as well as to build a road. A number of mechanized columns were used, the main drive being south from Fairbanks and the other north from the roadhead at Fort St John. Spearheads of these columns consisted of tractors and bulldozers.

The final junction occurred when Private Al Jalufka of Texas, driving a tractor from the north, met Corporal Refines Sims, Junior, of Philadelphia, driving a tractor from the south; Corporal Sims backed up his cat when he saw the trees falling towards him instead of away from him. Private Jalufka was at the opening ceremony at Lake Kluane, and Corporal Sims would have been there, but he was sick and his place was taken by another black soldier. Four enlisted men held the ribbon, two of them black and two white, a demonstration of racial harmony which was not always evident during the construction of the road. (Of the 11,000 U.S. servicemen, 3,600 were black in separate, segregated units.)

We spent more than one night at American army camps on our journey up the road and got little sleep, and as a result, we tried to stay, whenever we could, at civilian camps. While the U.S. Corps of Engineers drove the tote road through the forbidding northern wilderness in record time, civilian contractors working for the U.S. Public Roads Administration widened this pioneer route and refined it, lessening the grades and the curves and making it usable by ordinary vehicles. There were no tents at the civilian camps but wooden barracks or Nissen huts, which were warm and comfortable with hot and cold running water, but they were not easy to get into, since they were almost always full.

However, we did eat most of our meals at the civilian camps. The GI chow at the army camps was truly horrible. The food we were served was dehydrated or canned: dried eggs, powdered milk, even dried potatoes, and it had a strange chemical taste as if it had been chlorinated. We soon found out that the civilian camps had good, hearty meals, bacon and lots of eggs, real butter and milk, and fresh meat and vegetables.

Watson Lake, Yukon Territory, 15 November 1942:
The Battle of Stalingrad: A Russian broadcast says Soviet forces have begun an offensive.

The airport at Watson Lake was one civilian camp where we were able to spend a night, and it was there we heard the short-wave Russian broadcast, which was about the only news we could get in the far north. Watson Lake was a staging post for planes being flown to the Soviet Union, and the buildings were full of American ferry pilots; the Russians took over in Alaska.

Our stopovers at the military camps on the Alcan Highway were disillusioning, since most of us had the idea that the U.S. army represented luxury itself with the best pay and the best conditions. At least that was certainly the view in British Columbia, where pro-American sentiments were strong; we looked on California as the golden land and our role model. Yet here was the army exploiting the poor soldiers, most of whom were blacks or from the south, making them live in tents and feeding them awful, tasteless muck, while the civilian contractors treated their employees so well. Of course, the latter knew that if they did not do so, the cat-skinners would quit, despite the fact that they were making $25 a day, which was a lot of money then. The GIs had no such option; they were in for the duration.

It took us six days to travel in our unheated personnel carrier the 1,000 miles from Fort St John to Whitehorse, and although it would be an exaggeration to call it 'the worst journey in the world,' which we did, we cheered when we saw the first houses of the capital of the Yukon. Our vehicle had broken down on occasion and we had had to get out and push, which was better than sitting and freezing. I remember a long wait because a temporary bridge was being repaired; there was a line-up of trucks and we joined the drivers who were standing by a great bonfire trying to keep warm; it seemed hours that we stamped our feet and flailed our arms and toasted one side and then the other.

At Whitehorse I ran into an old friend, Richard L. Neuberger; he had been the *New York Times* correspondent for the Pacific northwest and Victoria was part of his beat, which was how we met. After the war Dick was to become a senator from Oregon, but now he was a captain in the U.S. army in charge of public relations. Dick Neuberger was not his sparkling self and seemed unhappy in his role as military spokesman. (The headquarters of the U.S. army's Alaska Highway project was in Whitehorse.) I quizzed him about the conditions in the American army camps, especially the terrible food: the dreadful dehydrated meat and potatoes and eggs, the dishwater coffee, and everything with a peculiar disinfectant taste. Was it saltpetre? The only explanation that he could give was that the quartermaster had to feed each man on so much a day, say 20 or 30 cents, which was adequate at home but not sufficient in the north. Another example of the mind-numbing bureaucracy of the armed forces. Another SNAFU.

The rest of our trip was largely ceremonial. We left in a long convoy of army trucks and cars for Lake Kluane, where the ribbon was cut and the highway declared officially open on 20 November 1942. The lake was chosen because, although it is in the Yukon, it is close to the Alaska-Canada border. Also, it's a beauty spot, 'the most beautiful place in the world' some say. Lake Kluane is in the midst of the St Elias range, the highest mountains in North America, and the snow-covered peaks rise 15,000 feet above its glacial waters, an emerald in a setting of huge diamonds. Unfortunately, we did not see Kluane at its best, since the lake was steaming in the -35°F temperature. It was just another cold, grey place.

As for the ceremony, it was like any other ceremony of its kind, except that the band was in a heated tent while the speakers, the dignitaries, were outside in the biting cold. A touch of colour was provided by a troop of Royal Canadian Mounted Police, who first paraded in their traditional red uniforms but soon put on their warm buffalo coats. It was so cold that Cliff Speer, the engineer, who was in a heated truck recording the proceedings, told me to see that no one kicked the wire to the mike since it was frozen stiff and would crackle. I had to introduce the speakers, the principals being the secretary of state for Alaska, E.L. Bartlett, representing the United States, and Ian Mackenzie, the minister of pensions and national health, Canada, and I was amazed and dismayed by the fact that they spoke at length, for a full twenty minutes each, despite the near -40°F weather. It was truly a chilling performance.

Others spoke – the American general whose troops built the highway was one – and they were as loquacious as the politicians. Major-General George Pearkes, the senior Canadian officer present, did not speak but stood to attention as if frozen stiff in his cavalry uniform. Since we had only one turntable, we had arranged for slight breaks in the program so that Cliff could change records. We had also asked for the band to wait a minute after the ribbon was cut by Messrs Bartlett and Mackenzie, so that I would have a chance to describe the ceremony. The breaks were observed but the band forgot itself, and I had time only to gabble, 'The ribbon's cut – the highway's open' before the national anthems stopped me talking.

In all the flood of words, which did nothing to warm our ears, as I wrote later, I could remember only one thing, and that was the description of the scene as 'an imposing wilderness.' That was what it was. Awe-inspiring too, hard and bleak, and uncompromising. I had to stand beside the microphone during the whole proceedings, and when I got out of the cold, it took me nearly an hour before I could get any feelings in my toes. At a lunch party following the opening ceremony in the newly built barracks nearby, where bear and moose steaks and the meat of mountain goats were served, toasts were drunk to the highway, not in champagne but, according to the account in my book, *Journey into Victory*, in coffee and water. On duty, the American army, like the U.S. navy, was grimly teetotal.

Looking back: the hard-packed snow was so cold that it squealed when you walked on it; I found that the same sound was made when you walk on shattered glass left by a V-2 hit on London. The northern lights, the aurora borealis, so brilliant against the dark sky, were streaming and dancing overhead, no fireworks could match them – did they crackle? I can't recall. And the lakes and rivers freezing and steaming in the November cold. We probably saw it at the wrong time of year, but the northern wilderness seemed dull and grey and empty and endless, 'nothing but miles and miles of nothing but miles and miles,' as one of the American officers was to say. In all the thousand miles we travelled from Fort St John to Whitehorse, we never saw a woman or an Indian or, for that matter, anyone else who was not engaged in building the road; but what was surprising was that we never saw an animal, not even a bird.

All of the hopes and expectations at the time of the opening ceremony, that this was going to be the road to Russia and eventually to Europe, may not have been realized, but the Alcan Highway, which is now paved, did open the north. It took the war and the United States army to do it, and if it had not been for them, it would have taken years to build the road, perhaps the ten years or more that the pre-war surveys had suggested. Any construction now would run into the objections and obstruction of the environmentalists, the Sierra Club, and the wilderness societies, and there would be court challenges by them and by the Indians, who would claim the land as their traditional hunting grounds. All of which would mean delays and add to the cost. The Americans invested $147.8 million in the construction of the highway, according to figures released after the war. They built it at their own expense – Canada contributed nothing – their only condition being that it should be a military highway under their control until the end of the war. (Ottawa did pay $108 million for the airfields, buildings, telephone systems, and other assets that the U.S. army left behind.)

We had to wait a day or so in Whitehorse before flying back to Edmonton. Because there was a tail wind, it took just three hours for the return trip, compared with seven days in the unheated, heavy-utility personnel carrier. Only the distance was not the same: it was a little more than 700 miles by air, whereas it was 1,000 miles by road. I recorded a fifteen-minute talk in Edmonton and then took the train back to Vancouver, since all planes were grounded, owing to a blizzard that cut visibility to zero. It was a white-out. When I reached Vancouver, it was raining. A delightful drizzle. I had left the 'true' North to the Americans, who would be standing on guard for the duration.

3

Radio Goes to War

Vancouver, 16 December 1942:
British Eighth Army drives towards Tripoli and junction with
Allied forces in Tunisia.

On the day that I returned to Vancouver from the Alcan Highway, there was a message to see the CBC regional director.
I stood before his large mahogany desk, on either side of which
hung two monumental totem pole paintings by Emily Carr. Ira
Dilworth was Emily Carr's good friend and patron and not only
brought her the recognition that was due her as an artist but
encouraged her in her writing and was her literary executor. The
desk between the totem poles was like a sacrificial table, and I
recalled standing before it on another occasion, when I had
overslept and the CBC had no morning news. Mr Dilworth, like the
stern teacher he could be, punished me by putting me on the night
shift, which put a crimp in my social life. This time I was not the
sacrifice. The regional director looked up from a pile of papers and
said, as if he were giving me some inconsequential directive, that
the CBC wanted me to go to London to join the overseas unit.

This was wonderful news – I had just been given the assignment that I had been seeking for three years and had given up hope of getting! My heart rose and I walked out of Mr Dilworth's office as if I were on a cloud with my head full of visions, very glamorous, of myself in uniform as a war correspondent. However, any idea of my spending Christmas of 1942 in London was quickly dashed. I had to get out of the navy; I had signed up and was awaiting the officer selection board, or whatever it was called, which still had not arrived. My request for a discharge had to go to Ottawa, and the land-bound captain of *HMCS Discovery*, the brick boat off Stanley Park, assured me that he would look after it, that it would take twelve days at the most, maybe ten days. It took more than three weeks.

It was only after I had got my discharge that anything could be done about transportation across the Atlantic – a matter that was entirely in the hands of the military. Ernie Bushnell wired that he was making the arrangements and that I could be leaving within a day or a week. So I went to Victoria to spend Christmas with my mother and father and to say good-bye. But it was more than three weeks, nearly four weeks later, that I was ordered to take the first plane to Ottawa. I was to get used to the uncertainties and delays of wartime travel, but at this time, with all the rapture and enthusiasm of my new assignment, I found the delays very frustrating. There had been farewell parties and I was still around. Was I really going overseas?

Now that I was back and waiting to go to London, the war news took on even greater significance. The British Eighth Army had won the Battle of El Alamein and was advancing towards the Allied forces that had landed in Algeria and Morocco. Rommel was being caught in a vast pincer movement. The CBC bulletins were full of this 'new front' and how North Africa could be a stepping-stone to the invasion of Europe, to the 'soft underbelly of the Axis.' The question was, what about the Canadian army, 'that dagger pointed at the heart of Berlin'? It could not sit idly by in Britain for much longer. I was afraid that my assignment might have come too late and that I would miss the great story of the Canadians going into action.

On Friday, 22 January 1943 I left Vancouver on a Trans-Canada Lockheed Lodestar. My flight was delayed ten hours. I had a seat on a plane that was supposed to take off at six o'clock in the morning, but we did not get away till nine o'clock. Then we left and returned to the airport three times. Something was wrong with the oil lines on the plane, and the mechanics could not fix it; the second and third times that we took off I could see the oil bubbling out of the wing. Finally, we got away at four o'clock in the afternoon on another plane.

We passed over the Rockies at sunset and, I remember, the jagged peaks were tipped with gold. It was bitterly cold on the prairies, -28°F Lethbridge, -36°F at Regina, -40°F at Winnipeg. There was a delay of six hours in Winnipeg, and we were put up in a hotel where we got some sleep before being roused for a seven o'clock take-off Saturday morning. A layer of clouds covered the whole of northern Ontario, but we flew over the clouds in the bright morning sunshine, only coming down into the mists and gloom of the earth at Kapuskasing and North Bay. At North Bay we learned that we were going to fly direct to Ottawa. A vast weather front was moving east and south across Ontario and had already reached and passed Toronto.

The clouds were so thick now that, though we climbed to 10,000 feet, we were flying in soup. An hour after we left North Bay, the stewardess answered the pilot's buzzer and came weaving back to tell the passengers, 'It's closed in at Ottawa, and we're heading for Montreal.' Here is how I described the rest of this extraordinary flight in my book, *Journey into Victory*:

A few minutes later she was summoned by the buzzer again.

'It's closed in at Montreal,' she announced. 'I dunno where. He said something about heading for Moncton.'

Through the cabin window there was nothing and we might have been flying anywhere or nowhere. The only note of confidence was in the roar of the engines, but above it was the buzzer's insistent signal.

'We're heading for Burlington,' she said.

The stewardess was a pretty, cheerful girl, and if she was worried she did not let the passengers know about it. Most of them were now getting nervous and were peering out of the window, trying to see through the impenetrable haze. There was a good deal of chatter about where we were going.

'Burlington – where's that?'

'Burlington Beach, near Hamilton?'

'No, Vermont.'

'In the United States?'

'Yeah, I guess it's closed in everywhere else.'

The two ferry pilots who were passengers on the plane discussed the possibility of landing in such weather.

'Goddammit,' said one of them, 'I've landed in stuff as thick as this. I took a chimney pot off but I got her down alright, and there was no damage beyond a scratch or two. The trouble with these commercial pilots is that they won't take chances.'

I made a serious attempt to read the magazine on my lap. It was open at a strange puzzle ... it was about ... a burial. I closed it up quickly and pressed my nose against the window and looked out into the fog. If it had closed in at Burlington where else was there to land, and how long would the gas hold out?

The first sight of Lake Champlain, the white reaches of ice that appeared out of the haze, was almost electric in its effect on the passengers. Everyone began talking and joking.

It was a near thing all the same, for ten minutes after we landed the snow began to fall. The fast-moving weather front had reached Burlington, Vermont, and the airport was closed in. We were the last plane to land.

I took a slow and very dirty train to Montreal. It was held up for an hour by a wreck, and I only just caught the last train to Ottawa; to cap it, this train hit a car at Vankleek Hill and was held up for half an hour. It was past one o'clock on Sunday morning that I finally got to bed at the Château Laurier Hotel.

At eleven o'clock in the morning, Donald Manson phoned and in his precise Scottish accent wanted to know what the hell had happened to me. 'Well,' he said, when I explained, 'You've missed the boat, but I guess we can get you on the next boat.' No, I knew no one in Ottawa, and Mr Manson, who was executive assistant to the general manager of the CBC, took pity on me, stranded in the capital on a Sunday, and I spent most of the day in his neat little brown house situated on Main Street between the Rideau River and the Rideau Canal. He told me that he had heard some of my broadcasts and liked my diction and my pronunciation; he felt that my voice was 'distinguished,' as he put it, not like that of the regular radio announcer, who had a common American accent and a sloppy, indistinctive way of speaking. I supposed my clear enunciation was due to my having been to an English public school, and I wondered whether this had had anything to do with my becoming a war correspondent.

There was no doubt that the CBC was an elitist organization, although Donald Manson himself came from humble origins in northern Scotland and liked to tell about it. He was one of the great pioneers of radio and public broadcasting in Canada. He had been with Marconi in Newfoundland for the first successful transatlantic wireless transmission in 1901; he had been in charge of the government's radio inspection service for many years; he had been secretary of the Aird Commission, whose report resulted in the formation of the Canadian Radio Broadcasting Commission, the forerunner of the Canadian Broadcasting Corporation. He was executive assistant to the general manager of the CBC when he entertained me in his home and was to become assistant general manager and briefly general manager before he retired in 1952.

Montreal, 3 February 1943:
Great Russian victory at Stalingrad; Field Marshal Paulus and remainder of Sixth German Army surrender.

In Montreal, I was asked to see James Thomson, the new general manager and another Scot, who rolled his Rs like a drum beat when he read me a lecture on my 'responsibilities.' At that time the headquarters of the CBC was split between Toronto and

Montreal, with a political headquarters, manned by Donald Manson, in Ottawa. The total number of people working at these locations, and across the country, as executives, secretaries, clerks, producers, directors, announcers, news editors, engineers, technicians, and such was a little more than 600.

When I was in Montreal, I was invited by Brooke Claxton to have a drink with him at his home, a beautiful eighteenth-century house on the slopes of Mount Royal. The Claxtons were old English Montreal, which was by no means an endangered species then. Brooke, a prominent lawyer, was an up-and-coming Liberal MP who was already parliamentary secretary to Prime Minister Mackenzie King. (He was appointed a cabinet minister in 1944 and, after he retired from the House of Commons, he became the first chairman of the Canada Council when it was set up in 1957; he was sixty-two when he died in Ottawa in 1960). Claxton paced up and down before the fire in the elegant drawing-room and said that he was concerned about the fact not so much that the United States army had built the Alcan Highway as that its presence on Canadian soil impinged, as he put it, on our sovereignty. He complained that the Americans gave out very little information, and he grilled me about what I had seen and learned. I said that I did not think that the Yanks would stay, that they had no love for the north, and that they were there just for the duration.

Another day and a half in a train took me to Halifax. I had hardly been there twenty-four hours when I received a note to telephone the shipping agent; it was quite late at night, but I got him at his home and he told me to be at the King's Wharf at half-past ten the next morning. A great liner, the *Mauretania*, was berthed by the Nova Scotian Hotel, where I was staying, but my heart sank when the taxi headed for the docks away from the fast transport. The handful of people in the dingy waiting room convinced me that I was going on a freighter, and the sign on the ship's deck, 'Danger – High Explosives,' and 'No Smoking' scrawled in chalk around the grey superstructure did not help me to get used to the idea.

The ship's name? My book, *Journey into Victory*, was subject to censorship, since it was published in 1944, and any identification, such as a ship's name or, for that matter, a unit's name, was blue pencilled. All I could say was that it used to carry newsprint and that it was a sort-of freighter-liner with accommodation for a dozen passengers. On this trip there were only nine of us, so we were comfortable enough, not overcrowded and sleeping in tiers, ten to twelve in an ordinary stateroom, as we would have been on the *Mauretania* and the other fast ships; but the cargo of ammunition and high explosives was never far from our thoughts. The fact that we were sitting on a keg of dynamite made the rule that you had to sleep with your clothes on seem rather ridiculous. OK, there should be no delay in getting the lifeboats away, but if we were hit in one of the two holds in which the explosives were stored, there would be no lifeboats to get away, nor anybody to get away in the lifeboats. But that was a navy rule, and ours was not to reason why.

Late in the afternoon of the day that we got on board, the freighter slipped away from the safety of the wharf, past the dirty grey waterfront of Halifax with clusters of ships clinging to its docks, out into the gloom of the open sea. Snow was falling and we could not see far, but we had a feeling we were alone. However, the next day we were relieved to find that, though we were the only merchant ship to leave Halifax, we were being escorted by two corvettes. Then we saw in the distance the unmistakable shape of an aircraft carrier, and we felt even better. Just after noon, we sighted the convoy: the whole horizon was covered with dots that grew into tankers and freighters, some forty of them, in a dozen columns of three to four ships; the columns were kept short to provide the minimum silhouette for the German U-boats. The aircraft carrier stayed with us for only a day, and the big convoy was left in charge of half a dozen destroyers and corvettes, which circled around the slow-moving cargo vessels, sometimes darting in and out, like sheepdogs looking after a flock of fat sheep.

Half way across, a storm struck; it caught up with the convoy, its great waves racing ahead, lifting the ships and dropping them into the troughs so they seemed to disappear. A hard core of hail formed the eye of the storm, and a light that was as bright as a rainbow overcame the darkness. The storm lasted for seven days; a mountainous wave crumpled the rear gun platform, another one stove in a lifeboat. There was one night when I got no sleep, partly because of the motion of the ship, the way we were being tossed around, but mostly because of the noise made by the waves smashing against the side of the ship. Even the chief mate said that once or twice during the night he thought that we had been hit by a torpedo.

All the passengers thought that the storm had kept the U-boats away. In the little saloon, with its chintz-covered chairs, the old squeaky gramophone, and no radio and no news, we never tired of talking about the convoy and the submarine menace. How many U-boats were there in the north Atlantic? Five hundred? Oh, no, half that number? Two hundred? There was speculation on the meaning of any change of course. One morning, the ships were running through pack ice, and we felt we must be near Iceland. Or Orkney and northern Scotland? All of this talk inspired the dyspeptic Ernie Burritt, who was returning to his post as head of the Canadian Press Bureau in London, to make a poor paraphrase of Churchill's famous saying: 'Never was so much said by so many who knew so little.' A favourite subject of conversation was the length of time the ship would take to reach England. Ten days? Eleven Days? Twelve days? It was well over fourteen days before we docked at Liverpool.

On arrival in London I was greeted by John Kannawin, the head of the Overseas Unit, and almost the first thing he said to me was 'Where's Paul Dupuis?' 'Why,' I asked. 'Isn't he here?' I knew that Paul Dupuis was supposed to have left Canada a week ahead of me; he was on the boat that I missed, but his ship had to return to Halifax and spent two weeks in Bedford Basin having its boilers fixed. So I learned eight days later when Paul turned up. Missing the boat could mean getting there more quickly.

When I arrived in London in February 1943, the CBC Overseas Unit was reduced to its bare bones. Besides Kannawin, there were Gerry Wilmot, who did features for the home services and looked after the broadcasts to the Canadian forces in the United Kingdom, and two engineers, Paul Johnson and Alec MacDonald. Bob Bowman had gone, and Rooney Pelletier, who had taken his place, had been offered a job with the BBC and wanted to go. An urbane and completely bilingual Montrealer, Rooney had found his spiritual home in London and became more British than the British; he affected an English accent and dress and, when I met him, was indistinguishable from other controllers of the BBC.

Someone had to be sent over quickly to relieve Rooney, and the CBC decided on John Kannawin, who was a fairly high-level official and had been in charge of the prairie region. They were able to get him a flight to London in November 1942, and Kannawin, in full flying gear, including an oxygen mask and parachute pack, sat or lay in the belly of an unheated, unpressurized Liberator Bomber, which took four hours to fly from Dorval to Gander and another eleven hours to Prestwick. Fifteen hours instead of fifteen days in a freighter. It was worth it, and Kannawin rejoiced in being a pioneer of transatlantic flight and having the mementoes to prove it.

Whether he was a temporary appointment was never clear; he was certainly not part of the restructuring of the CBC's Overseas Unit, with its emphasis on the News Service, and six months after his arrival in London, A.E. Powley, the senior news editor in Toronto, was sent over to take charge of the war correspondents. John Kannawin was not recalled, and, as might be expected, there were arguments and some hard feeling between him and Bert Powley as to their respective rights. It was typical of the CBC bureaucracy that they should be heavy on supervisors, on 'housekeeping.' The worst example occurred when I was the CBC correspondent at the United Nations in New York: there was a senior producer whose main job was to put me on the air. Overmanaging is endemic in bureaucracy.

Gerry Wilmot was a great showman and compère who looked after the entertainment of the Canadian troops. He had as his assistant Jack Peach, a raconteur with a dry sense of humour from Vancouver, but Jack had transferred to RCAF Public Relations before I reached London. Gerry also read the Canadian news over the facilities of the BBC for the Canadian forces and gained the reputation of being the fastest reader on the air. In fact, many British, who had no interest in Canadian news, listened just to marvel at the way that Gerry rattled along at 200 words a minute, so different from the measured pace of their own announcers. Wilmot always had a another person read the sports news; at first it was Jack Peach, and then a Corporal Smith from the RCAF. Whenever the corporal could not show, he would call on me. Now sports news should be done at a lighter, faster pace than the ordinary news, and I had a rather deep voice. I noted the way that Gerry would throw the mike switch off during the course of the newscast, cough and splutter, then on again *à toute vitesse*. I tried to follow suit. It was a challenging and invigorating experience.

This use of military personnel reached an extreme with Don Fairbairn, who had been a CBC farm commentator before joining RCAF Public Relations. He did almost as many reports for the CBC as any of the war correspondents, and A.E. Powley, in his book about the Overseas Unit, *Broadcast from the Front*, says 'we all considered [Don] one of us, although he belonged to the air force.' It is also an indication that the armed forces regarded the CBC Overseas Unit as its voice, which is no denigration of Don Fairbairn's many broadcasts. The fact of the matter is that in total war the war correspondents were propagandists. Censorship saw to that. Every report, every broadcast had to be passed by the censor, and there would have been serious consequences if any had been transmitted without the censor's stamp of approval. Letters were checked and any offending remarks were scissored out, and some arrived looking like cut-out paper doilies.

I was first of the new wave of CBC war correspondents to descend on London and the Overseas Unit. Paul Dupuis, with whom I was supposed to have travelled, was next; he was from the announce staff in Montreal, and he was to be the French-language equivalent of Gerry Wilmot in doing features and providing information and entertainment for the Canadian troops. Paul, who was a big handsome guy, knew hardly any English when he arrived in London, but he stayed on after the war to become a British film star, playing opposite Margaret Lockwood on a number of occasions. Andrew Cowan, from the talks department in Toronto, followed soon after; it was the beginning of an eleven-year assignment for him, since he was in charge of the London office of the CBC from 1946 to 1954.

In early May Bert Powley, who was to be our boss, arrived. It was not till towards the end of June that Matthew Halton got to London; he was to be the CBC's senior war correspondent, but he had been delayed because of finishing his book of memoirs, *Ten Years to Alamein*. Halton was already a famous journalist and broadcaster; he had been the correspondent of the *Toronto Star* and had covered the Nazi menace and the war from its beginning, his last assignment was with the Eighth Army in North Africa. At about the same time, Marcel Ouimet, Benoit Lafleur, and Paul Barrette, all of whom were with the Montreal news room, came over to join the Overseas Unit. They were to be the French-language broadcasters, although Marcel, who headed the news-room, which was a combined English-French news room in those days, could and did double in English.

Arthur Holmes had been Powley's companion crossing the Atlantic, and their convoy had run not into a storm as we had but into a wolf pack of U-boats; several ships, some said as many as fourteen, were sunk. Holmes was actually returning to London and the Overseas Unit, which he had helped to set up; he was the engineer who joined Bob Bowman on the *Aquitania* and crossed the Atlantic with the 1st Canadian Division in December 1939. He looked after the heavy disc-recording equipment – a standard studio unit weighing fully half a ton was all that was available – and it was with this equipment that Bowman recorded life on board ship and made the first broadcast from overseas.

The CBC described this broadcast, which was 'beamed' to Canada, as 'a unique departure in wartime news coverage.' It was certainly the first time that the actual sounds of a troop movement, of life aboard ship, of the men marching ashore, had been broadcast, mostly the result of the recordings that Art Holmes cut in the rolling motion of a ship at sea. It was an extraordinary feat, since, to this date, disc recording had been done only on a perfectly level turntable. Holmes was not content with being just an operator, and he designed the mobile studios and the portable recording units that we were to use at the front. He was a remarkably creative engineer, and much of the sucess of the CBC's coverage of the war was due to him. As Bert Powley said, 'It was largely through him that the CBC came to excel in broadcasting the sounds of battle.'

From the earliest days of the crystal set, Arthur Holmes was fascinated by 'wireless.' After high school he took a radio operator's course and worked for ten years on all manner of ships; he joined the Canadian Radio Broadcasting Commission, the forerunner of the CBC, when it was set up in 1933 and took further radio courses. He also learned to fly and had been offered a commission in the RCAF when he was assigned to go overseas with Bob Bowman. At the time, Holmes was the senior operator for outside broadcasts and had been in charge of the technical side of the 1939 royal tour. He should have become general manager or president of the CBC; after all, the corporation was run for years by engineers, Dr Augustin Frigon, Donald Manson, and Alphonse Ouimet. So why not Arthur Holmes? Was it because he was not in the establishment clique, not an elitist?

It soon became evident that there would have to be something better than the studio recording equipment if the CBC was to cover the Canadian troops in action, and it was fully expected that the 1st Division would soon be joining the British Expeditionary Force (BEF) in France. When Bowman and Holmes visited the Canadian camps in England, the only way they could get the heavy unit there so Bowman could interview the troops was in a van, and it was often difficult to hire a van. Holmes decided that if he was to assess what kind of equipment would be needed he would have to go to the front, and in January 1940 he toured the Maginot Line and the BEF positions, where the British were standing guard in trenches. Even in the case of the static phoney war, which he did not believe could last long, Holmes felt that the first thing that the CBC Overseas Unit should have was a vehicle that would have turntables and its own power supply: a mobile recording studio.

So he hurried back to London and arranged an early passage to Halifax. At the beginning of 1940 Canada was just tooling up for war production, but in the Ford plant at Windsor, Ontario, Holmes found what he was looking for – the chassis of a vehicle that was to become a regimental first-aid post, a small hospital on wheels. It would make an ideal mobile studio. He had one ordered, to be built to his specifications, the custom-fitted electronic equipment to be designed and constructed by the very capable engineering department of the CBC in Montreal. Holmes was greatly aided in the devising and construction of this radio recording van by Ernest Bushnell, director of programs; he had gone to London at the beginning of March 1940 to make arrangements for the CBC's coverage of the war, and he agreed with the need for a mobile studio. In fact, Bushnell kept sending messages to Holmes to hurry up with the vehicle and get it over in time to go to France with the 1st Canadian Division.

Just before he was due to return to Canada, Bushnell was disappointed to hear that the recording van could not be shipped before 1 May. It would not be ready in time for the Canadians' move to France, which, he was told, would be on 15 May; however, this move was postponed to 1 June. Bushnell reached Halifax on 12 May, about the same time that Holmes returned to London. On 10 May the Nazi Blitzkrieg struck. On 15 May Holland was overrun and the Dutch gave up; on 28 May the Belgian army capitulated. By 4 June the evacuation of the British Expeditionary Force from Dunkirk was completed. Arthur Holmes had arrived back in good time to pick up his pride and creation, the big, grey recording van, at Tilbury dock and drive it to London. He parked it by Broadcasting House. It was fully equipped, with three turntables, which meant there could be endless recording, as well as play-back facilities. As Powley wrote, 'One could dub from disc to disc, edit, and, in fact produce a finished programme ready to be fed into the short wave transmitters without leaving her spacious interior.' There was nothing like it in the whole of England. The BBC staff came down to gawk at the monster; they named it 'Big Betsy.'

There was a further delay in the movement of the 1st Canadian Division to France, but by 10 June it was on its way. The only Canadian formation to cross the channel, however, was the First Brigade, which landed at Brest; but after a few chaotic days, during which it never met the enemy, it was ordered to withdraw, and it was back in England on 17 June. Big Betsy was supposed to accompany the Canadians to France but was never given permission to leave London. Instead, the huge van did yeoman service on the 'home front.' It may have missed the Battle of France but it was in the thick of the Battle of Britain. The mobile studio, which had the very latest electronic equipment, gave the members of the Overseas Unit a great deal of freedom; if they could not get recording time from the BBC, they could use the turntables in the van; and they could go anywhere, at any time. I drove in Betsy all the way to Leith, the port of Edinburgh, to record the return of the first prisoners of war.

However, Big Betsy's greatest claim to fame was during the Blitz. Art Holmes, whom Powley described as being 'passionately addicted to the recording of sound,' was determined to get the whole ghastly symphony of the Nazi raids on a disc, the wailing of the sirens, the drone of the appproaching enemy bombers, the crack and crunch of anti-aircraft artillery fire, the slap and splatter of falling shrapnel, the whistling scream of the bombs, and the earth-shattering roar of the explosions.

So Holmes set out night after night in the big van for Hyde Park or Regent's Park, the best open spaces away from buildings that could come crashing down. He put the mike outside, on top of the van, and sat for hours inside, wearing the headphones and his steel helmet, listening to and recording the sounds of the Blitz; he said that he did not think it was particularly dangerous, because he figured the odds on a direct hit were long. He was more afraid of the shrapnel from the anti-aircraft guns tearing a hole in the van and smashing the equipment, but Betsy emerged scarred but unbroken. He wanted to get close to a bomb blast but not so close as to make the needle jump. His recordings of the Blitz were the finest ever made, and dubbings of them have been used and are still being used in films, without any credit ever being given to Arthur Holmes.

The Blitz overlapped the Battle of Britain, where the German attempt to knock out Britain's air defences was defeated by the 'few,' but it is generally said to have started on 7 September 1940 with a double raid, in the afternoon and at night. The saturation bombing of London went on for months, but the two heavy raids on the nights of 10 May and 13 May 1941 were really the last and were considered to be the end of the Blitz. After that, there were sporadic attacks – including, much later, the 'Little Blitz' in the winter of 1943–4 – but nothing to interest a recording fanatic like Art Holmes. He became bored. It would be a long time before the Canadian forces would leave Britain. That was apparent, and Holmes began to realize that Betsy would be too big to accompany the army into action, even at the level of divisional headquarters; a mobile studio was needed, but it had to be smaller, it had to be a vehicle that the forward echelons would accept. And, if they wanted to get the sound of battle, they would have to have portable recording equipment which could be carried on a jeep or, if necessary, manhandled to the scene of combat.

In the summer of 1941, after the German invasion of Russia, Holmes returned to Canada to work on plans for the new equipment that would be needed when the Allies went on the offensive. He found what he wanted in the army's HUP, Heavy Utility Personnel carrier, about the size of a four-wheel-drive station-wagon; there was room enough for three turntables, for amplifiers, for a regular sound mixer that Holmes said had four inputs, and for batteries and a charger unit. The HUP was converted into a mobile studio with all the facilities that Betsy had but half its bulk. The so-called portable recording equipment consisted of two large boxes weighing fully eighty pounds; it was usually carried on a jeep and, since it had no power source of its own, was run off the jeep's battery. The two boxes could be manhandled (as we later manhandled them into Sicily), and Art said that he had, with some assistance, actually carried them into action; they had to take along with them an automobile or motor cycle battery to provide power. The first box had a twelve-inch turntable and an amplifier with six or eight vacuum tubes (this was before transistors were invented); the second box held the motor generator and had two leads outside to clip on to a six-volt battery. With the HUP mobile studio and the portable gear, Powley said, 'no part of the battle-field would be inaccessible to our micropohones.'

When Art Holmes reached London with Bert Powley in May 1943, his work in re-equipping the CBC Overseas Unit was finished, and he was able to report that the smaller versions of Betsy, the HUP vans, as well as the new portable recording equipment, were on their way across the Atlantic. Eventually, there would be three of these front-line mobile studios: one in Italy, one in France, and the third held as a spare in London together with Big Betsy.

4

'Eyes Front' and All That

London, 1 March 1943:
Allies advance in Russia and North Africa but suffer heavy losses to U-boats in Atlantic.

O nce I had got my accreditation as a war correspondent from Canadian Military Headquarters (CMHQ), which was in the Sun Life building next door to Canada House, Trafalgar Square, I was sent to Burberry's in the Haymarket to be outfitted in a manner becoming my high status, or so I believed. Not only was there the walking-out uniform of an officer but a couple of battle-dresses that were also made to measure. The wardrobe included a smart Burberry raincoat with a detachable woollen lining and a 'British warm,' the stylish short overcoat worn by high-ranking officers, higher than the war correspondent's rank of honorary captain. There were also half a dozen khaki shirts, half a dozen ties, half a dozen pairs of socks, a Sam Browne belt, a peak cap, a wedge cap, and shoes, as well as riding boots and breeches. In *Broadcast from the Front,* Powley said, 'The cut and fit of the breeches had to be tested on a wooden horse that had been bestridden by generations of cavalry officers including, according to what one of our men was told, the great Duke of Wellington himself.'

I took the breeches but ordinary boots instead of the riding boots. Bob Bowman and Art Holmes accepted both, however, and there is a picture of them in full regalia, looking like a couple of jaunty cavalry officers of the First World War (at the beginning of the Second World War, British officers did dress like their counterparts of the First World War). Powley was horrified by the lavish way in which the CBC correspondents were being outfitted and put a stop to it, which, he admitted ruefully, was hurting himself as well as the later recruits to the Overseas Unit. I wore the raincoat for ten years after the war, and the 'British warm' into the sixties. I never wore the breeches; I thought my daughter, a keen horsewoman, would like them, but she said they were too heavy; I gave them away, and they are probably being used to this day; they would never wear out.

Such fine attire was to be worn in London or at a parade, not at the front. I was glad to have it, since I had landed with a suitcase and had only a tweed jacket and a pair of flannel pants; the trunk with the rest of my clothes was to follow overseas but never reached me; it must have gone down. I was issued a regular army battledress which was of a darker, coarser material than the Burberry one and had been treated with chemicals to protect against mustard gas. The authorities were still afraid of a gas attack, and all correspondents were issued with gas masks. (We had to carry them ashore with us when we landed in Sicily on 10 July 1943, but the troops soon got rid of these rather bulky bits of extra baggage and the beaches were littered with discarded gas masks. That was the last I saw of mine). Tropical kit, shorts and safari shirt, was also issued by the army.

I was not surprised at being dressed by Burberry, since I expected that war correspondents should get the best. After all, there were only half a dozen accredited British war correspondents in the First World War, and all were offered knighthoods at the end of the war, or so I read. As war correspondents we had the rank of honorary captain, which was a heritage of the First World

War and was not high enough in the view of Fred Griffin of the *Toronto Star*, who felt that the senior correspondents, such as he – he was older than most of us – should have the rank of honorary brigadier. I soon learned that in the Second World War the war correspondent was not an exclusive profession. That was apparent when I attended my first army briefing; the conference room was full of reporters, most of them in uniform – you could wear civilian clothes or uniform in England. There must have been a score of Canadian war correspondents when I got to London in February 1943, and more were on their way.

(The war correspondents' handbook, which was given each of us on accreditation, had abbreviated histories of Canada's participation in the First World War and in the Second up to 1943. It listed the Canadian casualties at Dieppe as 619 killed, 591 wounded, 263 missing, and 1,897 taken prisoner – actually, more than 1,000 were killed or died of wounds of the 5,000 from the 2nd Canadian Division who took part in the attack; only 2,200 returned to the United Kingdom. More than half the force was lost. There was no way of hiding the disaster, although the handbook tried to make the best of it by claiming that the Germans lost 170 planes, just 100 more than they really lost. The nightmare of Dieppe was always at the back of our minds when we thought about the next action, the coming invasion of Europe.

Aside from the abbreviated histories, and biographies of Lieutenant-General A.G.L. McNaughton, GOC-in-C of the First Canadian Army, and a few other senior officers, the handbook had some useful tips for war correspondents on saluting – salute only when saluted – and proper military behaviour – 'don't discuss religion, politics, or women' in an officers' mess. As for deportment when wearing a uniform: 'you will be regarded as a representative of both the newspaper profession and Canada, so don't slouch, keep your hands out of your pockets, don't smoke on a parade ground ...' It was apparent from this admonition that broadcasting was not yet recognized as a news medium by the military brass.)

We were few, however, compared with the British and Americans. Stewart MacPherson, a brash Winnipegger who was with the

BBC war-reporting unit, said that his group went on exercises like the troops and did mock coverage of mock battles. Stew was not the only Canadian to have joined the BBC as a war reporter; Stanley Maxted, a veteran entertainer whose roots went back to the CRBC and before, was another, and he was to gain lasting fame with his broadcasts of the ill-fated Arnhem jump. Stewart MacPherson stayed in London after the war and was for several years a star in British television before returning to Winnipeg; Stanley Maxted also stayed on and had leading roles in West End plays. There were so many war correspondents with the BBC that a wiseacre, possibly MacPherson, said that if there was a Nazi breakthrough, the BBC reporters could be called on to fill the breach. The great numbers of Second World War correspondents meant that they could not be held in the same esteem as their predecessors of the First World War. Still, they had glamour. When he was in London, Lionel Shapiro, who was with the North American Newspaper Alliance and later *Maclean's* magazine, lived at the Savoy Hotel, as did several American correspondents.

Although I could not claim such a prestigious address as Lionel's, I did live in some grandeur before going on the invasion of Sicily. Shortly after arriving in London, I met Wallace Reyburn, correspondent of the *Montreal Standard*, who said that I could have a room in the large flat that he shared with two other fellows. I jumped at the opportunity. It was enormous, occupying the whole top floor of a block of luxury flats in Portland Place. There were two wings, with two large bedrooms separated by a huge marble bathroom in each wing; the dining-room and drawing-room matched the bedrooms in size, and all rooms were luxuriously furnished. There was a separate apartment for the housekeeper, which included her own sitting-room. At a time when it was almost impossible to get a telephone, we had three phones, one in each wing and one in the large hallway.

The flat had been slightly damaged during the Blitz and there was fibreglass instead of glass in the windows; the owners had fled to the country and were only too glad to have someone occupy their flat. As a result, we could live in comfort and splendour, with a housekeeper who provided us with breakfast and dinner, at a whole cost for her wages, rent, food, and utilities of £14 a week, or £3-10-0 each.

London, 28 March 1943:
British Eighth Army drives the Germans from the Mareth Line, which BBC calls the last enemy defences in Africa.

Wallace Reyburn and I shared one bedroom wing while Gibson Parker and Desmond Sheen occupied the other. We were a congenial group with more or less the same interests, since both Parker and Sheen worked for the BBC's European Service. Wally had been on the Dieppe Raid and had written a book about it entitled *Rehearsal for Invasion*; he was the only correspondent with the Canadians to get ashore for any length of time. We used to talk about the raid while sitting in deep leather chairs in front of the electric fire in the drawing room; we wondered what had been achieved at Dieppe and what effect it would have on the coming operations. Now that the Mareth Line was broken, would it be Greece next? Or Sicily? Or Yugoslavia?

Gibson Parker used to bring back dubbings of programs he had produced for the BBC and play them on the combination radio gramophone in the drawing-room (there were four other radios in the flat, one in each bedroom). I remember one amusing evening when we listened to a recording entitled, 'The Briefing,' that Flight Lieutenant Jack Peach had made with his RCAF sidekick, Ray MacNess, which was a devastating satire on the American air force. Jack gave copies of 'The Briefing' as a Christmas present to every RCAF squadron in Britain.

John Kannawin had a top-floor flat on Harley Street, which, while not as grand as Portland Place, was a pretty good address. However, the catch was that the top floors anywhere in London could be got for a song, since they were the ones that would be demolished in any hit; the owners, like ours, had fled and would subsidize anyone to occupy their flats, 'even colonials,' as Kannawin said. 'Others of us,' Bert Powley noted in *Broadcast from the Front*, 'were dotted at a similar elevation around Marylebone, Westminster and Kensington.' The advantage of occupying a top-floor flat was that it provided a magnificent view of an air raid; it was quite a spectacle, with the flash of shell bursts and the searchlights trying to catch the bomber in a cone and the brilliantly coloured parachute flares dropped by the enemy over the target areas, the whole accompanied by the sound of a rolling barrage and the noise of the bomber's engines.

During the Blitz Arthur Holmes was bombed out of his apartment, which was an exception, being the one below the top floor; he had got it before the bombing began. Holmes was in bed at the time and he told me that the noise of the explosion was so loud that it did not register. 'I don't remember hearing it,' he said. 'I remember the room falling apart.' It was a direct hit, and though Holmes was lucky to be alive, he did suffer from the blast. His hearing was impaired and he was advised to learn lip reading, and ever after he insisted on standing in front of the person to whom he was speaking.

By the time I got to London, the CBC had more-or-less permanent quarters at 200 Oxford Street, the annexe of the Peter Robinson department store, which had been badly damaged during the Blitz but had been rebuilt for the BBC. We had a studio in LG2, the subbasement, which was soundproofed with blankets and cluttered with recording equipment, sleeping-bags, and a camp-bed; the deep underground studio was as safe a bomb shelter as the Oxford Street tube station, which was just across the road. There were offices upstairs and a desk for everyone. It had not always been thus.

When Bob Bowman and Art Holmes first came to London in December 1939, the BBC provided them with a small office in Broadcasting House; it was a 'cubby-hole of an office,' in the view of Ernie Bushnell, who found that the top BBC officials did not like having an independent CBC unit but wanted Bowman and company to join their war-reporting team. 'They were still treating us like colonials,' Bushnell said; he soon disabused the BBC of this imperialist scheme, although, he did agree to allow certain CBC personnel, such as Stanley Maxted, to join the BBC war-reporting team, but they would do so as individuals. The CBC Overseas Unit would be quite separate from the BBC.

The first CBC office, the 'cubby-hole,' was hit early in the Blitz, and the BBC found more space in one of its buildings in Langham Street. However, that office was demolished one night when no one was in it. The Germans were after the BBC, and, as Powley wrote, 'Broadcasting House itself, the prime target, stood like a battered Rock of Gibraltar with ruin all around.' The CBC was somehow found new quarters in Broadcasting House, but a parachute mine floated down and wrecked much of the building, including the CBC's new premises. The next move was to a girls' school in Regent's Park which the government had taken over for the duration, but within a few weeks the school was destroyed by incendiary bombs. Finally, in the summer of 1941 the CBC was given quarters in the newly rebuilt building at 200 Oxford Street, which was so conveniently located, not far from Broadcasting House and within easy walking distance of CMHQ, and Canada House – and that was where I found them when I arrived.

The upstairs offices were not very private, since the dividing walls, under the economies of wartime construction, reached only halfway to the ceiling; the conversation in one room could be heard in another. There was a woman next door who talked in superlatives over the telephone. 'My dear,' she would say, 'I have had a most frightful time – absolutely frightful. It was really too disgusting of his secretary not to let us know a little sooner. We had the maddest rush.' A clergyman who looked after the religious programs for part of the BBC's Empire Service had an office somewhere on the floor. He would ring up a colleague in Edinburgh every other day, it seemed, and could be heard throughout the building bellowing frantically into the telephone, 'Ah you theah? I say, ah you theah? Can you heah me?'

It was amid this noisy babble of voices that Andy Cowan and I sat down to plan our contribution to a new series of patriotic programs on the coast-to-coast network of the CBC to be entitled

'Eyes Front.' The producers in Toronto thought that an interview with a prominent person would be the ideal way of starting each show; it should be an informal interview, according to the directive, in the person's home, before his hearth. Obviously, they had Roosevelt's 'fireside chats' in mind. Andy and I agreed that the best possible person to open the series would be George Bernard Shaw. Who else? But how to get in touch with him? He had no phone at Ayot St Lawrence. We decided that we would have to write to him. We were not very hopeful, but we felt that if we devised some interesting questions, he might participate, especially since we would be going to his house to record the interview.

We worked all morning on the questions. Although Andy was a talks producer, I was the one who signed the letter and mailed it to G.B.S. Perhaps it was because I was a distant relative, my mother being a Shaw; then, too, I had had a brief encounter with the great man – or a non-encounter. When I was with the *Daily Herald* just before the war, there was a report that Bernard Shaw was suffering from anaemia, and I was sent around to Whitehall Mansions, where he had a flat, to find out if he was taking liver extract. I knocked on the door, which was opened by a nurse who politely but firmly told me that Mr Shaw was asleep – it was late at night – and that she could not comment on what medication, if any, he was receiving.

A couple of days later, the mail included a reply from Bernard Shaw: inside a stamped envelope neatly addressed to me in his handwriting was the separate sheet of paper on which we had typed the questions. Beside the first question, 'What do you think of Canada's war effort?' he had written in red ink, 'I don't think about it.' And beside the other questions and subquestions, which had to do with what was going to happen in the postwar world, he had written six times in red ink, 'I don't know.' His reply concluded with the following, also in red ink:

I have nothing worth listening to to say to Canada just now.
I never bore the public with impertinent messages.
In short, dear c.b.c., nothing doing.

G. Bernard Shaw
Ayot St Lawrence, Welwyn,
Herts.   13th. May 1943.

We chortled over the way he had turned us down, and I dined
out on Bernard Shaw's reply for years afterwards. At least he had
let us know promptly, and Andy Cowan and I were grateful. We
lined up a number of prominent people to introduce the weekly
'Eyes Front' programs, including H.G. Wells, Lady Astor, J.B.
Priestley, Harold Laski, and the dean of Canterbury. The producers in Toronto seemed pleased with the interviews; at least
they said nothing.

All the interviews were recorded on Big Betsy's turntables, with
the microphone on a long cord in the person's living room. I asked
Priestley if he would like to hear a play-back of our interview. He
gladly accepted, and he sat in the van with the earphones on and
listened to every word. Apparently, it was the first time that he
had ever heard himself. He had done countless talks for the BBC's
North American Service and had become the voice of wartime
Britain in Canada and the United States; while most of these
broadcasts were 'live,' many if not all of them must have been
recorded. Yet the BBC producers never invited him to listen to a
play-back; they may have been afraid that he would want to make
some change or do it again, or they may have simply conformed to
the general BBC attitude that it was not quite right to let a
broadcaster hear what he or she had said.

I rang up H.G. Wells. I remember hearing a rather high-pitched
querulous voice agreeing to the interview, but when I spoke of its
being informal, a fireside chat, he insisted that a list of questions
should be sent to him. Alec MacDonald, the engineer, drove the
recording van around to his house, one of a row of Regency houses
on the edge of Regent's Park and the only one occupied, since the
owners of the others had fled. We set up the microphone in the
dining-room, which was the front room and closest to the van.
Wells had my questions and his answers neatly typed out and in
a binder, with my part underlined in green and his underlined in

red. Most of the interview, which was five to six minutes long and is preserved in the National Archives, was about his novel, *Of Things to Come*, and his view of the future. I asked him if the war could go on for so long that the armies would degenerate into bands of ragged guerrillas fighting among the ruins, as they did in his book. H.G. Wells replied:

Unless a world wide equalitarian control is established, this is what the world may come to. My *Of Things to Come* was a warning rather than a prophecy.

P.S.: Would you mind explaining what you mean by a world wide equalitarian control?

H.G.W.: I think of it as something added to over and above the existing national and imperial governments. Plainly, this war cannot end in another Treaty of Versailles. A great number of things could only be put straight by world wide commissions holding authority from the governments engaged ... There is, in short, [the need for] the complete modernization of the economic life of the world. Existing competitive governments and competitive business organizations are incapable of this. A super control has become imperatively necessary.

As a Utopian socialist, Wells looked into the future and hoped 'for the disappearance of financial control and large fortunes, for an expiration of snobbism, for equalitarian good manners, [for] more collective feeding and less domestic drudgery.' After the recording, Wells offered us a glass of port; he had none, since he was a diabetic. 'You don't realize that you are talking to a famous man,' he said. 'I am president of the British Diabetic Association.' He seemed to treat his disease as clinically as a doctor would, in keeping with his desire to be known as a scientist rather than an author: he had a science degree from the University of London and had taught science before becoming a writer.

The greatest gift of science, in his view, was a ripe and pleasant old age. Wells was seventy-seven years old at the time of the interview and was enjoying life despite his diabetes. Science had made this possible, and he said: 'Not so long ago, a man was old when he was forty – old and stinking as well. His teeth, if not his body, were rotten, and he never had a bath. The mediaeval town was a filthy, evil-smelling place, a breeding ground for vermin and disease. Life was shorter, and it was lived much younger. Romeo and Juliet would never have been allowed to marry nowadays because they would have been under the legal age.'

'Eyes Front' was a delightful diversion. Most of my work with the CBC Overseas Unit was reporting on the Canadian troops, visiting their camps, and covering their endless exercises, which were rehearsals for the real thing, as all exercises were. But when would the curtain rise? When would the balloon go up? That is what the rank and file wanted to know. They had been waiting around too long for the battle to begin.

After Dunkirk and the fall of France, the onus for the defence of the United Kingdom had fallen on the shoulders of the Canadians, who were the only fully equipped troops left in Britain. They were the guardians of the island fortress, they held high the torch of freedom, or so the editorials said, and that was gratifying during the first few months when an attack was expected any day. It was not such a thrill when the danger passed, and the Nazis turned towards eastern Europe and the Soviet Union. The Canadian troops were stationed in the most vulnerable part of the country, the south coast, and they remained there for so long that the counties of Sussex, Hampshire, and Surrey became known as the Canadian country.

The morale of the Canadian army had reached its lowest point in the spring of 1943. According to an officer of the judge advocate general's branch: 'There are thousands of young Canadians who have become jail birds purely and simply due to the fact that they are fed up with sitting round doing the same old training all the time. They should be counted among the casualties of this war, but they won't.' Actually, when everything was considered, the number of crimes committed was remarkably low.

It was as if they were in a peace-time army, with all its dull and settled routines; only they were at war and far from home. Some of them had been separated from their families for more than three years, and it was therefore hardly surprising that marriages should break up. Not much was written about the heartbreak and anguish of the many Canadian women who were left behind and were abandoned. The only way the troops could stay in touch with their loved ones in Canada was by mail, and the Canadian army postal service was shockingly bad. (There were the programs that Gerry Wilmot did for the CBC English network, and later Paul Dupuis for the French network, which included messages from individuals in the armed forces, but nothing could replace mail.) I got to London in mid-February 1943 but I did not get a letter from my mother and father till 8 April, more than seven weeks later. The wire I sent on 15 February saying that I had arrived safely took a week to reach them in Victoria.

The Canadian troops in England were on the verge of mutiny over their poor mail service in the summer of 1942, according to historian Philip Smith. The trouble was that we were entirely dependent on the British and Americans to fly the mail across the Atlantic, and in his book *It Seems Like Only Yesterday*, an account of the first fifty years of Air Canada, Smith reported that in October 1942 there was a two-ton mountain of forces' mail piled up at Shediac, NB, unable to find passage with BOAC or Pan Am. This was a disgraceful situation, brought about by the contemptuous disregard for Canada by the major western powers. Not even the redoubtable C.D. Howe, minister of munitions and supply and Prime Minister King's wartime production czar, could pry loose a plane from the Allies to fly the mail to England. He tried to get four Douglas C-54s from the United States, but the Americans said they could not be spared. It was the same story when he approached the British; they turned down his request for the loan of a couple of Liberators.

Finally, Howe decided that Canada would have to fly its own mail to England; he impounded a British Lancaster bomber, which had been brought over to serve as a pattern for production at a Toronto factory. He had it modified to carry a few passengers and mail and with it inaugurated what was called the Canadian Government Trans-Atlantic Service, which was really the beginning of a Canadian international airline. The first non-stop flight from Montreal to Britain carried three passengers and 2,600 pounds of forces' mail in July 1943. After that date the mail service improved, and I noted that an airgraph that I sent to my parents on 6 August 1943 from Algiers was received on 27 August. Three weeks to a month was about the average length of time a letter took to cross the Atlantic, although by 1944 that figure was cut down to two weeks in most cases. One airletter of mine posted on 27 April in Italy was received in Victoria on 4 May.

On 1 March 1943, shortly after I arrived in England, I sent a PLT, a postal letter telegram, which cost me half a crown, to my brother, Sergeant Richard Stursberg, the best-trained soldier who never got overseas – he was turned down for active service because he was near-sighted and wore glasses! 'I want you to keep sending me a thousand cigarettes a month under the BC Overseas Tobacco Fund,' I wrote. 'This is the best fund of its kind in Canada as the cigarettes are shipped in bulk and insured. You put the order in Vancouver and all I get is a slip of paper which entitles me to go and draw a thousand cigarettes from British Columbia House [in London]. This way they cannot get lost.' I smoked and almost everyone I knew overseas smoked, and the government encouraged smoking by shipping cigarettes to the troops at little or no cost. We were not aware of the health hazards of smoking then, and, if we had known, it would have made no difference. Even those few who did not smoke took advantage of the governments' tobacco funds because cigarettes made good presents. Later, at the end of the war, they became a form of currency.

Food parcels were welcomed by the troops but took a long time to come, with the result that some items, such as oranges, which were not available to adults in Britain, perished. In an early letter home I wrote that I found the food in London to be 'surprisingly good.' 'It is rather on the plain side and I do miss such things as fruit juices and nuts as well as milk chocolates.' But when my mother sent me chocolates, they arrived as a sticky mess, and I asked her not to send any more. Canned goods were the best travellers, and they were much appreciated, especially the new canned meat called Spam. Delectable Spam – it was so much better than bully beef.

It was beautiful country, this south of England where the Canadians were stationed, especially in the spring and early summer time, and there were many great manor houses and mansions, the stately homes of song and story. They had been taken over by the government, and most of them served as billets for the armed forces. In fact, my visits to the Canadian camps became a tour of the stately homes – only they were not as they had been in their prime; all the furnishings had been removed, as well as the paintings, tapestries, and works of art, and the panelling and even the floors had been taken up, so that the rooms were as bare as barrack rooms. All the chandeliers were gone, replaced by naked bulbs.

Yet they still had some remnants of their stately selves. They varied from manor houses of brick and Elizabethan or Regency architecture to ducal palaces of stone and Classical or Palladian design; most had imposing gateways and long, tree-lined driveways leading through great parks which were still beautifully kept. I remember waking up in my camp-bed one morning and looking out the mullioned window at a stone mandolin player; it was a gargoyle on the concert room of a mansion that was a divisional headquarters. At another estate, which served as corps headquarters, there was a clock tower whose bells played a hymn every hour; my recollection is that it was 'Lead, Kindly Light.'

5

Ordeal of General McNaughton

London, 15 March 1943:
Canadians under General A.G.L. McNaughton in invasion test.
British say they achieved all objectives.

M y first real job as a war correspondent was Exercise Spartan,
the biggest manoeuvres ever held in Britain. There were all
kinds of exercises – too many, in the view of the Canadian troops,
who were tired of all this training for action that never seemed to
come; they varied from small demonstrations of a company or a
battalion to a full divisional landing practice on a cold, rain-swept
beach to Exercise Spartan, where whole armies were involved. I
remember the landing practice, not because of the wretched, chilly
conditions but because of the way that some British Tommies, in
what appeared to be regular conversation, used the four-letter
obscenity after almost every word and sometimes between words
– it was truly an 'extra-fuckin'-ordinary' performance.

Exercise Spartan (4–12 March 1943) pitted the 'Second British
Army,' really the First Canadian Army under Lieutenant General
A.G.L. McNaughton, advancing from a bridgehead in the south of
England, dubbed 'Southland,' against the enemy, a British army

commanded by Lieutenant-General J.A.H. Gammell and called the 'German Sixth Army' (shades of Stalingrad), defending 'Eastland,' the counties north of the Thames, and holding prepared positions around London. The object of the exercise, according to the official hand-out, was to 'practise the advance from a bridgehead and the control of air forces operating with the army.' However, Spartan was more than this prosaic military description, and there was excited speculation that it was the rehearsal for the invasion of Europe and the opening of the much-discussed Second Front. As the west of England, 'Westland,' had been given the role of a neutral country in the exercise, some correspondents thought that Spartan might be preparation for the invasion of Spain, since Portugal was a neutral country and France the enemy-occupied country.

It seemed to me that they were reading too much into the organization of these war games, and that making Westland a neutral country whose neutrality was to be respected was merely meant to limit the field of operation. Such limitation was needed, although it did concentrate the attacking Canadian army on fewer roads and made for horrendous traffic jams when the natural water barrier of the Thames was reached. The thousands of vehicles that make up an armoured corps stretched for miles and miles through the English countryside; the tanks, their motors roaring, lurched and skidded along the winding streets of the little villages and, wonder of wonders, did no more damage than knock a few bricks loose. But the tanks could not stay on the cobblestone roads; they had to deploy, and I watched half a dozen Canadian tanks chase some enemy armoured cars over the rolling farm fields; they flattened the hedges, left deep furrows, and mashed the new-grown wheat.

There were many such incidents, and, as might be expected, the farmers did not appreciate Exercise Spartan. I ran into a farmer who was literally speechless with rage: an armoured squadron had just disappeared over the hill after breaking down his fence and churning up his fields. He was carrying a shotgun, and he fumed: 'If they come back, I'll shoot them, so 'elp me, I will.' Of course, the farmers were recompensed for the damage done; in fact, compensation officers followed closely behind the marauding machines, cheque-books in hand. The cost? No one worried about that during the war.

Above all, Spartan was a test of the engineers with the Canadian army and their bridge-building skills. I watched them laying a deck on pontoons that had been manoeuvred into position across the Thames near Wallingford; their work was being constantly interrupted by 'dive-bombing' enemy planes; if the sappers did not take cover, they would be declared casualties by the umpires. A defending army always destroys communications as it falls back, and the umpires declared that gaps had been blown in most of the bridges and roads cratered, which kept the RCE busy. By the time the exercise was over on Monday, 12 March 1943, the roads and bridges in the countryside around London were littered with Bailey bridges. In fact, there were reports that the reason for the inconclusive ending – the Canadian army had entered enemy territory but was still some distance from the enemy capital of Huntingdon – was that the attacking force had used up its oil quota or had run out of bridging material.

It was a good story, Exercise Spartan: the military wanted publicity and to that end provided transportation and facilities and let the correspondents have a free hand in finding out what was going on. We lived with an army on the move, camped out, ate boiled bacon and hard tack for breakfast, and learned a lot that would stand us in good stead in the real war, especially how to read maps, since every signpost in England had been removed. I remember spending a whole day looking for a divisional headquarters, untying ourselves from convoys, and asking vainly for information; it turned out we had been given the wrong co-ordinates.

The removal of signposts at the time of Dunkirk and the invasion scare was surely one of the craziest defence measures ever taken; it was meant to confuse the enemy, but all it did was confuse and infuriate the inhabitants. Anyone travelling by train, the main means of transportation, could get lost and did get lost, since one station looked like another, especially in the blackout. We had maps and got around all right (except for that one day during Exercise Spartan when we were given the wrong coordinates), but returning to London in a vehicle was another matter: there were no street signs and we spent hours driving around in circles, trying to find out where we were.

When I was writing my final report on Spartan, John Kannawin came into the office and said to me that I had better go easy on what I was saying, since he had heard that the Canadians had not done well. I was shocked, because we had been told by General McNaughton that the Canadian and British forces under him had broken through the enemy front and all that was left was a hike to Huntingdon, but I knew that Kannawin had developed contacts in the BBC who were close to Whitehall. The subsequent conference at British GHQ, where the umpires' report was presented, more or less supported the Canadian army commander's claim. Yet it soon became apparent that Exercise Spartan was not a triumph for General McNaughton but his downfall.

It is hard to realize now the high regard in which General McNaughton was held in the early years of the war. There had been persistent reports that he would be the Allied commander-in-chief when one was appointed, and even up to the time of Exercise Spartan he was considered to be one of the men most likely to lead the assault on Europe. As a Canadian, he would be a logical choice because of American and British rivalries – or so it was said – and he had had a distinguished career. A brigadier-general in the First World War, he had commanded corps artillery and was credited with devising the 'creeping barrage,' although he always denied this. He was also a noted scientist, joint inventor of the cathode ray direction finder, and president of the National Research Council, 1935–9.

A charismatic figure, Andy McNaughton was more than the 'commander-in-chief,' as we called him; he was the father of the Canadian army. I wrote at the time, 'He was a hero, a legend to us, the soldier-scientist who was more of a scientist than a soldier and yet, we felt, would be a greater soldier than a scientist. He was what McArthur was to the Americans in those hysterical days after the fall of the Philippines, and yet he had never even had a Bataan. There was Dieppe, of course, but somehow we never connected McNaughton with that.' It could also be said that he was what Kitchener was to the British in the First World War, and a dramatic Canadian war bond poster of McNaughton had great emotional and sales appeal.

Richard S. Malone, the late publisher and editor-in-chief of the *Globe and Mail*, Toronto, was among those who built McNaughton up as the 'Kitchener of Canada' but after he became secretary to Colonel J.L. Ralston, the minister of national defence, was among the first to turn against him.

The publicity surrounding General McNaughton and the way that the press, not only the Canadian but the British press, played him up as a possible Allied commander-in-chief did not go down well with the military powers in Whitehall. Then, there was his insistence on the independence and integrity of the Canadian army and, as a result, he was being seen increasingly as a threat to the imperial war plans.

In 1963, when I was preparing a program on the twentieth anniversary of the landing in Sicily, the first Canadian action, I sought out the former chief of the imperial general staff (CIGS), General Sir Alan Brooke, who played a prominent part in McNaughton's removal as GOC-in-C of the First Canadian Army. Although unwell, Field Marshal the Viscount Alanbrooke (as he had become) agreed to a recorded interview in his home outside London. He was suffering from an embolism and had to keep his leg up on a footstool but otherwise was in full command. Lord Alanbrooke was considered to be the master strategist of the Second World War; he was said to have an iron will and was one of the few military leaders who could and did argue with Churchill and refuse to go along with some of his schemes. I got the impression that the former CIGS was anxious to talk about McNaughton; in a way it was like a testament, and it proved to be his last testament, since he died within a few weeks of the interview.

'I knew McNaughton from the First World War,' Lord Alanbrooke said, 'because he was my counter-battery staff officer, and he was absolutely brilliant. But the difference between a counter-battery staff officer and the GOC of an army is a hell of a step simply, and to my mind, he just couldn't make that grade there.

He was too much underneath the lorries looking at the shock absorbers or dealing with some rather junior person and not the senior ones.' His use of the possessive was peculiar, since Major Brooke, as he was then, and McNaughton, who was a lieutenant-colonel, were fellow artillery staff officers with the Canadian Corps in the First World War. Their relationship became strained; they had serious disagreements over the siting of guns, and, according to John Swettenham, McNaughton's biographer, from then on 'they had seldom seen eye-to-eye.' Lord Alanbrooke spoke of McNaughton's creating 'the greatest hoo-ha' over the 1st Canadian Division's landing in France in 1940. 'For some reason, I don't know why, he [McNaughton] was terribly upset in the way it was used, in the way it was broken up, to be put into ships, to be landed on the far side by brigade groups. I mean you can't put a whole blooming division [into a ship] and take it out like that. The first time I met him he went into a flaming rage about the way his division was being treated, and I said your division is being treated exactly and identically as every other division in the Second Corps, every other division in the [British] Expeditionary Force. Well, that pacified him.'

Alanbrooke was in charge of the forlorn British attempt, after Dunkirk, to help the French stave off the German advance, and his main task, as he said in the interview, was to extricate the battered remnants of the BEF and the few troops that crossed the channel to join him. Only the First Brigade of the 1st Canadian Division landed in France, and after moving some distance inland by train, it was turned around and sent back to England without making any contact with the enemy.

There was no mention in McNaughton's biography of any trouble over the 1st Canadian Division's going to France, but the general was upset over the way that Alanbrooke tried to break up the brigade and put smaller units under British command. He told Alanbrooke that the Canadians were not to be used as if they were British troops, and that they were to remain under Canadian command. He might have put it rather strongly, but the British commander never seemed quite to understand this. There was a revealing slip of the tongue during the interview, when Lord

Alanbrooke wondered when McNaughton was removed from his command by the 'Secretary of State for War.' He might have meant the Canadian defence minister, but then?

When he was CIGS, Lord Alanbrooke decided to test General McNaughton's ability to command an army in the field. 'I gave him one of the biggest exercises we had in England where there was a crossing of the Thames,' he said. 'That was Exercise Spartan.' Alanbrooke was supposed to have complained that, at a critical time during the manoeuvres, McNaughton had left his headquarters to help build a bridge, and that was not what an army commander should be doing. Apparently, this did happen, but John Swettenham said that the progress in bridging on that day was essential to the success of McNaughton's plan of attack, and that, in any case, the general was in constant touch with his headquarters. In the interview, Alanbrooke put it differently:

I went around to his headquarters, and I said to old Andy, 'Well, Andy, how are you getting on?' 'Oh,' he said, 'I'm having a hell of a day. I'm bridging the Thames.' I said, 'I'm delighted that you're doing that. Where are you doing it?' 'I'm bridging it here, and it's going to be the devil of a bridge,' he said. I said, 'Now, all right, your bridge is built, what's your object in having it there?' He said, 'What do you mean?' I said, 'You're not building a bridge in the blue without some jolly good object for it?' 'Can't you see it's a bridging exercise,' he said. 'And the whole thing is to get this bridge across the river here.' I said,'I don't see that it's much use putting a bridge across unless you are going to make use of it.' He had not got a plan of what he wanted to do with the ruddy old bridge. He got so locked up in the technical problem of building a bridge across the Thames that he had lost altogether the object of it.

Then, I remember the next thing he did, he moved the whole of the armoured division's supply column right across old [I Canadian Corps commander] Harry Crerar's lines of communication. Because I went to see him next. 'God, how am I getting on,' he [Crerar] said. 'I've got the whole of Andy McNaughton's armoured division coming across my lines of communication. I've just sent extra food for twenty-four hours to see us through.' He [Crerar] was in a hell of a state over this.

It was probable that Lord Alanbrooke was referring to the new and inexperienced II Canadian Corps, and the breakdown in communications led to a dreadful traffic snarl and virtual gridlock at the Thames. General Sir Bernard Paget, commander of the British Home Forces, wanted the II Corps commander, Lieutenant-General E.W. Sansom, fired, but McNaughton refused, saying that it would be unfair to blame Sansom for everything that went wrong, because he had a new staff and new equipment. Actually, McNaughton himself was responsible for much of the mess during Exercise Spartan, because he had insisted on having II Canadian Corps take part when it had only just been formed. It would have been better for him if, in the first place, he had accepted the experienced British corps that he had been offered. The trouble was that McNaughton seemed to feel that the main value of Spartan was in the training it provided, in bridge building, for example, not a test of armies in the field and of his ability to command. Lord Alanbrooke said:

He hadn't got it in him, McNaughton. He had the scientific side developed to a very, very, very high degree, and was streets ahead of most people. I know when he was counter-battery officer during the First World War, I never knew where the hell he was going to with some of his air burst ranging operations. With that all, he just missed, to my mind. But he took it frightfully badly, which hurt us all very much. We tried to put it to him, we saw his Secretary of State [presumably the defence minister, Colonel J.L. Ralston], explained it to him, he went into it, we saw Harry Crerar, we saw all, they all went into it. Then, finally he was removed back [home]. I couldn't get there myself but I sent a general especially to Liverpool to see him off [to Canada].

From the beginning McNaughton asserted that he had an independent command, and that his forces were not just another British formation. He made that clear in an interview that I had with him in the sixties, shortly after I had talked to Lord Alanbrooke. McNaughton felt that he was in the same position as the military representatives of the Allied powers in Britain. There was

a picture taken of him standing beside Churchill, with General
W.E. Sikorski, the Polish military leader, on his right and General
de Gaulle on Churchill's left. Just as the British high command
would not have interfered with the conduct of the Polish or Free
French forces, so, he asserted, they should not have given orders
to the Canadian forces, let alone have had him dismissed. Would
they have tried to fire Sikorski or his successor, Anders? he asked.
In fact, McNaughton claimed that such an action was a violation
of Canada's constitutional rights (Statute of Westminster). However, there was an ambiguity about his position – since another
group portrait of senior British army officers, taken about the same
time (1941) as the one of the Allied military leaders, shows a rather
glum General McNaughton standing in the back row, while General
Sir Alan Brooke is seated front and centre.

To add to these problems, General Montgomery refused to allow
McNaughton to visit the Canadian troops fighting in Sicily. Lord
Alanbrooke recalled that incident: 'Whether his application was not
in the form that would have been acceptable by Monty – he's a
queer fellow, Monty, at times – I don't know. But it was a mistake.
He [McNaughton] should have been allowed to, he should most
definitely have been allowed to have gone and seen them.' Montgomery's reasoning was that the 1st Division was just finding its
feet, and as he wrote in his memoirs, Simonds was 'young and inexperienced – it was the first time he had commanded a division in
battle.' Still, Monty's arrogant rejection was a humiliating blow for
General McNaughton, who saw it as part of an imperial plot.

Just as the BBC did not like an independent CBC overseas unit
in London, so the chiefs of staff in Whitehall were not really in
favour of an independent Canadian army; they might have given
it lip service when it was politically expedient to do so, but, by
their reckoning, it was an unnecessary formation, which only
hindered the proper and efficient use of the Canadian forces.
Although they would not say so publicly, their contention was that
the Allied war effort would have been best served by having the
Canadians in an overall British command.

When Lord Alanbrooke was asked about the Canadian government's reaction to the inclusion of the 1st Division in the invasion

of Sicily, he said that he was not sure 'whether Mackenzie King was being influenced by McNaughton against the breaking up, or the temporary breaking up even, of the Canadian army, in order to fit in [with the invasion plans], I don't know, but there might have been a slight friction then.' The former chief of the imperial general staff spoke of the Canadian army's being 'such a vivid thing the whole time with Andy,' and indicated that there was pressure to use the army as a whole in Sicily: 'He [McNaughton] couldn't see any good coming out of busting up his whole army in any way, and the last thing on heaven and earth that I wanted to do was to bust up his army, beyond fetching it in whole eventually. But I didn't see how the devil you were going to go and put the damn thing in as a whole to start with, without [its having] any experience at all.'

In the end, it was not so much Alanbrooke or Paget or the British high command who destroyed the Canadian army in all but name as it was the Canadian government. Ottawa was under increasing pressure, both civilian and military, to get the Canadian troops into action, and it jumped at the opportunity of their being included in the invasion of Sicily. General McNaughton was fully conscious of the need for battle experience and, after a half-hearted attempt to get his whole army written into the plans for the invasion, as Lord Alanbrooke implied, he agreed to the 1st Division and the First Army Tank Brigade's taking part in Operation Husky, the Sicilian Campaign. He did so on condition that they would be returned to rejoin the Canadian army for the cross-channel assault on Europe. He received repeated assurances from the British that these were only temporary detachments and that there would be plenty of time for them to be shipped back, since D-Day was a year away.

The Canadian government was overwhelmed with the outpouring of public pride and enthusiasm over the Canadians' being in action at last in Sicily and felt that it should reinforce such sucess by sending more troops to the Mediterranean; there was always the argument to be made that battle experience was needed. At first, the CIGS, General Sir Alan Brooke, was opposed, saying that shipping would not be available, but Ottawa insisted that Canadian participation be raised to the level of a corps. Mackenzie King appealed to Churchill. Finally, a way was found around the shortage of transportation: the British would leave behind their tanks and heavy equipment for the Canadians and the Canadians would leave behind theirs for the returning British, and a vast tonnage of shipping would be saved. The 5th Armoured Division and I Canadian Corps were dispatched to Italy in November 1943, and at the same time it was conceded that there was not much likelihood of their being returned in time for D-Day. The government's actions, which ran contrary to everything that General McNaughton stood for, were motivated by politics, the politics of the home front, but personalities were also involved.

Colonel J.L. Ralston, the defence minister, was like General McNaughton in that he had had an exceptional career in the First World War; he had commanded a battalion and been awarded the DSO and bar for gallantry. He was twice defence minister, from 1926 to 1930, and from 1940 to 1944, and in the late twenties he appointed McNaughton chief of the general staff. They had known each other for a long time but were never friends. Colonel Ralston was stiff and unbending, meticulous and demanding, and McNaughton found him hard to work with and would have resigned as CGS if the Liberals had not been defeated in 1930. In his second term as defence minister, Colonel Ralston believed that General McNaughton, as army commander, was making decisions that should have been made by him, Colonel Ralston. His criticism aroused the fury of Mrs McNaughton, which was the worst thing that could have happened, since she greatly influenced her husband, and the antipathy that the general felt for the minister turned to the deepest loathing.

Prime Minister W.L. Mackenzie King was a supremely success- ful politician, who held the record for length of service as first minister. The only time I saw him was in 1946, when he was the host of a Canadian reception at the Paris Peace Conference; short, bald, and pudgy, he seemed to me a courteous, old-world figure with his pince-nez and his morning coat, so different from the American representative, Jimmy Byrnes, or the Soviet Union's Molotov that he might have been from another century. How

Mackenzie King got to be prime minister and remained prime minister for so long was a mystery to me, for he was no orator; he could not rise to an occasion, and Leonard Brockington, who wrote speeches for him during the war, told me that the patriotic passages he inserted came out as flat as a recital of figures from the budget, that is, if Mackenzie King did not stumble and make them completely incomprehensible. (A lawyer, Brockington was best known as a public speaker; he was the first chairman of the CBC, an unpaid job, from 1936 to 1939.)

Yet Canada desperately needed the image of a strong war leader around which the nation could mobilize, as Dick Malone wrote in his book, *A Portrait of War*. Malone became a brigadier and the highest-ranking public relations officer in the Canadian armed forces and was known to us reporters ever after as 'The Brigadier.' Prime Minister Mackenzie King was hopeless as a hero-image, the Brigadier asserted, which was a statement of the obvious. But there had to be someone to fill the hole and that someone was McNaughton, and Malone was as responsible as anyone for the excessive publicity build-up of the army commander.

There was no doubt that the British high command played the major role in the dismissal of General McNaughton, and Lord Alanbrooke* took this fact for granted in the interview, but others were involved. Lieutenant-General Kenneth Stuart, the chief of the general staff, in Ottawa, had grave doubts about McNaughton's competence as a field commander, and so did Lieutenant-General H.D.G. Crerar, although his views might be considered suspect, since it was known that he was actively conspiring to have him

---

*Lord Alanbrooke used to visit Canada regularly after the war – the former CIGS had been made a director of the Hudson's Bay Company – but McNaughton refused to see him. He also refused to see Montgomery when he toured the country. Alanbrooke was a respected ornithologist, and in the late forties he made a field trip to Churchill. The Canadian forces in this northern outpost made elaborate preparations for the field marshal's visit, but when Major-General Jim Tedlie, who was then a colonel and commandant of Fort Churchill, met him, Lord Alanbrooke said, 'Tedlie, I hope you haven't gone to too much trouble. The only thing I want to see is the nesting ground of the Hudsonian Godwit.' According to General Tedlie, now retired and living in Sidney, BC, there was an ornithologist on the station, and they had no difficulty in finding the nesting ground of this rather rare bird.

ousted. They also resented McNaughton's celebrity status and his ostentatious ways. Malone described how the general arrived for his first meeting with Ralston, which happened to be at a hospital outside London, in 'a convoy of staff cars with pennants flying and a motorcycle escort.' He was acting as if he were the supreme commander. It was all so un-Canadian.

Both Prime Minister Mackenzie King and the defence minister, Colonel Ralston, shared General McNaughton's vision of the Canadian army as a national symbol of sovereignty and independence, but with them it was not a magnificent obsession. As politicians they had to pay attention to public opinion, and the Canadian people were becoming increasingly impatient with the army's sitting around doing nothing in England and were demanding action. It was all right to send the 1st Division to Sicily – that was to have been a temporary assignment to gain battle experience – but to insist that Canadian participation in the Mediterranean Theatre be raised to the level of a corps was to break the army in two.

On this issue of splitting up the army, Colonel C.P. Stacey, the Canadian war historian, came down firmly on the side of McNaughton, saying that he was absolutely right and Mackenzie King and Ralston were absolutely wrong. In fact, what they did was 'absurd and silly.' 'The only way a country of Canada's stature can hope to exercise any influence in a coalition war or to maintain effective control of its own forces,' Colonel Stacey wrote in his memoirs, *A Date with History*, 'is to keep these forces as concentrated as possible, not to scatter them around the world.' Furthermore, the battle experience gained in Italy was not passed on, since the 1st Division did not rejoin the army as originally planned, and the Canadians entered the Normandy campaign as green troops.

The way that the McNaughton affair was handled showed that the Canadian government accepted British suzerainty, and that, if the chief of the imperial general staff, General Sir Alan Brooke, felt that General McNaughton was not fit to command an army in the field, he, McNaughton, had to go. It could not happen now, but the Second World War was a transitional time for Canada as a nation: there was the assertion of sovereignty but not of real independence. As J.L. Granatstein and Desmond Morton wrote, in *A Nation*

Forged in Fire, 'psychologically Canada remained [during the Second World War] the colony it had legally been at the beginning of the First World War.' That was precisely the condition that we found ourselves in when we were in London during the war. We were still British subjects, but I should add that most Canadians accepted their lowlier dominion status and, despite grumbling, were proud to be part of the British Empire. The Canadian armed forces were patterned after and meant to fit in with the British armed forces, even to the extent of having tea instead of coffee!

No constitutional crisis was involved and, while McNaughton raised the issue, he never pursued it. It was his fate to be a man before his time, a premature nationalist.

London, 22 November 1943:
General A.G.L. McNaughton is expected to announce his retirement as the commander of the First Canadian Army; the BBC said that he would be leaving for reasons of health.

I had returned to London in the middle of October 1943, and the news that Andy McNaughton was quitting did not come as a surprise, because there had been rumours to this effect for some time past. After the 5th Canadian Armoured Division and I Canadian Corps had left for Italy, we heard reports to the effect that General Sir Alan Brooke had told General McNaughton that there was really no need for the Canadian army headquarters now, that it might as well be disbanded. Apparently, General Sir Bernard Paget had been much more explicit, suggesting that the First Canadian Army should be reorganized into a British-Canadian army and that a British general should be put in command. While we suspected that the information about these imperialist manoeuvres was being leaked by McNaughton's staff, there was no way of confirming it, and, in any case, censorship would have prevented any reporting of it.

As might be expected, this proposal was too much for Mackenzie King and Colonel Ralston; while they acknowledged the supremacy of the British high command, they knew that there would be a political storm at home if they accepted their advice, and they insisted that a Canadian be in command of the First Canadian Army even if it was only a shell. Eventually, Lieutenant-General H.D.G. Crerar succeeded General McNaughton and commanded the army, which had more British and Allied troops than Canadian, in the campaign in northwest Europe.

Shortly after Christmas 1943 the McNaughtons left the large house in Leatherhead, Surrey, that they had occupied for so long, to journey home. I covered their departure: thousands of Canadian troops lined the road and the general got out of the car and crossed from side to side shaking hands. There were cheers and cries of 'come back soon.' It was an emotional scene. As Colonel Stacey said in his memoirs, General McNaughton was the only Canadian general who was loved by his men.

On his return to Canada, it was expected that the former army commander, who still was greatly respected, would become the first Canadian-born governor-general. In September 1944 Lieutenant-General McNaughton was gazetted a full general, which was regarded as a significant step towards Rideau Hall. However, his promotion and the prospect of a vice-regal appointment did not assuage the bitterness he felt over his removal from the army command. All great men have their weaknesses, and Andy McNaughton's was that of hubris. It was his excessive pride, coupled with a desire for revenge, that warped his judgment and allowed the wily Mackenzie King to use him as a pawn in the power game he was playing over the conscription crisis. McNaughton agreed to take Ralston's place as defence minister and find the reinforcements that were so desperately needed overseas without resorting to conscription. He failed.

During the short time that he was in the government, however, McNaughton did have his revenge on the imperialists. At the end of 1944, there was a request that I Canadian Corps be used in an operation against the Dalmatian Coast; this was Churchill's scheme to attack the 'soft underbelly of the Axis' and develop an exclusively British theatre of operations. McNaughton made it absolutely clear, according to his biographer, John Swettenham, that the Canadian Corps was to remain in Italy and would leave only to rejoin the Canadian army, which was in the Netherlands. The British were furious. As the master strategist, General Sir Alan Brooke headed the planning of this venture and he appealed to Churchill, who sent an angry note of protest. But Mackenzie King, with McNaughton at his back, rejected it. I Canadian Corps rejoined the First Canadian Army in the middle of March 1945, and for a little more than a month in the last stages of the war, the Canadian army fought as a national army, not as a mixed Allied force.

Instead of being the first Canadian-born governor-general, McNaughton became a defence minister, and a defence minister who could not be elected. He was no politician. He could not win a by-election in the Ontario constituency of Grey North, where he was defeated by a little-known local Tory, Garfield Case. When the general election took place a few months later, in June 1945, he ran in the Saskatchewan constituency of Qu'Appelle and lost again; Mrs Gladys Strum of the CCF won, and McNaughton came third and last. The soldiers' vote went heavily against him. He had forfeited their trust. After this second rejection, he had to resign. It was a sad climax to a remarkable career.

6

Into Action without a Mike

London, 13 May 1943:
Tunis and Bizerta fall. Axis forces in North Africa surrender.
Way now opened for the invasion of Europe.

It was ironic that I should be wounded during a demonstration of a river crossing in England and come through the real war with its real battles without so much as a scratch; but life, as well as history, is full of ironies. 20 May 1943: a bright and sunny day on the green and pleasant downs, and the demonstration by Canadian troops had the atmosphere of a sporting event, with the spectators, including the Duke of Gloucester, standing in a roped-off area above the river. Smoke shells were dropping in front of us to cover the infantry landing from rubber boats. I believe that they were being fired by mortars from across the water over our heads. At any rate, one of them, perhaps because it was a dud, fell short and hit me.

The next thing I knew I was on the ground; I had the sensation that I had been struck a smashing blow on the head, but when I found I could not move my legs, I realized that I had been hit on the back. For a moment panic gripped me. I thought, 'My God, my back is broken.' The words were as clear as a banner headline in my consciousness. But then I felt pins and needles in my legs and I could wriggle my toes and move my foot. The fin of the smoke mortar shell had cut my cap, the full weight of the shell falling on my shoulder and back. As I wrote at the time:

If I had been standing a little straighter I should have been killed. Instead, sudden death struck me a glancing blow which did no more harm than a very bad bruise. I had a swelling on my back about the size of a football.

While I lay on the ground, the pain making a strange pattern in my mind, a thought kept popping up. Finally it burst through the wire-netting frames that seemed to enclose my brain. 'This is so stupid,' I said as they lifted me on a stretcher, and I repeated it again, 'This is so stupid.' Colonel Stewart, the medical officer who attended me, must have thought that I was becoming delirious, because he said very firmly that it was not stupid. But I was worried over the possibility of being laid up for months and missing the coming show. At the time I did not know that I had no broken bone. I felt as though every bone in my body was broken.

Standing next to me when I was hit was Lieutenant-General E.L.M. Burns; I found this out much later when I was the CBC correspondent at the United Nations and the general had just been appointed commander of the United Nations Emergency Force (UNEF) in the Middle East. He recalled the incident when we met in New York. General Burns, who was the most taciturn of men, became almost loquacious. The military officers watching the demonstration were alarmed at what happened, he said, since it was within a few feet of the Duke of Gloucester. But, Burns went on, with obvious satisfaction, the duke did not flinch; he lowered his field-glasses, looked down at me, said, 'Good Lord,' and returned to surveying the demonstration. I could have told General Burns that His Royal Highness was in no danger because he was one of the few people standing under a corrugated iron roof. The duke did send his equerry, a hearty Guards officer, around to see me when I was in hospital.

It was in the Canadian hospital that I got an inkling of coming events. One of the orderlies, an older fellow who always seemed to have the latest gen, came into the ward and stood at the end of my bed; he knew that I was a reporter and he was pleased with himself because he had news for me. We were all going to be moved to another hospital, he said. When? Why, tomorrow. This hospital was packing up, all the staff were being reboarded, which meant that they were going overseas. No, no, this was not an exercise, not a practice, it was too serious a business, it had to be the real thing. The next day we patients were taken in a convoy of ambulances to another Canadian hospital. I did not stay long; I left shortly after a doctor performed an aspiration on my back, withdrawing some of the liquid caused by the heavy bruise.

My back was still tender and I carried a pillow everywhere I went in London. It would have been awful to have missed the show, as I thought I would after I was hit, and I was glad to be out and about. There was an undercurrent of excitement and expectation during those warm June days when the double summer time stretched the daylight till midnight. The Tunisian campaign was over, and Africa had been cleared of the enemy. Now the next blow had to be at Europe.

I had stopped using a pillow or I had lost it, when John Kannawin told me one morning – it was a Thursday – that he was thinking of going to Scotland on a golfing holiday that weekend. But he was worried that there might be some 'startling development,' as he put it – we were used to talking in code: walls had ears. We both agreed that it was unlikely to happen for a few days, if not a couple of weeks. I went to the theatre that night and did not get back to the flat till late; Wally Reyburn told me that Kannawin had been ringing all evening and wanted me to get in touch with him as soon as I got in. When I called him back, John asked me if I would go on the golfing holiday with him. I was puzzled because he was quite insistent, but I said, no, I wasn't interested. So he gave up and said that he would talk to me in the office the next morning.

In the security of the CBC's underground studio, Kannawin

explained that what he was trying to tell me over the phone was that I had to leave that night (Friday night, 11 June, 1943) to join the 1st Canadian Division, which we knew was in Scotland, although this information was supposed to be hush-hush. I grinned sheepishly, embarrassed that I had been so dense. Kannawin and Bert Powley, who had also been informed, knew no more, except that Canadian Press and the Canadian Broadcasting Corporation had priority positions for whatever was going to happen, and no other correspondents were included. I had to pack and clear out of the flat without Wally's knowing – he usually worked there but fortunately that morning he was out – and I told the housekeeper that I would be away some days on manoeuvres.

At CMHQ, where I went for the secret briefing, I told them about the interview with H.G. Wells, which was set up for that afternoon; it was to be recorded and held for release on 'Eyes Front' in a couple of weeks' time. Major Bill Abel, a large, bald former advertising manager, who was head of army Public Relations, said that I should go ahead, that the delayed broadcast would make a good cover for my movement. I was flattered that I had already reached the stage as a war correspondent that I needed a cover; I didn't realize at the time that it was really a tribute to radio.

So I did the interview with H.G. Wells and afterward, since it was well past five o'clock, hurried back to 200 Oxford Street, where I had left my belongings after getting them out of the flat. I ate a quick supper at the BBC cafeteria, which smelled of boiled cabbage and was noted for its sawdust sausages and dried-egg omelettes. Ugh! I repacked my bags in our LG2 studio, which was used not only for recording but also for storage, and said good-bye to Kannawin and Powley. At half-past seven, a Canadian army car delivered me up and drove me to Euston railway station, which was a seething mass of troops. There I found my priority travelling companion, Ross Munro of Canadian Press, a tall lanky fellow who was the most experienced of the Canadian war correspondents. With him was a conducting officer, who was to take us to our destination.

It was a miserable journey. There were no sleepers, and for a time we thought we were not going to get any seats, but our porter found some space in a compartment, and after an argument with an RAF officer, we sat down squeezed together. It was quite hot in London, but it grew colder as we sped northward. The train was blacked out so that we could not read, and we were wedged so close together that sleep was almost impossible. For what seemed interminable hours, we sat stiffly upright staring through the dim, smoke-filled haze of the single, blue light in the compartment at the shadowy figures opposite.

What sweet relief it was to reach our destination and get off the train in the early hours of the morning. But that feeling did not last long, since we found ourselves alone in the cold and gloomy confines of what must have been the station for Troon, because that was where we spent the next day and night. Finally the conducting officer got us a lift in a station-wagon to the hotel that the 1st Canadian Division had taken over as an officers' mess; there we were told that we were not expected till later, the usual excuse when the army fell down on arrangements. Another SNAFU! After a couple of hours' sleep and breakfast, we were taken to the quartermaster stores in a stable outside the town and issued tropical kit. This was proof, if we needed any, that we were headed south. We repacked our bags.

Since we had nothing else to do, we took a stroll through the town, which was a seaport and resort within easy reach of Glasgow. I bought a couple of books for the expedition ahead, Tolstoy's *War and Peace*, and *The Seven Pillars of Wisdom* by T.E. Lawrence – I found the latter heavy going but I got through it. There was so much time to spare at the front: what did they say about war, that it was 90 per cent being bored to death, and 10 per cent being scared to death? Somehow these two volumes survived the bashing around in a kitbag and today have a place in my library at home in West Vancouver.

The next day we travelled to the port and boarded a large tender packed with troops. It chuffed across the green, wind-swept sea towards a line of transports silhouetted against the grey sky. We passed by the towering stern of the first one and then another

and another and another; I had counted seven, eight, nine great
ships by the time we berthed alongside one of the biggest. The
troops, who were loaded down with packs and full equipment,
staggered and jostled their way up the gangway into the maw of
the ship.

Our transport was the *SS Marnix Van Sint Aldegonde,* a Dutch
East Indiaman, and reminders of its past colonial glories could be
found in the lush tropical decoration of the lounge and dining
saloon and the Balinese boys who waited at table. Concrete gun
posts broke up the wide sweep of the lido deck, however, and the
swimming pool had been turned into a storage area, while assault
landing craft instead of lifeboats hung from the davits. The lower
cabins had been torn out to make room for mess decks.

The officers could imagine themselves on a pleasure cruise.
They occupied the staterooms – Ross Munro and I had one – and
they ate in the dining-room, where the food served by the Balinese
waiters was plentiful and good. The men, however, were herded
together in mess decks, sleeping in hammocks and eating off long
wooden tables over which the hammocks rode at night. Despite the
most rigorous cleaning, the mess decks smelled.

Most of the 3,500 aboard the *Marnix* were soldiers, but there
were sailors, Royal Navy commandos to man the assault boats, and
RAF crews to take over any captured airfield. The Royal Canadian
Regiment, which was to be one of the assault battalions, was the
only full unit on the ship, but there were fragments of other units,
mostly British. As might be expected, Ross and I identified with
the RCR; we got to know the young officers of the regiment; we
used to have long discussions about the war and its aftermath, but
mostly we talked about life at home. We played bridge or poker
with them in the first-class lounge, which was a bit shopworn but
still retained some of its grandeur. While the troop-ships were in
the Firth of Clyde – which they were for more than two weeks –
the bar was open, and since a pink gin cost twopence halfpenny,
or about a nickel, there were some rousing parties.

They were an eager lot, the RCR officers, but their enthusiasm
for action was tempered by concern because none of them had any

battle experience except for Strome Galloway, a captain then, who
had been on attachment with the British First Army fighting in
Tunisia. The man who was looking forward most to meeting the
enemy was the second-in-command, the ebullient Major Billy Pope;
by contrast, the commanding officer, Lieutenant-Colonel Ralph
Crowe, seemed subdued, but he was as much of a daredevil. Both
men were killed in the first two weeks of the landing in Sicily. The
padre, Rusty Wilkes, was a wonderful, warm-hearted guy, who was
a great comfort to the men in the bloody combat.

After the first rapture of being aboard, it was difficult to keep
the men occupied, cooped up as they were on a ship for so long. We
had one horrible landing exercise; there was to have been another,
but it was put off because of bad weather. On the preceding
afternoon the troop-ships moved down the Ayrshire coast, and, in
the early hours of the morning while the moon was still shining,
I joined the RCR as they were loaded into the assault craft; ours
dropped with a soft plop into the sea. I remember feeling something sharp under me but there was such a squash – we were
packed like sardines into these boats, which looked like sardine
tins – that it took me half an hour of persistent wriggling to find
out that I was sitting on the edge of a spade. And the knowledge
did me no good because I could not move.

It was not rough, but we were in the assault craft for fully two
hours and there was a swell. A few of the men were sick and, since
they could not move, there was nowhere else for them to vomit
except over their fellows. At last we felt the boat crunch against
the sand, and we filed down the ramp, stepping thigh-deep into
icy-cold water. I could see red tracer bullets chasing each other out
to sea and bright flashes of explosion on the horizon, all the stage
effects of a real invasion. The assault troops pushed inland, but I
decided to stay on the beach and watch the rest of the division
land. It was raining and windy and, wrapping myself in a gas
cape, I found a place in the dunes that was a natural observation
post.

Although I was wet and cold, I dozed off, to be awakened by
the roar of planes. It was dawn, and Hurribombers and Boston

bombers were sweeping low over the beaches. 'Enemy air raid,' a loudspeaker boomed across the sands. 'Enemy air raid. Everyone take cover immediately.' From the gaping bows of the large LSIs (landing ships infantry) came long lines of troops. 'You men on the beaches,' the loudspeaker sounded peremptory, 'Lie down. Can't you see you're being attacked?' The poor fellows had waded ashore in water up to their necks in some cases and now they had to fall flat on the wet sands because of the simulated air raids. All of the 20,000 troops who took part in the exercise were soaked through when they returned to their ships in the afternoon.

In some ways a practice could be worse than the real thing; this was certainly true in my case, because I landed in Sicily without getting my feet wet and the weather was Mediterranean fine instead of a chilly Scottish downpour. It was probably a good policy to make the exercises as tough and as realistic as possible, although that fidelity was not appreciated by the participants, judging from all the angry and anguished cursing that I overheard.

That exercise and a route march on the Isle of Arran were the only activities outside the cramped quarters of the trooper. The days dragged on, and we became more and more impatient. Every morning we woke up to find fewer ships around us; the aircraft carrier and the strange-looking vessel that carried landing craft had gone. But we were still stuck in the Clyde. An insidious rumour began filtering through the *Marnix* that this was just another rehearsal. Ross Munro, who had experienced many postponements and disappointments in his years covering the Canadian forces, made a bet that we would be back in London within a week.

On the afternoon of 28 June 1943 Ross and I were summoned to the headquarters ship for a conference with Major-General Guy Simonds, the commander of the 1st Canadian Division. He was a lean, wiry fellow who modelled himself on his hero, General Montgomery, even to the way he spoke. Simonds was incisive but had not much to say except that we were joining the Eighth Army for an important combined operation in the Mediterranean and that we were setting sail that night. We spent so much time being shown all the gadgetry in the headquarters ship that we almost missed the *Marnix*. By the time we reached it, its anchors were up and all its sally ports battened down, except for one. Our convoy was already moving, and within five minutes of my scrambling up the ladder, the ship had fallen into line. We passed through the opening in the anti-submarine boom and were on our way at last.

It was on the third day out that we were briefed: we found out that we were going to invade Sicily. We would be landing on the southern tip, Pachino Peninsula. I noted that it was 1 July, an appropriate time for Canadians to learn of their first great mission of the war. There was no cheering, no whooping it up, although the troops in their mess decks did whistle at the size of the force involved, altogether half a million men. They were more mature, these Canadian soldiers, than their fathers, who had looked on battle as a great and glorious adventure; they knew that it would be a grim and bloody business. Normal training was impossible, so the men spent most of the time above decks getting a sun tan while the troop ships sailed past Gibraltar into the blue Mediterranean Sea: it could have been a cruise. There were a couple of alerts but no attacks.

The weather had turned hot and the fan was going full blast in the cabin as I typed a letter to my parents. I knew they would be worried about the coming action. 'It may be dangerous – I can't really tell,' I wrote, 'I'm going to take care of myself, but the story is worth the danger. It's probably the biggest story of all. At any rate I'm not worrying. As a matter of fact, I'm looking forward to it.' This was the kind of letter that so many of the officers and men aboard the troop ships were writing their loved ones. I was very careful of what I said, that I was 'on my way to foreign parts with some Canadian troops,' but I need not have been. My letter, dated 7 July 1943, was not received, according to the notation written on it by my mother, until 15 September 1943, long after the Sicilian campaign was over. This was the kind of censorship by delay that so frustrated the armed forces.

Around Cape Bon, North Africa, we entered the assembly triangle that was bounded by Malta to the north and Tripoli to the east. At first we were disappointed not to see a single new ship, and then, as we headed northeast towards Sicily, there it was, the greatest armada that the world had ever known. Ships as far as the eye could see, big ships and little ships, warships and troopers and freighters and swarms of landing craft, and they had set sail for this venture from ports in Africa and the United Kingdom and from as far away as Canada and the United States. Altogether some 2,500 ships, we had been told in the briefing on the *Marnix*: the force involved was so great that fully a third of the British and American merchant marine was being used. It was a formidable sight, but our pride and confidence were tempered by an ugly change in the weather.

It began with a breeze that turned into a gale in the early afternoon. Whitecaps flecked the waves, which were growing in size. The big ship began to roll and it was difficult to stand up to the wind in the forecastle. The storm grew worse, and we began to wonder whether the landing would not have to be called off: H-Hour was 3 a.m. The seas were so heavy that they seemed to swamp the destroyers near us as we sailed past the brown sandstone cliffs of Malta. There was a sick feeling of uncertainty about whether Husky, the code name for the invasion of Sicily, would have to be postponed. Yet, as evening approached, it became apparent that there would be no change in plans. Perhaps it was too late to turn back now.

The ship was creaking and heaving as we went down to dinner. The tables in the dining saloon were covered with snowy white cloths, and the dinner was just as good as usual and the Balinese boys just as attentive. I made a note of what we had: consommé, poached salmon, stewed steak with boiled potatoes and carrots, apple pie, cheese, and coffee. Major Billy Pope referred to it jokingly as 'The Last Supper,' according to Galloway, which, in retrospect, was rather sad. It was to be the last sit-down meal for some time, and it was extraordinary to go from this dinner in these luxurious surroundings into action. The assault troops were blackening their faces and making preparations for the landing on the beaches of Pachino Peninsula.

By nightfall the wind had dropped to a breeze but there was still a heavy swell, which made loading the landing craft a difficult manoeuvre. The storm delayed operations: the assault troops of the RCR, who were to go in under cover of darkness at 3 a.m., H-hour, did not get away from the ship until 5 a.m., when it was daylight. This could have been disastrous, but there was little resistance. Strome Galloway, who, with his waxed moustache, looked like a Guards officer, called the landing 'almost bloodless.' I went in with the second wave, my portable typewriter wrapped up in my lifebelt so that it would be unsinkable.

Pachino Peninsula, Sicily, 10 July 1943, 6.30 a.m.:
This is London calling. The Allies are invading Sicily. British, Canadian, and American troops have landed on the south-eastern beaches of the island.

It was the radio in the galley of the landing craft. One of the crew – I could not tell whether he was with the army, navy, or air force, since they all wore the same khaki uniform in a combined operation – was astonished: 'Now, how did they get the news so quickly?' he asked. We passed a monitor whose heavy gun was belching flame, but the other warships had stopped firing. It was fantastic, this invasion in broad daylight without any opposition! Where were the enemy planes? The gunners were scanning the horizon, squinting into the sun, but there was none. Some of the landing craft that had taken in the assault troops were returning, and we shouted at them, 'What was it like?' Each bosun yelled back: 'Nothing. Nothing at all.'

Twenty years later, Lord Alanbrooke was to say of Sicily, 'We got less opposition than I had expected.' He believed that the speed with which the invasion was carried out meant that the Germans never got themselves properly organized for it. The storm on the afternoon before D-Day might have had something to do with the enemy's lack of response. It must have affected the airborne operation, which was the only real casualty of the landing. 'We dumped them all in the water,' Lord Alanbrooke said. The gliders were let adrift too early, which was possibly because the severe headwinds were not taken into account. The experience paid off, however, and the field marshal asserted the gliders were an outstanding success in Normandy, where the best flight landed in the dark within 150 yards of its target.

I landed in Sicily without getting my feet wet. A large amphibious vehicle called a DUKW came alongside the LSI when we ran into a sand bar and took us ashore. Already anti-aircraft guns were on the beach, and a bulldozer was widening the entrance to a small lane. Landing craft, including large tank-landing craft, kept coming in and offloading troops and guns and tanks. There was a great array of ships in the waters off Pachino Peninsula, a stretch of poor farm land that had been turned into the busiest port in Sicily. A combined operation was confusion, organized confusion. I recall that I didn't know quite what to do. There was no transportation, no one to report to. Ross Munro had landed earlier, but I could not find him on the crowded beach. So I sat down on the sand and began to write my first story. It was scorching hot; and there was nothing in the sky, not even a cloud.

That night ashore we knew we were at war; the German planes that had left us alone in the daytime made several raids when it was dark. After a hot and dusty journey, mostly on foot, to the airfield that had been one of our first objectives, I had come back to the peasant's hut that was advanced divisional headquarters and was trying to get some sleep there when all hell broke loose. We were worried not so much about the enemy bombs but about the rain of steel splinters from the massed anti-aircraft artillery both on shore and on the ships. There was no place to shelter, the hut had a straw roof, and our steel helmets seemed so inadequate; an officer standing beside me had a large gash slashed in his shoulder. When the raiders were not around, there were unseen marauders in the sandy soil to keep me awake, and between the fleas and the flak, and the fleas were worse, I got no sleep.

The next morning my waist was as red as raw beefsteak, and with an acquaintance, Major Hébert, who was just as badly bitten,

I went for a swim to assuage the irritation. A row of barrage balloons floated over our heads, and the beach seemed busier than ever with more men and supplies being landed. I teamed up with Pilot Officer Bob Francis, an RCAF PR who was with the 1st Canadian Division, and we thumbed a ride to Pachino, the first European town to be captured. It was a cluster of low buildings glaring white in the sun, with a population of some 20,000, and running it was Lieutenant Charles Papalardo, a Sicilian-American with the Allied military government. His assistant was a huge American paratrooper, Private Hank Likowsky, who had been blown off course by the storm on the eve of the invasion and had landed in the Pachino area.

We met Lieutenant Papalardo in the fly-blown hotel where he was staying, and while we were talking, there was a burst of anti-aircraft fire. I went on to the balcony and saw three Messerschmitts banked low over the town and heading north. They had just strafed the airfield. We had dinner in the hotel's dining-room, where a curtain of glass beads kept out the sunlight. It was a simple meal, the best the hotel in this poor place could do for the commandante: macaroni and cheese and fried potatoes, but I can remember still the cucumbers and tomatoes in vinegar. It was a delicious treat, the first salad I had had in weeks.

During dinner, the Fascist mayor came to see the military governor, 'a lickspittle,' Papalardo called him, but he had got us the local senator's house, and we would not have to sleep in the hotel. It was Allied policy to work with the local administrators, and without exception all were card-carrying Fascists. The senator's house was the finest building in Pachino. It had some comfortable bedrooms and even bathrooms with flush toilets, but there was no running water or electricity. I sank into the soft luxury of a double bed and was just dozing off when the anti-aircraft guns opened up. One of them was firing in the square just outside my window. Enemy planes were raiding the airfield. The noise seemed to start my flea-bites itching, or it may have aroused unseen inhabitants of the senator's bed. At any rate I got very little sleep.

The next day I was determined to reach the front. I got a lift to Ispica and arrived in time to see my flea-bitten friend, Major Hébert, take over the town on behalf of the Allied military government. I thumbed another ride and a few miles further on came upon Ross Munro with our conducting officer, Captain Dave Maclellan; we greeted each other with whoops and cries of 'Where the hell have you been?' They had just got a jeep – prior to which they too had had to thumb their way around – and were cooking up some lunch in a farm field beside the road. There were five of us, including a couple of fellows from the army's film and photo section, and we all piled into the jeep with what kit we had been able to retain after the landing, which was not much – I had my typewriter and a blanket. Still it was quite a load, and one photographer had to sit on the hood.

We had not gone far when we almost ran down a civilian car in which there were two Canadian officers and two Italian officers; we followed it down a side road into an olive grove and were thus present at the formal surrender of the first Italian general. He was Major-General Achilles d'Havet, who was a portly old man, looking grey and tired, in contrast to the lean, vigorous appearance of General Guy Simonds. However, d'Havet knew the fine points of military etiquette and insisted that he be allowed to keep his pistol, saying that his coastal division had only nine battalions and was opposed by a whole corps: the odds were overwhelming. It was a question of being gracious to a beaten enemy and General Simonds gave in and merely asked for the ammunition; he must have regretted losing the pistol as a souvenir.

After we left the olive grove, we passed columns of Italian prisoners, who had fallen into our hands with the capture of General d'Havet's headquarters at Modica. There were thousands of them, and they were only too willing to cheer and raise their fingers in the V sign for the photographers. It was a nice drive to Modica on a hard-surfaced road, and we came upon only a few signs of war: a dead horse here, a blown-up road block there, and, in one village, a burnt-out Canadian truck, beside it the body of the driver covered by a white tarpaulin on which flowers had been laid. But we never did reach the front during the first phase of the Sicilian campaign. When we caught up with the forward Canadian troops, they were resting, having been bypassed by the British, who were carrying on the advance.

I had a good sleep that night, wrapped up in a blanket on the hard dry ground in an olive grove. The benzedrine we had taken for the landing must have worn off and I had got used to the fleas and the flak – there were air raids again. We were at corps headquarters, and the next morning I recall feeling almost exhilarated when General Montgomery walked over and shook hands with us. I wished I had had a microphone to record what he said to us and the pep talk he gave the troops. (Later, I did record an interview with General Simonds). Monty said the reason for giving the Canadians a rest so soon after the landing was because they were becoming sunburned, but I wondered whether that was just a pretext and the real reason was that he wanted to get to know these new troops or rather to get them to know him. He played the role of a military superstar and the men loved it. An Eighth Army officer, part of whose duty was to censor the mail, told me that the amount of hero-worship for Monty in the letters of private soldiers was astonishing.

The fact that I had no microphone or recording equipment meant that I was acting not as a radio reporter for the CBC but as a newspaper reporter. I was doing what Ross Munro did for CP, and he had Dave Maclellan as his copy boy and the close cooperation of the military authorities as far as transmission was concerned. As a result, he was able to scoop the other agencies. The army PR, which was full of former newspapermen, acted as an adjunct of the Canadian Press and, at first, did not pay much attention to the newfangled medium of radio. Ross was a hard worker and he would sit every evening, usually under an olive tree, hammering away at his portable typewriter until it was dark, and I felt that I had to keep up with him, until I got a wire from the CBC saying that my telegraphic dispatches were too long for broadcasting and I should keep them shorter.

We had a brief rest of a couple of days or so, and then the 1st

Canadian Division was on the move again. We passed through the British troops (51st Highland Division) in a small town called Vizzini, and pressed on without much opposition until we reached the foothills of Mount Etna, in the very heart of Sicily. There, the Canadians ran into the Germans: elements first of the Herman Goering Panzer Division and then of the 15th Panzer Grenadier Division of Afrika Korps fame – and the going got tough.

My memory of that rapid advance – we did 100 miles or more in four or five days – was of the powdery white dust that made the sunburned soldiers look deathly pale, like ghosts. I wrote at the time, 'Clouds of dust hid us in our jeep as we darted in and out of the convoys, and sometimes it was as thick as a fog, and we would have to slow down because we could not see ...' The dust was white, and the sun was white hot too, and when we were held up in a traffic jam, the heat penetrated my bush shirt and shorts and seemed to burn through to the bone. Thank God for our control of the air, for the dust, the clouds of dust churned up by tanks and trucks, made us an obvious target, but the Luftwaffe did not dare attack in the daylight. The advance went on day and night, and at night the dust was eerie. Yet it was a thrill to be part of this drive northward towards the European mainland, past Italians raising their fingers in the V-for-victory sign: we felt we were making history.

At Valguanera, a battle began in the full heat of the afternoon sun. We reached a ridge from which we could see the hills where the Germans were holding out. Our guns opened up and shells screamed overhead; I could hear the chatter of machine-guns and the heavy thump that mortars make. I could see the Canadian infantry, dark specks against the brown hillside, and the flaming splash and pop of distant explosions. It was more of a skirmish, rather than the great set-piece battles that I was to witness, but there were casualties, and the next day we returned and saw graves being dug in a sun-baked field for ten bodies lying in a row, wrapped up in grey blankets; according to the chaplain, they were two officers and eight men, who had been killed in the battle yesterday.

The Panzer Grenadiers were finally driven from the hills, but the advance had been slowed to a crawl. I had received a cable from the CBC saying that I should leave the front to make some voice broadcasts about the invasion of Sicily from the nearest radio station, which was at Allied Force headquarters in Algiers. The wire left it up to me as to when I should make this move, although it suggested that it should be as soon as possible. I knew that the Eighth Army's strategy was to turn east at Leonforte in the middle of the island to attack the main German defence positions before Mount Etna, leaving the western slopes of the volcano and the Nazis there to the Americans. The Canadians had been slowed down by the enemy rearguards, and I felt that I could go to Algiers and return without missing much, as long as I could make good connections.

7

First Sound of Liberation

Malta, 22 July 1943:
American troops take Palermo, capital of Sicily. Axis forces fall back to defence line before Mount Etna.

B efore leaving the front, I saw some of the fighting for Leonforte. We drove through Valguarnera, past the stinking remains of a dead horse in the main square, across a burning hot valley where our twenty-five-pounders were firing in the open, since there was no cover. As I remember, Leonforte was an ordinary enough place, but, unlike most Sicilian towns, it was not on a hilltop but in a narrow defile. Although the Canadians had forced their way into Leonforte early that morning, we were not able to get within a mile of the town because of the heavy mortar fire on the road. Not even ambulances were allowed beyond a wrecked villa that had been turned into a regimental aid post. The Germans were holed up in the caves that pock-marked the steep cliffs on either side and were in a dominant position. There was bitter house-to-house fighting, and, quite clearly, it was going to take some time to secure Leonforte.

I had obtained my travel documents, marked Priority Two,

which was about as high as a war correspondent could expect, and set out for the coast with a liaison officer who was returning to the rear echelons of the Eighth Army. At Syracuse, I found a tank-landing craft which was leaving for Malta; once on board this large vessel, I had a shower which was my first wash in weeks.

Valletta, the great British naval base and capital of Malta, was in ruins, but its people had survived the Axis bombing by taking shelter in the large caves beneath the port; most were still living there, because there was nowhere else to live. It was a thrill to be in Malta, brave little Malta, the George Cross Island, which could not be vanquished. We had heard so much about Malta. George 'Buzz' Beurling, the great Canadian ace – I think I met him in London, but there is no record of an interview with him – was credited with shooting down more than twenty-eight planes, most of them in defending the island against the mass attacks of Italian and German bombers between June and October 1942. Beurling liked to make out that he was a cold-blooded killer, but according to his biographer, Brian Nolan, he used to have nightmares of the air battles. Beurling was the 'Falcon of Malta,' the title of the British edition of his biography. Then there was my cousin, Bob Dafforn: he was over six feet, six inches in height, really too tall for the cramped quarters of a Spitfire's cockpit, but he was determined to be a fighter pilot. He survived the Battle of Britain and was wounded in the Battle of Malta and invalided home; he recovered and was back flying, only to be killed in a training accident.

If it had not been for the likes of Beurling and Dafforn, and had Malta fallen, the course of the war, certainly in the Mediterranean Theatre, might have been very different. There could have been no invasion of Sicily without this historic island fortress having first been secured. My memories of Malta were of the sweltering heat and the brown sandstone colour of everything – the cliffs, the buildings, the ruins and the dust – sandy brown compared with the white limestone dust of Sicily.

At Luqa, near Valletta, the famous airfield from which the Battle of Malta was fought and won, it was stiflingly hot. The inside of the Dakota transport plane while it was on the ground was like an oven. Randolph Churchill was sitting in a bucket seat across from me. Nobody knew what the prime minister's son was doing in this area, and nobody seemed to like him. Sweat poured off us and Randolph became more and more testy and blasphemous with the delay in the take-off. There were wounded on the plane, in tiers of stretchers in the forward section, and their suffering in this awful heat must surely have been worse than ours.

I got to Algiers the next morning, just two days' travel from Leonforte. So far, my connections had been good. Andrew Cowan was there and so were two of the CBC engineers, Paul Johnson and Alec MacDonald. They had brought some of the portable recording equipment with them and were awaiting the arrival of the first of our vans. Andy was covering Allied Force headquarters and was able to show me around the extensive press and radio set-up. I went to work describing the Sicilian campaign from the beginning, the storm the day before the landing, the surrender of the Italian troops, the advance through the heat and the dust; I did several long voice reports and made up for all the telegraph dispatches that I had sent. The broadcasts went by short wave from Algiers to London and were then beamed to Ottawa, where they were received, re-recorded, and put on the Canadian networks.

Algiers, 25 July 1943:
Mussolini and his Fascist government fall; Marshal Badoglio takes over and will open negotiations for an armistice.

The news of the Italian coup came as quite a shock, and there was great excitement in the correspondents' room and a barrage of questions that the briefing officers could not answer. Years later, Lord Alanbrooke, when I interviewed him, admitted that he had not expected the Fascists to collapse so quickly, although it had been apparent from the first few days of the Sicilian campaign that we were fighting not Italians but Germans. It had come as such a surprise, the British field marshal said, that they were not able to get things organized quickly enough to take advantage of the situation. He agreed there had been a plan to land an airborne division on Rome; the Allied war machine was so ponderous, however, that nothing was done for more than six weeks! By that time the Nazis had rescued Mussolini in a daring operation and the Wehrmacht occupied all major Italian cities, including Rome.

If an airborne division had landed on Rome within a week or two of Badoglio's taking power, the war might have been shortened. Thus this incredible delay was the SNAFU of all SNAFUs. It was worse than the next grade in the vulgar barrack room rating, that of the FUBAR (Fucked Up Beyond All Recognition), and qualified as a TARFU (Things Are Really Fucked Up), the ultimate SNAFU, when the situation was so bad that superlatives and sarcasm were redundant. There might have been another explanation for this TARFU, and that was that the Americans were not really in favour of a full-scale campaign to knock Italy out of the war. They regarded the Mediterranean Theatre as a costly diversion and wanted to concentrate all their forces on the cross-channel invasion, and the development of a real second front.

The British airborne division was being reorganized after fifty of their gliders were, as Lord Alanbrooke said, 'dumped' in the sea, and only twelve of a force of more than 130 reached their target. This disaster did not improve Allied relations, because the British charged that the American pilots of the tow planes cut the gliders adrift five miles off shore. (The censors ensured that not a word of this recrimination got out.) Many of the paratroopers of the U.S. 82nd Airborne Division who were dropped in support of the American Seventh Army, which landed to the west of the 1st Canadian Division, were blown off course by the previous night's storm and came down in the Eighth Army area. I met one of them when I visited Pachino on the second day ashore. The 82nd had regrouped and was ready and available, and General Eisenhower did think seriously of using it to seize the airfields around Rome, but the Allied commander-in-chief was not one to take risks. He should have struck immediately; instead, he conducted secret and complicated negotiations with Badoglio until it was too late and the Germans had taken over Italy.

Actually, the original plans for Sicily did not envisage going much beyond the island, and this was a reason why General McNaughton felt fairly confident that the 1st Canadian Division and the First Army Tank Brigade would be returned to him after they had gained battle experience. It was the British who insisted on the Italian campaign and the Americans who reluctantly went along. This time Churchill had more than eloquence to make his point; he posed the question of what would happen to the troops when Sicily was conquered, which could be by the middle of August. They could not stand idly by waiting for the cross-channel operation which was not slated to begin till May 1944. Churchill was quoted as saying that this inactivity would have 'a serious effect on relations with Russia who was bearing such a disproportionate weight [of the war].' As was to be expected, Lord Alanbrooke would not comment on Allied differences; however, he was scornful of a U.S. proposal to attack the Cherbourg peninsula at the same time as Sicily was being invaded.

When I heard the news of Mussolini's fall, I became even more anxious to get back to the front as soon as possible. I redoubled my efforts, and, as I said in a letter to my parents, 'I worked like hell getting off four fifteen minute broadcasts and two [broadcasts] of three minutes as well as an article for Maclean's Magazine which the office [CBC] seemed to be insisting that I do,' and after less than three days, I was able to leave Algiers. Paul Johnson and the recording gear were to fly back with me, but Paul had received a Priority Three and could not get on the first plane out. I had the equipment put on my Priority Two travel papers, however, and so by myself I had to manhandle across Africa the two heavy boxes in which the disc recorder was housed. When I arrived at Tunis, I left the so-called portable machine – it was portable on a jeep – at the El Ouina Airport and thumbed a ride to the Majestic Hotel, where the rest of the Canadian war correspondents were billeted.

Most of these correspondents were beside themselves with frustration over the endless delays in getting to Sicily; they were mainly representatives of independent Canadian newspapers, who had been told when they came out that they might not get to the front immediately because the number of correspondents with the fighting troops was strictly limited during the early phases of the campaign. I remember seeing Bill Wilson of the British United Press and Lionel Shapiro, who was representing the North American Newspaper Alliance, in Sicily in the middle of the campaign; as agency correspondents they had priority positions, although lower than than those of Ross Munro and me. The other reporters had been warned, but their impatience and anguish were understandable, since they were sitting in Tunis while the priceless story of the first real Canadian action was going on just across the water.

Ralph Allen, who had just been released from the army to become the Toronto *Globe and Mail*'s war correspondent, could not see anything funny in the situation, but Wally Reyburn, with whom I had shared the luxury apartment in London, was his usual humorous self. He told me that he was writing another book. 'Yes,' he said, 'The title's going to be *Last Man into Sicily*. It should be a best-seller. But maybe a better title would be *I Was Not in Sicily*.' Sholto Watt of the *Montreal Star* was not one to succumb to tensions; he insisted on living well. Leaving the complaining to others, he had a comfortable room with a balcony where he spent much of the day lolling around in the sun as if he were at a resort.

At dinner that night in the Majestic Hotel, which had been taken over by the British military authorities as an officers' hotel, an orchestra played; it struck up 'Lili Marlene,' which we knew as the Afrika Korps song that had been taken over by the Eighth Army and had become the song of the Mediterranean Theatre; we had even heard the peasants in Sicily humming and singing 'Lili Marlene.' Wally beat time with his fork and said that I was crazy to have left Sicily and that I wouldn't get back. While I denied this and said that I had the general's order to return, I began to wonder whether he might not be right. The reaction at El Ouina Airport when I applied for plane travel to Sicily had been very negative. It was difficult, the fellows in charge of transport told me, very difficult. The engineer and the equipment were quite out of the question, but they would do their best for me. God, I thought, what if I were to be stuck here with these crazy corre-spondents!

The next morning I was at the airfield bright and early, but there was no development. It was very difficult, they repeated, but they should have something definite by noon. At lunch time they had nothing to report, but they assured me they were doing their best. It meant that I had missed any opportunity of getting to Sicily that day. I was becoming desperate and even thought of going by boat, but that would have taken a week – far too long with Mussolini kicked out and Badoglio acting like a Pétain and ready to give up. In the afternoon Paul Johnson arrived; he had waited around Algiers airport all the day before without any luck but had got away that morning.

We had to move the recording equipment, those precious two black boxes that I had stashed at El Ouina, to the hotel; and so Johnson and I went back to the airfield. I was beginning to hate the place. My travel orders were with air transport, which was an American show, and, as a last hopeless gesture, I decided to try the Royal Air Force. At the counter a clerk examined my creden-tials and said, 'Where would you like to go, sir? We have aircraft going to Palermo and Cassibile.' 'Cassibile,' I replied, hardly believing my ears. The clerk asked what was my weight, and then said to be at El Ouina at quarter to seven the next morning. 'Oh, yes, that's all, sir,' he said. It seemed all too easy; I felt there must be a catch somewhere. But I had the good sense to return to the counter and explain to the officer in charge that I was a broad-caster and that it was necessary for me to have an engineer and recording equipment with me if I expected to do my work properly. Could I bring the engineer and the equipment with me the next morning on the off-chance that there might be room for them on the plane? 'Oh yes,' the officer said. 'There should be room, as we've got two planes going to Cassibile tomorrow.' Paul and I stole out of the hotel early the next morning and silently flew away to Sicily. We did not want to tell anyone in case we did not get away, and we kept our fingers crossed until we were airborne.

Cassibile was on the coast near Syracuse, a couple of dusty

runways laid down on what had been farm land. It served the Eighth Army all right, but there was no jeep, no car, no transportation for the high-ranking officers on board the plane, let alone for a couple of unheralded travellers with their strange luggage. We sat on the portable recording equipment in the blazing sunlight, watching stretcher cases being lifted out of the ambulances into the hospital planes and wondering how we were going to reach the Canadians, who were more than 100 miles away. Some of the wounded had the red shoulder patch of the 1st Canadian Division, and we decided that our best bet would be to ride the empty ambulances back to the front.

So we did; and riding with us was a tall, lean, thirty-year-old officer, Lieutenant-Colonel Dan Spry, who had been sent to Sicily to take command of the Royal Canadian Regiment, whose former commanding officer, Lieutenant-Colonel Ralph Crowe, had been killed in the recent fighting. Dan was anxious to know all about the battalion he was taking over. He pumped me for what information I had, which was not much, but it was a pleasant way to pass the time. (Dan, who was the son of a general, was to become the youngest general in the Canadian army when he was given command of the 3rd Division in 1944.) We had lunch at an air evacuation centre, a clearance point for the wounded being flown to Malta and Africa and only a few miles down the road from the Cassibile airfield. We took another ambulance to a Canadian general hospital that had just been set up in an insane asylum outside Syracuse; according to Matron Agnes MacLeod, it was the first Allied hospital opened in Sicily. A third ambulance took us to a casualty clearing station that was closer but still far from the front. We spent the night there, sleeping on stretchers in the ambulance.

The next day we got a lift in an ammunition truck as far as divisional headquarters. The recording equipment in those two black boxes bounced around with the artillery shells in the back of the vehicle as we drove over secondary roads through the sun-scorched hills to where the Canadians were, and Paul Johnson was afraid that the delicate cutting head might be broken. But it was not, and that evening I made the first recording from the front.

In the eight days that I had been away, the Canadians had advanced a little more than eight miles. Leonforte had been cleared after a couple of days of bitter house-to-house fighting, and the 1st Division had then turned right, according to plan, to advance up the road leading to Mount Etna, the next objective being the medieval town of Agira perched high on a mountain cone. The Germans had fallen back in good order, however, and were entrenched in the surrounding hills; they put up fierce resistance. The Royal Canadian Regiment ran into trouble at Nissoria, a small town on the way to Agira, and it was there that Lieutenant-Colonel Crowe had been killed. Air support was used for the first time, Allied medium bombers blasted the enemy positions, and the whole of the divisional artillery laid down a devastating barrage. After five days of hard fighting Agira fell, and two companies of the PPCLI (Princess Patricia's Canadian Light Infantry) marched up the cobblestone streets to the cheers of the populace.

(The only known occasion when heavenly hosts were said to have intervened in the Second World War was at Agira. There were several such claims in the First World War, the best known of which involved the Angels at Mons. An Italian, Guiseppe di Franco, was in the hilltop town of Agira during the battle. He saw that the Royal Twenty-Second's advance had been brought to a halt by heavy enemy fire. Then, he says, a great light appeared, and the Virgin Mary took command of the Vandoos and led them to victory over the Germans. He wrote an account of this miracle in a book entitled *La guerra in Sicilia, e i segni celesti in Agira (The War in Sicily, and the Heavenly Signs in Agira)*. Sr di Franco presented a copy of this 150-page book, published in Rome in 1950, to Yvon Beaulne, who was a secretary at the Canadian embassy in Rome at the time.)

Paul Johnson and I and the recording equipment reached the front the day after Agira was taken, and, according to the official history, this was the Canadians' biggest battle of the Sicilian campaign. The Canadian cemetery at Agira is the largest in Sicily. When we got to the camp, we heard that the pipe band of the Seaforth Highlanders of Canada would play 'Retreat' in Agira that evening, and I was determined to record this. We drove up the steep road to the old town square and parked the jeep with the recording equipment beside the steps of a Romanesque church. I had to act as a producer as well as a reporter, since we had only one turntable and could not do any editing. However, the pipe major was only too pleased to cooperate, and the priests in their shabby black robes who were going to ring the church bells fell over themselves to oblige me and ring them when I gave the signal. As I said in the broadcast:

... I am standing on the steps of the ancient church in the main square of [Agira]. Directly in front of me is the pipe band of the Seaforth Highlanders which is going to give a concert ... Besides hundreds of townspeople there are scores of Canadian soldiers perched on the top of carriers and trucks parked near the church ... At the end of the street, over there, you can look across the yellow sunburned valley and see the hills where the Germans are. You can see the smoke of battle as well, and hear the rumble of the guns. The bells of the old church are going to ring out before the pipers begin playing ... And there they are ringing now, the church bells of Agira ... And now the band under Pipe Major Edmund Essen of Vancouver ...

So there was the perfect victory sound: the Seaforth High-landers' band playing 'Retreat' and the bells of the newly captured town of Agira ringing out. The CBC described it as 'the first actuality ever broadcast from a freshly liberated area in the Second World War.' In his book, *Broadcast from the Front*, Bert Powley wrote of this radio report that 'a friend in the BBC, who had been listening to an incoming transmission, walked up to my desk and said: "Congratulations. You've got the first sound out of conquered territory."' In their regimental diary the Seaforths proudly recorded that their pipe band's concert in Agira was 'heard in London and broadcast over the BBC.' Actually, the BBC used my report in the Home Service and the European Service, and thus the Seaforths could have heard it on the following night. The BBC was entitled to use any of the CBC war reports or programs in any of their services except those heard in Canada; this was a quid pro quo arrangement, since we used their receiving and transmitting facilities.

At the time, I had no way of knowing that my first broadcast from the front was to be such a scoop. All I knew was that I had got Paul Johnson and the recording equipment into Sicily in good time for me to act as a radio reporter, and well before the campaign ended. The fact that we arrived just after the Battle of Agira, and just before the Seaforths celebrated this victory by playing 'Retreat' in the town square, was good luck, although persistence had paid off. It was proof again that if you want something badly enough, you will usually get it.

This was the first sound of liberation, and the poor, government-financed CBC had bested the wealthy U.S. networks, a remarkable feat in itself but not a very difficult one, since the Americans had a rule, apparently carved in stone, that there could be no recording of news programs. This self-denying ordinance went back to the thirties, when radio, and particularly radio news, was under constant scrutiny by the powerful newspapers; there were charges that broadcasters were faking and distorting news by means of recordings. In order to silence their critics, the U.S. networks made a public pledge that all news programs would be done 'live' and therefore there could be no accusations of fakery or distortion. The restrictive effect of this covenant became apparent with broadcasts from overseas: Hitler's triumphal entry into Vienna was at 11 a.m. Austrian time, which was 6 a.m. New York time and 3 a.m. San Francisco time, and there could be no delayed transmissions. Yet there were Ed Murrow's famous broadcasts of the London Blitz, but they were not recorded; the CBS correspondent happened to be on the air live when sirens sounded and the bombs fell.

But what about the BBC? The British had no such inhibitions about not recording news. I thought about this when I learned that when I broadcast 'Lili Marlene,' *the* great song of the Second World War, it was the first time that the tune had been heard in Britain, let alone in Canada and the United States. It was after the Sicilian campaign had ended that I made this recording. The Canadian war correspondents were billeted in a large villa on the slopes of Mount Etna. At night we would watch the flames erupting from the great volcano. There was not much to do, since we were between battles, and I thought of recording 'Lili Marlene,' which had intrigued me ever since I heard the Italian peasants singing it in the fields. So I arranged for the piece to be played by a little municipal orchestra in the town of Ionia on the Straits of Messina. This time, we had our front-line recording van, and Alec MacDonald drove it to the coast and parked it by the house that served as a makeshift studio. I think I paid £1, about $5 then, for the performance.

As I said in my commentary, the Italian words were a literal translation of the German, about the girl the soldier left behind, as were the English words (until Tin Pan Alley screwed them up) and 'that's because I think they appeal to soldiers of all nations, to German and Italian, to American and British and Canadian.' I gave what I knew of the history of the song, which was sketchy; I came to know much more about it later and even met its composer, Norbert Schultze, in Berlin.

The lyrics were written by a German minor poet, Hans Leip, but when the song was first recorded in 1938, it did not sell. The name was changed from 'Lili Marlene' to 'Lied eines jungen Wachtpostens,' 'The Song of the Young Guard,' to cash in on the war, but it was a time of jingoism and 'Wir fahren gegen England' had much more appeal, although the change in name did eventually lead to the song's great popularity and fame. In 1941 the Nazis turned Radio Beograd, which they had just captured, into a forces station for the newly formed Afrika Korps; the officer in charge of programming went through a stack of records he had received from Radio Vienna and came upon 'The Song of the Young Guard.' He thought it would be appropriate for 'lights out,' 10 p.m.; he played it three nights running, but he was not impressed and took it off.

But the song had made its mark. The war was two years old, the soldiers were far from home in the African desert, and it was time for a sentimental song.

'Lili Marlene' was then played every night at 'lights out'; it became the lullaby of opposing armies, since the Eighth Army as well as the Afrika Korps and its Italian allies tuned into Radio Beograd. Lale Andersen, who made the original recording and whose husky, music-hall voice thrilled the troops, became a star and sang 'Lili Marlene' in Berlin's Kabaret Der Komikar. Norbert Schultze told me that he did not make much money out of the song, however, that it became a hit too late, when there were shortages in Germany, and, as a result, only a few thousand discs could be pressed. When I was in Berlin at the end of the war, I was given a copy of the original recording, but the name had been changed to 'The Song of the Young Guard.'

The BBC used my 'Lili Marlene' piece, with the Sicilian orchestra thumping it out and the young tenor making it sound like an operatic aria, after the nine o'clock news, the most prestigious time, and apparently it caused a sensation. There were letters to *The Times* berating the BBC for airing this enemy song. I was surprised that the BBC should have used my piece; I had assumed that they would have broadcast the song long before I made my recording for the CBC. After all, it was no secret, and there had been reports about this extraordinary song and how both sides in the North African campaign turned their wireless sets to Radio Beograd to listen to 'Lili Marlene' before going to sleep. Why, then, did the BBC war correspondents not record it, as played in the officers' hotels in Tunis or Tripoli, or as sung by Tommies in the desert army?

Although the BBC had no inhibitions about recording news, they did have inhibitions about appointing engineers as war correspondents. During the Second World War, anybody – be he or she a politician, scientist, fashion writer – who wanted to visit the war zones was usually accredited as a war correspondent; it was easier that way for the military. I mention 'fashion writer' because several were put into uniform so that they could cover the Paris couturiers who opened for business in the winter of 1944–5. Engineers, however, were another matter to the class-conscious controllers of the BBC, whose romantic notions of war correspondents went back to Churchill in the Boer War. To make a technician an honorary captain, oh, no, that would never do! They tried to overcome the effect of this snobbery by devising a recording unit that a correspondent could operate by himself without the help of an engineer. Wynford Vaughan-Thomas, an ebullient Welshman whom I knew and admired, went ashore at Anzio in January 1944 with a disc recorder that operated on a spring and had to be wound up. He never told me how it worked; perhaps he was too loyal. As far as I know, that was the first time that such a device was used by a BBC war correspondent. Later on, I saw one of these spring-wound disc recorders; it was certainly portable, since it weighed no more than ten or fifteen pounds, but it looked like a plastic toy and had no fidelity whatsoever. When it worked, which was not often because the reporter kept forgetting to wind it up, it was good only for the voice and could not record the sound of battle. (There was no such thing as tape in those days; the first time I came across tape was at the United Nations in the fifties.)

On the other hand, CBC war recordings were of the highest quality, owing to the expertise of the engineers, who not only operated the machinery but kept it in perfect running order, and to the very latest in electronic equipment that Art Holmes and the CBC provided. My piece on 'Lili Marlene,' which I had a lot of fun doing, was amusing and entertaining and an antidote to the grim battle reports. It got a lot of publicity; so much so that it tended to overshadow my work as a war correspoondent, and I was in danger of becoming known as the man who broadcast 'Lili Marlene.' It was included in a CBC 'museum' of outstanding radio broadcasts that made the rounds of the fall fairs; the others were Churchill's riposte 'Some chicken, some neck,' King Edward VIII's abdication speech, the Dionne quintuplets singing 'There'll always be an England,' and Frank Willis's Moose River Mine disaster report. Of all the hundreds of war recordings in the National Archives in Ottawa, this one of mine – which was really a filler because there was no news of the fighting – has been rebroadcast the most. It tickled the fancy of Max Ferguson, who used it periodically in his radio programs.

After Agira, the next objective for the Canadians was Regalbuto, a small town strategically located in the valley leading to the great and forbidding mass of Mount Etna. The Germans had rushed up two battalions of paratroopers, and they put up a strong defence in the heights on either side of the town; for Regalbuto, unlike Agira, was on a hump surrounded by high hills. There were no cheering crowds when we entered Regulbuto shortly after it was captured, no silent people in front of their doors raising their fingers in the V sign, nobody at all; for the town had been torn apart by the Allied air force. Houses were gaping open and beds and chairs hung crazily from shattered second floors; some buildings looked like dollhouses with their fronts ripped off and the rooms and furnishings exposed. Rubble filled the streets to such an extent that a bulldozer had to clear a way for our jeep, and I saw for the first time how a heavy bombing attack could actually delay the advance.

The next day I visited the Forty-Eighth Highlanders of Toronto, who were on the steep, stony slopes on one side of Regalbuto. An officer told me that the Loyal Edmonton Regiment was across the sunburned expanse of the Simeto Valley on a mountain almost opposite us. And that was where the real fighting for Regalbuto was taking place: on the heights on either side where the German paratroopers were dug in. The town was obviously a much easier target for our bombers than the enemy positions high in the hills, and while close air support could be of great assistance to the infantry, the mountainous terrain of Sicily and Italy made it a hazardous operation. From where the Forty-Eighth were, the countryside was laid out like a map: there was the great volcano which rose darkly above a stormy sea of burned yellow hills, and there was Aderno, the key town on the road that skirted the base of Mount Etna.

We were watching a column of Canadian armoured cars and tanks slowly climbing up the brown thread of a road across the valley towards where the Edmontons were, when there was the sound of planes overhead. We paid no attention, thinking they were ours, until the drone of their motors changed to a roaring scream and then we dived for cover in a rock-strewn ditch. They were ours all right and they were attacking us. One of the soldiers who had been following them through his field-glasses said that they looked like American planes, a whole squadron of them. They strafed the dusty ridge held by the Toronto regiment, but fortunately they missed and no one was hurt; but they did not miss Regalbuto. I did not mention this attack on our troops by our own planes in my book, *Journey into Victory*, because the censors felt it would be bad for morale, although they let me say that the planes bombed Regalbuto a day after the town had been taken and that a number of civilians and Allied soldiers were killed.

As soon as I saw that Regalbuto had been hit and was covered by a pall of smoke and dust, I ran down the steep slope to our jeep and started off for the town. More rubble and debris had fallen into the streets, and some soldiers were already clearing the main square. There were scenes of horror: a hand, white and lifeless, sticking out of the rubble; a girl on top of the wreckage of her house, crying and waving her arms in despair. Two Canadian soldiers tried to comfort her, and one of them said that her mother and father were buried under the tons of broken masonry. Three American GIs stood by their jeep staring at the girl as if hypnotized. They had been driving into the town when the planes struck and they said that they saw the aircraft had United States markings. They were bewildered and angry at what had happened.

This was the first time in my experience that our troops were attacked by friendly planes, but not the last time. It was not always the fault of the airmen: sometimes they were given the wrong coordinates, and one Italian hill town looked so much like another from the air. Then, on the other side of the coin, I saw Canadian anti-aircraft gunners opening up on American planes, which did everything to show their identity. It was probably impossible to eliminate this sort of insanity entirely, especially if the air crews were green and the troops fresh, but there was no doubt that it was extremely bad for morale, not to mention good feelings between allies.

Paul Johnson and I took the recording equipment with us wherever we went in the jeep, and I made good use of it describing the fighting in the parched, sunburned valley leading to Mount Etna. It was terribly hard going because the Germans were putting up a stiff rearguard action and had to be cleared from every hilltop position. The problem with mountain warfare in this fearful heat was drinking water. The men had to carry so much water that they could not take any rations and often went hungry for days.

(Mules had to be used to supply the Canadian troops fighting in the stifling heat on the slopes of Mount Etna. A Mule Transporter Company was formed by the RCASC (Royal Canadian Army Service Corps) and put under the command of Captain L. 'Jack' Jackson, formerly of the Lord Strathcona Horse. Approximately 250 mules were requisitioned and a platoon of ninety animals was assigned to each brigade on the evening of 4 August 1943.)

It was little more than a week after the victory celebration in Agira that the Canadians took Aderno and cracked the German defence line before Mount Etna. The enemy, in danger of being outflanked, withdrew from the major city of Catania on 5 August and two days later pulled out of Aderno. The smell of death hung over the ruins of the town, which must have been a pretty place once, nestling at the foot of the volcano; there were bodies lying in the streets, horrible nightmare bodies with black faces and thick grinning lips. As I said in my broadcast report: ... 'There is nothing left in Aderno but death, dust and ashes. You remember the phrase that Prime Minister Churchill used in a speech a few months ago. Well, I saw its grim reality in this town which was one of the key positions in the so-called German Etna line. I have never seen such destruction. There were parts of the town that were simply wiped out ...'

The Canadians came out of the line at Aderno, and I was ordered to Algiers to cover Allied Force headquarters, but before going I went for a swim in the Simeto River. It was a delicious

experience, splashing around in the swift-flowing water, and I
remember thinking how peaceful the valley was now: there were
goats grazing on the dry yellow grass, and in the distance some
peasants were threshing wheat. I also got General Simonds to
review the work of the 1st Canadian Division during the campaign.
That was the last use I made of the portable recording equipment
that we had triumphantly borne to the front some ten days before;
I left it in Johnson's charge, to be taken over by Matthew Halton
and Marcel Ouimet, who were replacing me in Sicily. The military
authorities had finally accepted the need for broadcasting in
French, and therefore the CBC needed to have two correspondents
at the front. By the time they arrived, Halton and Ouimet could
report only on the British and American forces, since the Canadians were out of the action. But they were there for the expected
invasion of the mainland of Italy, in which the Canadians were to
play an assault role.

At Allied Force headquarters in Algiers, a bell used to ring in
the passage outside the long, crowded correspondents' room just
before a communiqué was read. It was a very insistent bell,
designed to drag a reporter away from an argument with a censor,
no matter how righteously indignant he was. It rang twice on 17
August 1943, the day that the Sicilian campaign ended. The
coloured pins had marched across the huge wall map of Sicily at
the end of the correspondents' room and had almost met at the top,
so that we were not surprised when the briefing officer announced
that American troops had reached the outskirts of Messina at eight
o'clock the night before. There was a rattle of typewriters and a
rush of agency men to the counter where a censor stood, rubber
stamp in hand, to pass the flashes as they were handed to him. A
public relations officer shouted above the din that each of the
broadcasting networks would have a minute on the air in half an
hour's time.

The five of us – CBC, BBC, NBC, Columbia, and Mutual – drew
from a deck of cards for the order in which we would go on the air.
We sat on a wooden bench in the small, newly built studio, which
was just down the corridor from the correspondents' room, and

followed each other to the mike on the blanket-covered table, waiting a few seconds for the American operator to establish contact with London, New York, or Toronto. That was the first bell in the morning; the end of the Sicilian campaign was still to come, and the correspondents settled down to wait for it. The British missed their tea in the Regina Hotel and the Americans their drinks in the Allied Officers' Club at the Alletti Hotel because the second bell was not sounded till ten o'clock that night.

General Eisenhower, who looked fit and cheerful, held a news conference the next day at his residence, a white building that Americans called the 'White House,' overlooking Algiers; he was dressed in a plain khaki shirt and trousers without any rank badges or ribbons. The Allied commander-in-chief apologized for having predicted that the Sicilian campaign would be over by 5 August; he was almost two weeks out. But then I found that most soldiers were optimists. The coloured pins were removed from the map, which became bare and uninteresting, and a monocled British officer announced that there would be no further communiqués on Sicily.

We could relax and go swimming around the bay on the fine sandy beaches of Guyotville. A French colonial capital, Algiers was really a stuffy place, but it did have a number of large whorehouses that were frequented by the British troops but out of bounds for the Americans. In fact, British Military Police patrolled the red-light district, and I recall one MP, who was posted outside a brothel that was as big as a hotel, telling me that the average time a Tommy spent with a girl was less than five minutes. There was the Casbah, which Hollywood had glamorized, but I found it a dirty, stinking place and was revolted at the sight of running sores on the feet of Arab children; I remembered what H.G. Wells said of a medieval city.

It was dull, but then I was invited on board HMS George V and asked to speak to the ship's company on the Sicilian campaign. The 45,000-ton British battleship was docked in Algiers harbour; besides her ten fourteen-inch guns, she had an array of 'Chicago pom-poms,' or multiple anti-aircraft guns. (This was one of the reasons it was so dangerous to be out of doors during an air raid on Algiers; in addition to the *George V*, there were other warships in the harbour as well as all the guns ashore. This meant the city had to endure a hail of steel splinters from the flak, much heavier than any I experienced in London.) The public relations officer on this huge battleship was a Canadian (perhaps that was why I got the invitation); he took me to dinner in the wardroom, which was as large as a dining saloon on a liner, and there was another one for the captain and the senior officers. I spoke over the public address system from a well-appointed studio near the bridge.

There was not much news, but I kept busy doing several fifteen-minute broadcasts and another 2,500-word article for *Maclean's* magazine, the second in a couple of weeks. Altogether, I wrote half a dozen articles on the war for *Maclean's*, which was then the leading periodical in Canada. I did not like covering Allied Force headquarters in Algiers: it reminded me too much of my work as a news editor in Vancouver; rewriting a communiqué was not so different from rewriting agency copy. Therefore, a week or so after the end of the Sicilian campaign, I was delighted to hear that I was to return to the front. Looking back now, I am not sure whether the order came from the CBC or from my friend, Royd Beamish, who was in charge of Canadian army PR in Algiers, and I did not ask any questions. I wanted to be in on the invasion of Italy. Ernie Burritt of Canadian Press, who had crossed the Atlantic with me, was in Algiers, and we were to travel together. Transportation had been arranged, we were on an hour's stand-by notice, but days went by and there was no call.

When we inquired, we were told that east-bound planes were filled with high-priority personnel being rushed to Sicily at the last moment, and there was a backlog of eight days. The map of Sicily had been taken down from the wall at the end of the correspondents' room and a map of Italy was being pieced together. We were at our wits' end when Wing Commander Rod MacInnes, chief of RCAF Public Relations in the Mediterranean Theatre, made what we thought was a silly remark: he said that if we could get to Tunis, there would be no trouble getting a flight to Sicily. But how would we get to Tunis? Rod, who was to become a vice-president of Air Canada, said that he would drive us.

It was crazy: it was some 600 miles to Tunis. But there was no other way. We started off before dawn the next morning in a 1,500-weight truck that bore the yellow desert camouflage and appeared to have fought a personal battle with the panzers of the Afrika Korps. It was a day and a half's journey and Rod drove all the way, past the beautiful city of Constantine, built on either side of a gorge, past Bone. We slept in the truck under the stars in the black African night – or tried to sleep. I rolled up in a tarpaulin cover and used a haversack as a pillow and got a fitful rest. We were off at dawn the next day through the Medjez Valley, where some of the fiercest fighting of the Tunisian campaign had taken place. There were shell craters and bomb-blasted buildings, but the valley was strangely silent and empty now. I noticed that the graves were in neat cemeteries, unlike the graves in Sicily, which were dotted along the roadside.

We reached Tunis at noon and were told that the first plane to Sicily was not leaving till the following day. It was scorching hot, and we went for a swim in the Mediterranean; that night, we stayed at the RCAF villa that was run in sumptuous style by Italian prisoners of war. At El Ouina Airport early the next morning the transport officer shook his head. There was no room. We tried the Americans, who were across a field in a black building beside some burned-out hangars, but no joy there. So back we went to the British building, forlorn and frustrated, and the transport officer looked up and said two passengers had not turned up. We were on board the only plane leaving for Sicily that day.

An RAF officer met us when we landed at an airfield near Catania. MacInnes had alerted him to the arrival of a couple of Canadians, but he had expected RCAF types. He gave us lunch during which we learned that the 1st Division was near Messina. A succession of lifts took us up the coastal road that was clogged with traffic; we passed convoy after convoy. It was dusk by the time we began to see Canadian signs along the roadside, and almost dark when we reached divisional headquarters. Major Bill Gilchrist, a senior Canadian public relations officer, greeted us. 'My God,' Bill said, 'you certainly time things right. We're invading Italy tonight. Jump into the jeep and we'll go and see the fireworks.'

8

Broadcasting on the Run

Strait of Messina, 3 September 1943:
British and Canadian troops under General Montgomery cross
the Strait of Messina and land on mainland Italy.

D usk had given way to darkness and night was in full control
with all the majesty that a vigorously enforced blackout gave
it when we left divisional headquarters and drove along the
twisting coastal road towards the loading beaches. There was no
moon and we could feel and hear much better than we could see,
and we felt the closeness of the houses and heard the whispered
voices of the Sicilians sitting at their open doors and on their
narrow balconies, chatting as they had done every evening of their
lives, but this was the night of the invasion of Italy.

Then we saw a strange fire burning brightly in the encircling
darkness and giving a sheen to the oily blackness of the Mediterranean. We saw it whenever we swung out away from the houses
along the coast and the gently lapping waters of the tideless sea.
We took a closer look and noticed that the fire seemed to rise and
fall like a revolving beacon, and decided that it must be something
burning across the narrow strait on the mainland. We crept along,

past the grey, shadowy forms of trucks, and came to a halt. A voice said, 'I'll lead you across the next crater,' and we followed a pinpoint of red light.

Somehow we found the white villa on the left-hand side of the road which was the headquarters of the Canadian assault brigade. Across the road from the villa, the olive trees ran down to the loading beaches, and on the white sand sprawled dim forms of men in battle equipment. They were members of the Carleton and York Regiment, which was one of the two assault battalions, the other being the West Nova Scotia Regiment. The British 5th Division was landing on the left of the 1st Canadian Division. Most of the men were asleep, and those who were awake smoked and talked in hushed tones as though they were afraid that they might be heard across the dark Strait of Messina in the darker mass over there that was Italy.

It was a tense time for the assault troops, the waiting hours before an invasion. They joked about the rumours that were going the rounds that night, beach rumours they called them. They had seen the fire on the mainland – it had gone out now, but it had burned just across from us, above the shore they were going to attack. They had heard that it was an ammunition dump set ablaze by the 'Eyeties' in preparation for withdrawal; that would account for the way it flared up all the time. The men felt that the fire was a sign that the landing would be a pushover, but then it might be simply another rumour. A fellow who was probably an officer whispered in my ear, 'I don't know whether it's a sign that they're not expecting much trouble, but we're only carrying twenty [wooden] crosses with us.'

There was a low throb of engines and the shapes of landing craft began to appear on the water. A tall, lean figure sat down in the sands among the dim, grey forms of the soldiers. It was only after he began to tell us about the assault plans that I realized he was the colonel of the Carleton and Yorks. He said the Canadians were going to land on the very toe of Italy just north of the important port of Reggio. The two assault battalions were his own and the West Nova Scotias; they were to take the town and form a beachhead. The Vingt-Deuxième, the French Canadian regiment known as the 'Vandoos,' would pass through them and attack the two forts above the town; it was believed that there were some old Italian coastal guns in one of the forts and some modern German eighty-eights in the other. Another Canadian brigade was to land and turn south to take the airfield just below Reggio.

While the colonel was talking, a loudspeaker on the beach boomed out, 'Landing Craft Number Seventeen, come into shore slowly.' A faint shape began to take form, then a crunch and a clanking sound was heard as the boat let down its ramp onto the beach. A naval officer approached us and said, 'The guides are ready to take the men on board the boats, sir.' The colonel got up and shouted, 'Number Seventeen. All ready. Let's go.' We stood up and watched the men file by into the gaping mouth of the landing craft. They were heavily laden and their feet sank into the sand; some of them seemed to be still half asleep. The poor fellows, I thought, they would be stuck in the cramped quarters of the landing craft for hours: H-Hour was not till 4.30 a.m. and it was only just past midnight.

The miles of beach and olive groves were as crowded as Sunnyside Beach in Toronto on a hot summer day. We moved among the assault troops, searching for the CP and CBC correspondents who were going to cover the attack and, more by luck than anything else, found them. I exchanged a few words with Matthew Halton, who was kind enough to congratulate me on my reporting of the Sicilian campaign. It was the first time that I had met him, and we stayed only a few minutes. In the darkness I could not really tell what he looked like.

We made our way back to the road and and after a number of inquiries found the red villa the roof of which offered an excellent vantage point from which to observe the invasion. Somebody, presumably the owner, was living on the ground floor, and I was surprised that people had not been cleared out of their houses along this part of the Sicilian coast, which served as the springboard for the attack on the mainland. It was just past one o'clock in the morning, and the 500 guns massed in the hills around

Messina were not going to open up on the shores of Italy until half-past three. Perhaps it was the divan bed in the villa, so beautifully soft and springy; at any rate, I was tired and I lay down, and the next thing I knew, Ernie Burritt was punching me in the ribs. I suddenly became aware of a rolling thunder of noise – and I dashed up onto the roof. I described the scene in my broadcast:

... Almost with the first shots, half a dozen searchlights were switched on – they were pointed vertically and their beams made a beautiful column of light. The searchlights served as markers on which the landing craft could take bearings. The hills north of Messina were lit up by the flames of the guns which were brighter by far than the brightest sheet of lightning. The noise became a rolling, roaring, endless thunder. Our artillery was sweeping the toe of Italy with a broom of fire and steel. We could see the flickering flashes in the darkness across the strait where the shells burst. Now and then there was a glow in the sky where the guns had set fire to a building, and once there was a bright burning patch that sent up little onions of light ... At half past five, the guns stopped. The torrent of shells on the Italian mainland ceased just as quickly as it began. The dawn was lighting up the Calabrian hills and within a few minutes I was able to pick out the shapes of landing craft along the Italian coast. There was a smell of cordite in the air and over the Strait of Messina hung a long thin cloud which had been manufactured partly by the guns during the night, partly by the smoke-screen laid down by the landing craft as they went into the beaches ...

As soon as I could, I got down to work and did a fifteen-minute piece for the CBC on the barrage and crossing the Strait of Messina, of which the above was an excerpt. As I said in a letter to my parents, the invasion of Italy was 'a cinch for me as I have been covering it from the rear.' I missed all the gut-wrenching tension of taking part in the assault – Matthew Halton did that – and yet it turned out that I had the best eyewitness account, since the landing was an anticlimax. There was no opposition, there was no reply to the concentrated artillery fire. The enemy had with-drawn, and the inhabitants of Reggio Calabria must have known what was coming and had very wisely taken to the hills. The landing was a 'piece of cake,' as the British would have said. The Canadian troops walked ashore, and there was no one there, just an empty landscape that appeared war-torn because of the shell holes and burning buildings.

Although the Messina barrage proved to be quite unnecessary, it was a magnificent if expensive spectacle. Assuming that the artillery fired at the rate of one round every minute for two hours – and the 5.5-inch medium guns as well as the field guns, the twenty-five pounders, could be fired at the rate of two rounds a minute – then some 60,000 shells had been wasted on the deserted coastline of Italy. It is impossible to say how much the cannonade in the early hours of 3 September 1943 cost, and expenses were of no concern during the war. Still, Allied Intelligence must have known that the 100,000 enemy troops who had escaped from Sicily and withdrawn across the Strait of Messina were not going to defend the toe of Italy. The last Germans to leave Reggio, a battalion of the 29th Panzer Grenadier Division, had pulled out fully two days before the British and Canadians landed.

Yet this was the first attack on the mainland, on 'Fortress Europe,' which the Nazis claimed was impregnable, and even if Intelligence was right, and the enemy had pulled out, one would have expected rearguards to be left. Instead, the Germans contented themselves with blowing bridges and cratering the steep, twisting roads through the mountainous Aspromonte. General Montgomery was not taking any chances, however, and ordered the Messina barrage. Some Eighth Army officers who were on the roof of the villa with us on the night of the invasion said that it was a greater sight than the night barrage at El Alamein, which opened the way for the desert victory.

Monty was a flamboyant figure and set a sartorial style at the front that must have made the more traditional British officers blanch. He wore the black beret of the armoured corps with two badges, as well as other unusual headgear such as the wide-brimmed Anzac hat, suede shoes known as 'desert boots,' a cravat, and, in the winter, sweaters, corduroy trousers, and a sheepskin coat. As might be expected, his way of dressing was copied by the lesser ranks; parachute silk was favoured for a cravat, and I remember my delight in finding a piece suitable for my own wear. The Eighth Army commander became a dress model even for American GIs, who took to wearing fancy scarves until their spit-and-polish officers put a stop to such unmilitary attire. However, Monty's dashing appearance and his eccentricities belied the fact that he was a cautious commander who did not usually take risks. He would not launch an offensive until he had two or three times the number of men and munitions as the enemy. This was why the troops had such confidence in him: they knew that when they went into battle, they would have overwhelming support.

What made a great general? We would argue about this at night while camping in the open during an advance and drinking vino out of our metal canteens under the stars, or more prosaically in some battered Italian villa when the front was static. Montgomery was the greatest field commander that the British had had for a long time – since the Duke of Wellington, someone said. How did that come about? The other commanders had all the executive and organizational abilities that he had, and yet he had succeeded where the likes of Wavell and Auchinleck had failed. We wondered about this and came to the view that luck counted for a lot, as it did in other careers, but perhaps more so for a four-star general. There was no doubt that General Montgomery was lucky: he arrived in North Africa at just the right time, when the tide had turned and the Eighth Army was getting all the men and equipment and air support that were needed to defeat the Afrika Korps.

On the day of the invasion I talked to a number of Canadian sailors who had manned the landing craft that took the Canadian troops into Italy. Every one of them was amazed at the lack of resistance on the beaches. One of the seamen described the way the boats zigzagged through the smokescreen and suddenly found a hole in the mist and grounded ashore; he was proud of the fact that they had landed the troops without getting their feet wet. The sailors were thrilled by the artillery barrage, calling it the most wonderful thing they had ever seen. It had done a lot of damage

to Reggio: it looked as if someone had swept the roofs off all the
houses in the city; there were at least two ships sunk in the
harbour. Their only taste of action was at about noon when some
enemy planes made a half-hearted attack on the hundreds of boats
off the beaches and disappeared as quickly as they had come; one
of the fellows said scornfully that they must have been Italian
planes. I met the Canadian sailors at their camp, which was by the
sea on the outskirts of Messina, and as I said in my report:

... From where we were sitting, chatting, we were in sight of the loading
beaches which are still crowded with motor transport. There were long
rows of vehicles moving slowly over the sand and then bumping up
ramps into the yawning stern of scores of landing craft. There were
lines of soldiers on the beaches as well ... It looked like pictures of the
beaches of Dunkirk, only there were no geysers of water from the
bombing, no smoke from burning supply dumps. The Mediterranean
was blue and unruffled. This was indeed a Dunkirk in reverse. And
along the coastal road long convoys were moving past the giant ger-
aniums that are in bloom in Sicily now and the purple azaleas toward
the loading beaches ...

Three hundred beds had been cleared for casualties in the
Canadian General Hospital – it had moved from the old insane
asylum at Syracuse to much better quarters in a beautiful modern
sanatorium near Messina – but when I went there the day after
the landing, there was exactly one patient. He was an Army
Service Corps driver who had gone ashore long after the assault
troops and had been wounded by shrapnel during the enemy's
feeble air raid, and he was rather overcome by the amount of
attention that he was receiving from the underworked nurses. A
little later I returned to the hospital and found that it had received
three more patients from Italy. Two of them had broken bones
from falling out of trucks, while the third was a Canadian sailor,
a good-looking boy with a curly blond beard who grinned rather
sheepishly and admitted to having been kicked by a horse. 'I was
in the crew of a landing craft,' he said. 'We were ashore on a beach

near Reggio and saw some horses. One of the fellows had the idea of going for a ride. I guess I must have got on the wrong end.'

After we had visited the hospital, there was not much to do, because the main story was with the Canadian troops driving up the boot of Italy. The roles were reversed now, and I was with the rest of the Canadian correspondents who remained in Sicily, while Matthew Halton and Marcel Ouimet were with the priority correspondents who landed at Reggio and were covering the advance. There were about twenty of us, including conducting officers, and we were billeted in a villa that belonged to a macaroni millionaire (so I said in a letter home) on the slopes of Mount Etna; it was a huge place with wide verandas, but it had no running water or electric lights.

We were told that we would be joining the advancing troops when the bulk of the 1st Canadian Division had crossed into Italy; but movement was very slow, since there was only one winding, twisting road that was cut into the steep eastern side of the Italian 'boot' and the retreating Germans had all but wrecked it. The sappers worked day and night to repair the blown bridges and the large craters in the road. The British 5th Division and the Canadian Army Tank Brigade had the only other road along the rugged western coast, and that had been just as badly damaged by the enemy. It was a pleasant enough if boring interlude in the villa on the slopes of Etna, and at night we would sit in the garden, drinking vino and watching the pyrotechnics of the erupting volcano.

Mount Etna, 8 September 1943:
Italy's capitulation is announced by General Eisenhower. As agreed, the main Italian fleet is surrendered to the Allies.

We heard the news on the car radio in the CBC's studio van. Paul Johnson had gone with Halton and Ouimet and taken along the portable recording equipment so that they could report on the Italian invasion, while Alec MacDonald had stayed behind with the van. Evidently the armistice had been signed on 3 September, the day the Canadians landed, although it did not go into effect until 8 September. Now we understood why there had been so little resistance. In fact, I talked to an Italian prisoner who had been captured at Reggio, and he said that his outfit had been told that the armistice had been signed and that there was no need to fight.

The news of the Italian surrender was greeted with wild celebrations in Sicily. The slopes of Mount Etna were lit up like a Christmas tree; bonfires burned and nature itself seemed to join in the party as the volcano sent its flames soaring into the night sky. Crowds gathered and sang 'Mama, Mama,' a catchy popular tune that had taken the place of the Fascist 'Gionivezza' in the hearts of the people. Canadian soldiers joined in the fun, firing tracer bullets into the air and breaking open cartridges and lighting trails of gunpowder. In one village there was dancing in the street to the music of an unusual band made up of a mandolin player, a violinist, and a Scottish piper. Bottles of wine appeared, and toasts were drunk to the Allies and a 'Free Sicily.'

The next day, we heard on the van's crackly little radio in the CBC van that another landing had been made by the Allies at Salerno, a seaside resort south of Naples. This one, as we had expected, was no pushover: British and American forces encountered fierce German resistance and fought for days before securing a bridgehead. Shortly afterwards we received our movement orders and began our long, five-day journey to the front.

The landing craft were now being used as a fast ferry service, and it took us only half an hour to cross the Strait of Messina. We drove in convoy through the mountains over the wild volcanic plateau known as the Aspromonte to the east coast. The road was little more than a dusty dirt track, worse, it seemed to us bumping along in the CBC recording van, than the route the Canadians had followed in Sicily. Although all the bridges had been blown by the Germans, in most places the engineers had built diversions across the dry river beds; that was fine now, but I wondered what would happen when the rains came. This was the 'Maple Leaf Highway,' complete with signs that had become so familiar to the Canadian soldiers, the gold maple leaf on a red background, with warnings and instructions to drivers and admonishments to the rank and file:

If you can pee that yellow stream
It means you've taken your mepacrime.*

Along this dirt road, we passed lines of Italian soldiers heading in the opposite direction. They would lean on their sticks – and all of them seemed to have sticks – when we drove by, hefting their rucksacks higher up on their shoulders, not speaking, not greeting us, not even calling out for a cigarette. They seemed far too intent on the journey that lay ahead of them and had halted only to avoid the clouds of dust from our wheels. They were quite different, these Italian soldiers, from those we we had seen in Sicily. There were no grinning Canadian guards with these men, and there was no military order about them. They were trudging along, without puttees, with their coats over their shoulders and their caps on the backs of their heads; some of them were lugging battered, old suitcases or cloth bundles.

It was a sobering sight; for what we were seeing was the disintegration of a large part of the Italian armed forces. These men were not prisoners of war, and their sullen mood was in sharp contrast to the happy-go-lucky attitude of the prisoners in Sicily. They had not been captured in any battle or rounded up by the Allies. These Italian soldiers had simply quit. They had left their camps or barracks when it was evident that their units had broken up: their officers had gone, the whole paraphernalia of command had disappeared, and the cookhouses were closed. They were going home, and there was a grim determination about these stragglers on the desert track over the Aspromonte to return as quickly as possible to their families and the life they used to know. Looking at the ragtag remains of a once-great army, I wondered if our

---

*Mepacrime, an anti-malarial drug, also known as Atabrine. Later in the war, Palludrin was developed, which did not have the penetrating yellow pigment.

soldiers would have behaved in this way if they had suffered the same shattering defeat as the Italians. The Germans never did. They fought to the last, and when they surrendered, as they did in Holland, their iron discipline held even in the POW camps.

We finally caught up with the Canadians as we left the east coast and swung back into the mountains. Among the first troops I saw were some members of the Royal Canadian Regiment who were standing by their carriers, taking a break. When I told them that we had just driven hundreds of miles during the last few days, they said, 'That's all we've been doing, just trekking along.'

In their hasty withdrawal from the toe and the boot of Italy, the Nazis had forgotten to destroy the telephone lines. As a result the Canadians could and did telephone through to enemy territory. They would ring up a town forty miles or so ahead and get the mayor or another official on the other end of the line and ask him how many Germans there were in the area. Sometimes they were fooled in these telephone conversations. One mayor informed them that there were 2,000 Germans in his town, but when our troops arrived there, they discovered that there had never been more than a company of Nazis near the place. They were ready to shoot that mayor, who must have been an unreconstructed Fascist, but he had disapppeared.

The Canadians met no real resistance until they reached Potenza, more than three weeks after they had landed on the beaches near Reggio. They engaged in a short skirmish with some Nazi paratroops before taking the provincial capital, some seventy miles inland from Salerno and Naples. Up until then it had been a victory parade, each hilltop town greeting them as conquering heroes and insisting that they stay long enough to eat and drink. The 1st Canadian Division finally came to a halt in the brown hills around Potenza: it had to regroup. After advancing more than 400 miles from the toe of Italy, its units were somewhat scattered, and there was fully 100 miles between two of the brigades.

We caught up with Matthew Halton and Marcel Ouimet at Potenza; the Public Relations camp was in the Appenines not far from the city, in a chalet that had belonged to a Fascist sports club. There was quite a large corps of Canadian correspondents with the 1st Division now. It included most of those who had languished in frustration in Tunis during the Sicilian campaign, as well as the three 'old men': Fred Griffin, the veteran *Toronto Star* correspondent, who had come up with us; the grandfatherly Bert Wemp of the *Telegram*, a former mayor of Toronto; and the great storyteller Greg Clark, an amiable gnome with a scatological sense of humour. At the same time, a message that had evidently been making the rounds for seven weeks in the Mediterranean Theatre finally caught up with me (on 23 September); sent on 12 August, it instructed me to return to London. Bert Powley was always of the view that I had somehow been able to avoid receiving it; my explanation was that fortunately I had been able to keep one step ahead of it, and that communication near the front was, as he knew, very slow. At any rate, before making my way back to Algiers and London, I had time to get to know Halton, whom I had met so briefly on the loading beaches in Messina. I found him to be a good companion and, as I said in a letter to my parents, 'it's an honor to be the running mate of such a famous and experienced correspondent.'

Halton was a great raconteur, and he entertained us with accounts of his exploits as a foreign correspondent and a war correspondent: he had seen the rise of Hitler, had been involved in the Spanish civil war, and had covered Munich. He had spent a year and a half with the Eighth Army during the battles that raged back and forth across the Western Desert and culminated in the victory at El Alamein. Matt spoke in the dramatic manner that was the hallmark of his broadcasts and was his natural way of telling a story. Originally a newspaper correspondent, he soon adapted to broadcasting and, as Powley said, became an addict of sound, or actuality; some of his broadcasts from Ortona and Normandy and among the finest examples of radio reporting.

Halton covered the Finnish war, and it was one experience that affected him deeply and that he had some difficulty rationalizing. In his reports he had extolled the 'brave Finns' for the way they had stopped the first onslaught of the Red Army, but in the end they had lost, while the Russians, whom he had scorned for their blundering aggression, were now our friends and brave Allies.

It was in Algiers, while waiting for travel orders to return to London, that I had a run-in with Canadian army Public Relations. Major Bill Abel and his assistant, Captain Eric Gibbs, had come to Allied Force headquarters on some sort of inspection tour – CMHQ officials liked to get out in the field so that they could say they had been at the front. They accused me of disregarding my travel orders and making off with the seats intended for some high-ranking officers when I got Paul Johnson and the equipment into Sicily on a RAF plane. At first I thought they must be kidding, but they were serious. Perhaps these piffling travel charges were just a pretext to get at me for the complaints I had made to the CBC about the army's Public Relations officers and how they favoured Canadian Press.

Yet it seemed to be more than that. They were really angry with me; Bill's face was red and there were beads of sweat on his bald pate. I got the impression that they seemed to resent me personally as an upstart, which I suppose I was, and an outsider from the wrong part of the country who had somehow got all the breaks. There was something, too, about my name: it was a German name, but so was Eisenhower's, but that made no difference to those two desk-bound patriots. (During the First World War some of my British relatives changed their name.) I suspect they thought I was Jewish, but my grandfather, who left Germany in the 1860s, was a devout Congregationalist, and an uncle, Dr Otto Stursberg, was for forty years a Christian missionary in India. At any rate, we had a heated argument, and I told them that in their comfortable quarters in London they knew nothing about the problems of a correspondent, and a radio reporter at that, in a war zone. I was incensed and I used rather strong language, which was foolish because it did me no good in the end.

While I was in Algiers, I received the first sound of battle. The recording was made by Marcel Ouimet and Paul Johnson during an attack on a small Italian town. They had parked the CBC van on a hilltop, from which Marcel, holding the mike, could look back about 1,000 yards at our guns and forward about 2,000 yards to the town that was to be taken. (Paul was in the van at the controls.) It was a perfect vantage point, and Ouimet could see the Canadian infantry moving forward behind the barrage. The recording had everything, as Bert Powley said in his book: 'the gun fire, the whistling of the shells overhead and the distant detonations as they exploded. To make things perfect, a few squadrons of Spitfires roared directly over the microphone, by happy chance in the few intervals when the guns were silent.' Marcel did not attempt to describe the action and only afterwards dubbed in his narration.

I let the correspondents at AFHQ know about the battle recording. Most of the big names, such as Dan De Luce of Associated Press, Reynolds Packard of United Press, and Pierre Huss of International News Service, were still there, and practically all of them gathered in the studio to listen to it as it was relayed to London. They were impressed. The English version of the broadcast – Marcel Ouimet did both a French and an English version – was used by the BBC after the nine o'clock news, and it was heard in the United States through the Mutual Network, which picked it up from the BBC's North American Service. It so excited the syndicated New York columnist Walter Winchell that, Powley said, he wrote about 'tanks rumbling by, Spitfires going overhead to the attack. Nazi and British shells whizzing by his ears,' and 'the young Canadian correspondent standing his ground till the Nazis fled.'

At last my travel orders came through; I left Algiers on 13 October in a Dakota transport plane and flew to Rabat on the first leg of the journey to England. I was stuck there for four days, waiting for a flight. Every day and sometimes twice a day I would visit the airport, only to be told that people with higher priorities were ahead of me. Once I had visited the souk, the Arab market, there was not much else to do or see in Rabat. I was put up in a small tourist hotel, and I remember that the restaurant had no butter, so for breakfast I ate dry toast and the little Moroccan eggs that were about the size of pigeon's eggs. When I did get off, I found I was on a BOAC aircraft the windows of which were covered with steel shutters. (Apparently all civilian planes had to be blacked out.) I did not like not being able to see out; I had the sensation of flying in a coffin. I was greatly relieved when we landed safely in Gibraltar, because I knew the runway was short – it was there that Sikorski was killed when his plane could not come to a halt and crashed into the sea.

We stopped in Gibraltar for five hours and had dinner at the Bristol Hotel, which was crowded with officers in transit. I bumped into a couple of old friends. One of them was Odie Smith, whom I had not seen in ten years, since we were on the McGill rowing crew. Odie was a captain with the engineers and was on his way somewhere; I remembered him as having a bad stutter, but with all the drinks and the camaraderie at the hotel, he could not have been more eloquent. As I wrote home, 'the Rock [of Gibraltar] was like a stage setting at night as it was lit up by huge searchlights.' So was the Bristol Hotel, with its windows shining on the narrow street that led up to the Rock. I was sorry to have to leave the party and board the blacked-out plane, which left at 11 p.m. (The fact that it was considered safer to fly at night accounted for the five-hour stop-over.) The flight was a long one because we made a wide sweep of Portugal, but it was longer still, since we ran into a storm and did not land in the west of England till ten o'clock in the morning. Eleven hours in that flying coffin!

The last part of the journey was by train; it was so crowded that I stood or sat on my bags in the corridor. I got to London and the CBC at 200 Oxford Street in the evening, but, at that, I was ahead of Andy Cowan, who had left Algiers some time before me. He got a passage on a navy ship but when he did not turn up several days later, we wondered where he could have got to. Perhaps the warship had been diverted to southeast Asia. Then we would have to get him accredited to Mountbatten's command! But we were only kidding, and Andy showed up about a week after I had arrived.

I stayed with Bert Powley in his Harley Street flat, which was big enough to provide a temporary haven for returning CBC correspondents. There was no chance of my getting back to the luxury flat that I had left to go on the Sicilian campaign, but I was lucky enough to run into Stanley Maxted, who told me that I could have his flat because he was leaving. It was a bachelor apartment in a modern block – it even had central heating – within walking distance of the BBC and 200 Oxford Street. The rent was 3 guineas ($15) a week.

I met Stanley at The Cock, the local pub for the CBC Overseas Unit and the BBC's North American Service. The Cock was a pleasant pub – not old and famous like The Cheshire Cheese and The Bell, not one of those fancy, modern cocktail bars full of chromium and bright leather upholstery. Just a pleasant pub. The lamps had red shades that gave off a warm light, and the brass pots and pans hanging over the bottles behind the bar had a deep, rich shine, so that if there was no fire in the grate under the picture of the revelling monks, it did not seem to be cold. We would stand around one of the empty beer barrels that had been up-ended on the carpet to serve as tables, chatting and drinking the Scotch ale the pub had on draft.

Besides Maxted, other Canadians with the North American Service who frequented The Cock included Stew MacPherson, the giant Byng Whittaker, and J.B. 'Hamish' McGeachy, an incomparable commentator and a delightful and amusing drinking companion. Among the Americans with the service was Elsa Knight Thompson from Seattle, a talks producer with a passionate interest in international affairs. Then there were Manfred Lachs, who was briefly with the BBC's European Service, and George Weidenfeld, who was a commentator on European Affairs with the North American Service. Manfred was a young Polish lawyer, a gold medallist, who was to write part of the indictment for the Nuremberg War Crimes Trial. After serving as Polish delegate to the United Nations, he was a member of the International Court of Justice for more than twenty years. Weidenfeld was a brilliant Viennese student who was full of anecdotes about international politics, of which he had an amazing grasp. He became a leading book publisher in Britain and was created a life peer in 1976. One of George's quips that I noted seemed to typify the upside-down world of the war, where the Soviets were our Allies and the Italians had become our 'co-belligerents.' 'Did you know,' Weidenfeld said, 'that the King of Italy has conferred the Order of "Santissima Annunciata" on Stalin? That makes Joe his cousin, and now Joe can call him Victor. I don't think the Soviets are at all pleased about this. At least they haven't said anything about it.'

My simply furnished, one-room apartment was a perfect workplace; there was no telephone, no radio. When I signed a contract with Harrap's for my war correspondent's book, *Journey into Victory*, I took three weeks off – I was owed some holidays – to write the second part of the book on the Sicilian campaign; the first part on the Alcan Highway was already written. I used to get up at eight o'clock in the morning and bang away at my portable Hermes typewriter until I went to bed at midnight; occasionally I would take time off to see a Mickey Mouse movie. I had to go out for some meals, but otherwise I fed myself in the apartment. When I had been in the luxury flat, I had turned over my ration books to the housekeeper, but now I used them to get two eggs a week, two ounces of butter, and bacon and ham, which were on points. Bread was off the ration, and there were lots of powdered milk and dried eggs, but I could not make anything edible out of them.

However, I knew of a little restaurant in Soho that made fine omelettes out of dried eggs. Restaurants were strictly controlled in Britain during the war; they could not charge more than 5 shillings (a little more than a dollar) for a three-course meal. At that price, most eating out was awful, but there were so-called British restaurants where I could get a very decent dinner for this amount. Restaurants could charge 5 shillings for extras, such as rolls and butter and/or coffee, however, and that was how fine establishments like Prunier's or Rules or the White Tower could keep going.

The winter of 1943–4 was the time of the Little Blitz, the vain attempt by Hitler to retaliate for the saturation bombing of his cities. I should have taken cover in the cellar, but I never did;

when the noise of the raid seemed to be coming closer, I would leave my apartment and sit on the lower stairs until the all-clear sounded. The best air-raid shelters were the tube stations, and they were fully used during the Little Blitz. Oxford Street station was just across the road from the CBC office, and there were tiers of metal bunks on its deep underground platforms.

Coming back late at night, I would have to edge past people bedded down on these bunks, men, women, and children. As the train pulled out, I would see the familiar wartime posters, 'Walls Have Ears,' and 'Careless Talk Costs Lives,' and the tribute to the Soviets, 'London Salutes Lion-Hearted Leningrad.' Most of the people were asleep; I wondered how they could sleep with the noise of the trains, but I suppose they got used to it, and the trains did stop running around midnight. There were some who slept there, more than 100 feet down in the bowels of the earth, every night, Little Blitz or no Blitz; perhaps they had been bombed out and had nowhere else to sleep. It was dangerous to be on the streets during a raid, not because of the bombs but because of the rain of steel splinters from the massed anti-aircraft artillery.

One of the most dramatic events I covered was the return of the first Allied prisoners of war at the end of October 1943. (Under article 68 of the Geneva Convention, nations at war were required to repatriate men who were seriously ill or badly wounded, as well as non-combatants. The first exchange was supposed to have taken place in October 1941, but it was cancelled because the British refused to go along with German demands. It was two years before a new repatriation agreement was finally reached. The POWs were examined by members of a Swiss medical commission, and those found not fit for further combat were transported to Sweden, where they were to board a ship to take them to the United Kingdom. An RCAF officer, Don Morrison, who was shot down in November 1942, said that they passed trains carrying returning German prisoners of war.)

It took us a couple of days to drive in Big Betsy from London to Leith, the port of Edinburgh, where the British and Canadian POWs, some of whom had been captured at Dieppe, were to disembark. Harold Wadsworth was the engineer assigned to the job, and another engineer, Joe Beauregard, who had just joined the Overseas Unit, came along for the experience. Harold did most of the driving, but he let Joe take the wheel of the big recording van while we were going through York, and Beauregard was a terrible driver. I recall the nightmare vision of Joe scattering the cyclists and almost running down several of them. (Joe Beauregard was with me in Italy; he was a very good fellow, a competent technician who later became a broadcaster in Montreal, but his driving never improved.) We crossed the border into Scotland and spent the night at a comfortable and cosy inn near Berwick-on-Tweed. The next day, 25 October 1943, we reached Edinburgh and got set up on the dock at Leith in good time for the first repatriation of 4,000 sick and wounded Allied prisoners of war.

It was a thrilling scene, the great Swedish liner, *Drottningholm*, moving slowly, almost imperceptibly, alongside, its decks crowded with hundreds of khaki-clad 'walking wounded,' who were shouting and singing, 'Roll Out the Barrel,' and the crowd crying and cheering on the dock. There were Union Jacks everywhere and the flags and bunting brightened the dark and grimy port. It made a great actuality program, twelve minutes and forty seconds long. I was pleased with my work and felt that it was my most successful 'ad lib' job. 'In fact,' I wrote in a letter to my parents, 'my stuff was used in the BBC Home Service in preference to their own man's, which was quite a boost for me.' On reflection, I think the BBC might have used my report rather than their own because our recording was of a much higher fidelity, so that some of the credit should go to the engineers, Harold Wadsworth and Art Holmes, who designed the equipment.

New Year 1944. The CBC Overseas Unit gave a cocktail party in the council chamber at Broadcasting House on New Year's Eve, and many of us continued the celebrations at The Cock. This would be the year the war would end, the Victory Year, 1944, and everyone drank to that. At the beginning of January I was told that I would be returning to Italy; Matthew Halton was coming back, and I would be taking his place.

Opening Alcan Highway. Ian Mackenzie, minister of pensions and national health, and E.L. Bartlett, U.S. secretary of state for Alaska, cut the ribbon at Lake Kluane, Yukon, on 20 November 1942, a bitterly cold day. Peter Stursberg is the hooded figure by the CBC mike, describing the frigid ceremony.

SUPPORT OUR FORCES
and THEIR LEADERS
Honour your pledge
"Buy WAR SAVINGS
CERTIFICATES - Regularly

Above: Exercise Spartan. Ablutions in the field: from left to right: conducting officer, CBC engineer Paul Johnson cleaning his teeth, war artist Lawren Harris shaving, and Peter Stursberg also shaving

Facing page, top: This poster of General McNaughton as Canadian war leader had great emotional appeal.

This photograph, taken in February 1941, shows General McNaughton with Allied war leaders, Polish General Sikorski, on his right, Churchill, and General De Gaulle.

Off to Sicily. Before setting sail, war correspondents Ross Munro, Peter Stursberg, and Lionel Shapiro go to a briefing aboard the headquarters' ship on the River Clyde.

Sicilian battlefield. Through this photograph, which illustrated one of his
war articles in *Maclean's* magazine, the author met the west coast artist
Gordon Smith. Smith is the wounded soldier in the foreground.

Above: CBC van reaches Italy. Standing in front of the vehicle are, from left, Matthew Halton, conducting officer, Marcel Ouimet, CBC engineer Alec Macdonald, who brought the van from Sicily, CBC engineer Paul Johnson, and Peter Stursberg.

Facing page, top: Broadcast from Ortona church. The author is shown reporting from the shattered belfry of the twelfth-century cathedral of San Tomasso, which claimed to have as a relic the head of Saint Thomas, the twelfth and doubting disciple.

Benoit Lafleur (left) is shown here listening to a play-back of his report that Joe Beauregard had recorded on the CBC portable equipment which was mounted on a jeep.

Cassino reduced. The ultimate in war's destruction, the town and the monastery had been bombed and blasted into the rock, and one had to go close to distinguish the rubble and the ruins.

The Hitler Line. War artist Charles Comfort's dramatic depiction of Canadian troops storming the steel and concrete fortifications of the Hitler Line, the last barrier to Rome. Shown up-ended is a Panther tank turret.

Above: Meeting before the Rhine. In rear: Chief of Imperial General Staff Alan Brooke and 21st Army Group Commander Montgomery, both of whom were field marshals; in front: Canadian army commander General Crerar and Churchill. This photograph was given to the author by the general's son, Peter Crerar, as a souvenir; the general had had it autographed.

Facing page, top: Interview with Squadron Leader Jack Charles on the occasion of his winning a £150 purse for the thousandth enemy plane brought down by his squadron. Charles, a Battle of Britain pilot, was credited with eleven of them.

Peter Stursberg (left), engineer Art Holmes, and librarian Miss M.R. Bridgeman listen to play-back of recordings in CBC Overseas Unit's office at 200 Oxford Street, London.

Above: Liberation at last. In the towns and cities of Holland huge crowds greet the Canadian troops as conquering heroes.

These happy Dutch girls and at least one boy go for a joyride on a Canadian armoured car.

Three Canadian soldiers survey the bomb-blasted Gedechneskirche; it has not been rebuilt, remaining as a monument to the destruction of Berlin in the Second World War.

Art Holmes shows Premier George Drew of Ontario the battle honours on the recording van that was returned to Toronto after service in northwest Europe.

Paul Morton. The *Toronto Star* war correspondent was parachuted behind the enemy lines in Italy, only to be disaccredited, disbelieved, and dismissed. His was the most daring and dramatic achievement of any reporter, but it led to personal tragedy.

Twenty years later, Peter Stursberg listens to his 'Lili Marlene report,' part of a travelling exhibit of outstanding radio broadcasts that visited fall fairs; this photograph was taken at the Central Canada Exhibition in Ottawa.

9

Underground at Anzio

London, 1 January 1944:
In a New Year message, General Eisenhower, supreme Allied commander, says: 'We will win the European War in 1944.' There are predictions that it could be over in four months.

It was a sombre time, that January in London, dark and dreary, as I remember it. There was the 'Little Blitz,' with German planes attacking every other night, or so it seemed, but the raids were more of a nuisance than anything else. It was the blackout that was so depressing, the blackout that went on for fifteen hours a day from four or five in the afternoon to seven or eight the next morning. The blackout combined with a pea-souper fog meant that one had literally to feel one's way along the street, touching the wall or building on the side of the pavement, creeping along and trying to avoid ghostly figures that appeared suddenly out of nowhere. The pea-souper had an acrid stench and was so filthy that I found my handkerchief to be black with soot. Yet the mood of the people was upbeat; it was one of weary confidence, as one American observer put it; for the British were enduring their fifth wartime New Year. As if sensing the mood, the BBC and the

London press were full of exhortations about 1944: it was a time of opportunity, as a leader in *The Times* said, 'when all the endurance of the years of adversity is about to be rewarded.'

The Cock tavern was a friendly oasis in the desert of the night. There, the progress of the Allied war effort was discussed over mugs of Scotch ale: the Russians were going great guns, they had recaptured Kiev and had freed Leningrad, but the advance of the Anglo-American armies in Italy had ground to a halt. The bitter battle for Ortona the Canadians had fought and won, but all attacks on Cassino had failed. The best that the British and the Americans could do was to bomb the cities of the Reich, the British at night and the Americans in daylight; the RAF in a series of raids on Hamburg had created a fire storm that had incinerated 50,000 civilians and made 800,000 homeless. It was a horror story that passed without much notice.

Hamish McGeachy and the other commentators and propagandists of the BBC's North American Service were much more interested in the foibles and foolishness of the Allies. It was a psychological release from the positive attitude they had to take in what they said about the war effort. AMGOT was the acronym used for Allied Military Government in Occupied Territories, until some linguist pointed out that AMGOT was a Turkish obscenity; then it became AMG. But piles of posters and mountains of writing paper and other bumf had to be destroyed.

Perhaps the most amusement was generated over the Allied paper money, a sample of which was brought to the pub and was handed around. The Italian lira notes had become worthless and were replaced by this Allied scrip that had the appearance of game money rather than the real thing; around the edges of this scrip were printed the Four Freedoms: 'Freedom of Speech,' 'Freedom of Worship,' 'Freedom from Want,' and 'Freedom from Fear.' The Four Freedoms were the brainchild of American politicians and were first mentioned by President Roosevelt in his 1941 state of the union address; Churchill reluctantly agreed to them and, strangely enough, so did Stalin, and they became a wartime slogan. I remember that the Four Freedoms were printed in English on one side of the Allied scrip; I cannot recall whether they were in Italian on the other side, but they must have been. There was much mirth when Hamish pointed out that some smart 'Eyetie' might take 'Freedom from Want' as a pledge and demand compensation from the Allies.

Nothing more on Halton's return: he was probably having priority problems getting back, as I had had, and was stuck in some way-station like Rabat or Gibraltar on the half-circle flight around Portugal to England. Travelling in the war zone was always a gamble. Meanwhile, there was a lot to do in London. Aside from broadcasting assignments, I had to work with Harrap's people on the editing of the book. Also, old friends from the Pacific Coast who were with the Canadian forces overseas looked me up whenever they came to London on leave, and it was great to see them and get all the latest news and gossip. Sometimes the news was grim: I heard that three or four of the fellows with whom I had palled around, including Jack Trace, were listed as missing in action, which usually meant that they had been shot down over Germany. Jack had been such fun, always ready for a party in Victoria, but he was a rear gunner in a Lancaster bomber, and the chances of survival for a rear gunner in night raids on the Reich were about the same as those of a fighter pilot in the Battle of Britain.

One of my assignments was to visit the so-called 'Beauty Shop' in East Grinstead, just outside London, where the remarkable plastic surgeon, Dr Archibald McIndoe, remade the faces of Battle of Britain pilots and other airmen who had been badly burned in combat. Dr McIndoe, a genial New Zealander, told me about the work, how he and his associates were able to replace eyebrows, lips, even noses; then he turned me over to his Canadian assistant, Dr Ross Tilley of Toronto, an RCAF squadron leader (major), who, according to McIndoe, was a 'whizz' at remaking hands.

I was shown through the special hospital facility that was housed in a couple of temporary buildings. Most of the patients were sitting or walking around. There was one young fellow whose nose seemed to be growing out of his arm, which was supported in a kind of cradle, and another who had no eyelids and pink, shiny scars for cheeks, where skin was being grafted. I had seen a lot of dead bodies, but the sight of this terrible disfigurement made me feel faint, and Dr Tilley told me to sit down and put my head between my legs. I was not going to admit to such weakness, however, and blamed my discomfort on the hospital smells and the close, heavy atmosphere indoors. Dr McIndoe said that the 'boys' had to undergo dozens of operations, but none of them wanted to leave or go out on the street until their faces had been properly fixed up.

By now the streets of London were crowded with American troops, but they tended to hang around Picadilly Circus and the Windmill Theatre, where there was a mild strip show, and we saw hardly any of them at The Cock tavern. There was lots of entertainment that winter, which helped to relieve the long hours of the blackout. The West End theatres opened early, most performances beginning at 6:30 p.m., and according to letters home, I saw Oscar Wilde's *An Ideal Husband,* the musical *Panama Hattie,* and at the Haymarket, Congreve's *Love for Love.* The theatres were quite cheap, but the dinner dance at the Berkeley Hotel was not; I wrote to my mother and father that it cost £3 ($15) each for my partner and me, and compared it with £1 ($5) we had paid for a dinner dance at the Empress Hotel in Victoria or at the Hotel Vancouver.

Matthew Halton got back at the beginning of February, and I told my parents to stop sending food parcels because I expected to be leaving soon; but my departure was delayed till towards the end of the month. Art Holmes returned about the same time as Matt, and I was delighted that he agreed to take over my bachelor apartment while I was away. Finally, the movement orders came through, and I took the train to Glasgow, where I boarded the *Almazora,* an old Royal Mail boat that had been saved by the war from the 'boneyard'; it never made the same impression on me as the *Marnix* had done.

I heard that the *Marnix,* which was part of a convoy carrying the I Canadian Corps to Italy, went down in the Mediterranean. Art Holmes was on that convoy in November 1943, and his ship was also sunk; he told me that he was having dinner with Lloyd Moore, another CBC engineer, when there was a 'terrific explosion that seemed to lift us out of our seats and then the lights went out.' Everybody grabbed his lifebelt and felt his way to the dining saloon door, but Art had misplaced his and spent a few minutes finding it. When he did, he could not find the door but crawled over the wreckage and through a window on the port side, which was deserted because of the heavy list. He got to an open deck just in time to see the next attack on the ship. The JU-88s came over at mast height, and all the guns in the convoy opened up on them with tracer bullets and shells. Art got the impression, with the coloured tracers converging in his direction, that 'it was me and not the planes they were shooting at.' Although two troop ships and an American destroyer were sunk by the Luftwaffe, there were few casualties and Art and Lloyd were soon rescued.

My return trip to the Mediterranean Theatre was uneventful; there were no raids, perhaps one or two alerts, but nothing memorable. It was a 'rest cure,' as I wrote home. There was good accommodation on board, good food, no liquor. I shared a cabin with Joe Beauregard, the CBC engineer and 'demon' driver. I spoke to the troops in the mess decks, as I had done on the last voyage, only this time my lecture was about the Sicilian campaign, whereas last time it was on the building of the Alcan Highway.

We had more entertainment than on the *Marnix*, since there were two ENSA (Entertainment National Service Association) companies on board. As well, there were a number of Canadian nurses, at least two of whom had been married while serving overseas. Which reminds me of wartime romances. Just before setting sail for Sicily, Ross Munro had married a Canadian nurse in England, Helen-Marie Stevens, known as Stevie; Paul Johnson did the same: his bride, Jacqueline Johnston, was with the WD (Women's Division) of the RCAF in London. My future sister-in-law Mildred Robertson was married 'in the lines,' as a wedding at the front was called. Her hospital had moved to Bari and her husband, Captain William Wright, was with the Royal Engineers in Italy. A marriage 'in the lines' was a traditional affair, with a wedding cake and a shower of rice as the newlyweds set off in an army truck for a seven-day honeymoon on the Isle of Capri.

It was a dull, rainy day at the beginning of March when the ship reached Naples, and the beautiful bay of song and story looked grey and forlorn; the visibility was so poor that we could scarcely see the outline of Vesuvius. The port was crowded with troop ships and warships, their camouflage grey matching the colour of the water. There were freighters, the mass-produced U.S. Liberty ships, unloading tanks and guns and other war supplies, and the streets of the city were full of jeeps and military vehicles. Naples had been badly bombed by the Allies before it was taken in October 1943, but the buildings on the main street, the Via Roma, seemed to be more or less intact; they were dark and dirty, however, with peeling paint and boarded-up windows. The Canadian army Public Relations had a large and comfortable flat in the middle of town, and, since they had an Italian chef who had worked for the king, the food was exceptional. People used to drop in for lunch, and at one meal I met the Canadian war artists, Will Ogilvie and Charles Comfort – the latter was to become director of the National Gallery in Ottawa.

On 7 March 1944 we left Naples for the front; it was a long, cold drive over the Apennines, where we met ice and snow at the higher elevations – so different from the sunny Italy that I remembered from the year before – to the Adriatic side and to the Ortona area, where the 1st Canadian Division was in the line. The PR was with divisional headquarters at San Vito, a wretched little town a couple of miles from Ortona, and that was where Joe Beauregard and I found the other members of the CBC team in Italy, Benoit Lafleur, the French-language reporter, and Lloyd Moore, as well as the van and the portable recording equipment. The CBC had somehow acquired a small apartment above a shop that made spaghetti – I figured that Art Holmes, a great scrounger, must have been responsible for this gem of accommodation; it had the only interior plumbing in town. There was no central heating, of course, but Pietro, whose wife, Maria, ran the spaghetti enterprise, used to bring up a pan of smouldering charcoal to warm us up until we could no longer stand the suffocating fug.

Shalto Watt of the *Montreal Star*, who appreciated his creature comforts, was the only other occupant besides the four of us. The apartment had a main room, which was used as an office and living room and two smaller rooms where we set up our safari beds and bedrolls. I remember a delicious spaghetti feast that Maria cooked up for us – we had been able to get some flour and a can of bully beef for her. The PR mess was in a nearby building, and so were the Beaver Club for other ranks and the Officers' Club, where one could get a drink, usually vino (whisky and beer were on the rations and were handed out at the messes), and there were weekly tea dances. In a letter to my parents, I referred to our partners at these dances as the 'local lovelies.' The Beaver Club, the Officers' Club, the tea dances, and other amenities were a sign of a static front, and the 1st Division had had its headquarters in San Vito since December 1943.

Ortona was badly banged up as a result of the battle, but the rubble had been cleared from the streets, and the town looked livable and had become a rest area for troops who were out of the line. There was a twelfth-century cathedral in Ortona, the church of San Tomasso (Saint Thomas), which had the distinction of housing the skull of Saint Thomas, the twelfth and doubting apostle. Apparently Ortona's greatest son, the Navigator Acciuole, who was probably a pirate on the side, had sailed as far as India, where he found the tomb of St Thomas. He thought nothing of digging up the saint's remains and taking the skull back to his home town. This relic was credited with having performed all kinds of miracles, including converting oranges into cannonballs to fight the Turks. We could not see the place where St Thomas's skull was buried: it was under a pile of stones and rubble, because the church had suffered a direct hit and a large hole had been torn in the domed roof. The cathedral's great bell had survived, however, and I thought the belfry was a suitable place from which to do a broadcast on the dedication of the Canadian cemetery at Ortona.

When we visited the front line, which was a couple of miles north of Ortona near a muddy stream called the Arielli, the Royal Canadian Regiment was on guard duty. We had to make our way on foot up a rise to battalion headquarters, located in a stone farmhouse; we were told that, had we driven, our jeep would have brought down enemy shell fire. Lieutenant-Colonel W.W. Mathers had taken over command of the RCR from Dan Spry, who was now in charge of a brigade. We went to an observation post in a nearby barn, from which we could see, over a shattered vineyard, the slit trenches of our forward positions and, across a ditch, those of the enemy. It was eerily quiet, and Willie Mathers wanted it to remain that way – which is why he had insisted on our leaving the jeep under an olive tree some distance away. This was static warfare, and there was no point in arousing the enemy.

That did not mean that there was no shooting. As I said in a broadcast, 'static warfare is still warfare': in some ways it was worse than offensive warfare. Nightly patrols were sent out to meet the insistent demands of Intelligence for prisoners. This was a vicious game of hide-and-seek, of ambush and fire-fights, with resulting casualties. On occasion the dead could not be collected, and Strome Galloway said that months later, after the Battle of Cassino and the withdrawal of the German forces, the graves detachment picked up the bones and laid them to rest in the Canadian cemetery at Ortona. Those who returned unscathed from these patrols got as a reward an inch of rum in an enamel cup. The troops manning the slit trenches, which were only a few yards from the enemy, could not move from their cramped quarters in daylight, and the foul weather, the freezing rain, and the chill winds meant that they were often up to their knees in icy water. It was only at night, when the mule trains brought up their rations, that they got a real meal.

It was a very different war from the one that I had known only a few months before. I wrote in a letter to my parents that the situation seemed to me to be much closer to what it must have been like in the First World War. The Italian front in March 1944 looked like pictures of the Western Front. There were the same ruined farmhouses, the same shell holes full of water, the same broken, leafless trees. It was trench warfare again, and the slit trenches and foxholes of the Second World War were even worse for the occupants than the deep interconnected trenches of the First World War had been. As I reported to the CBC in the middle of March that year:

... On the other side of the Apennines – and by the way they divide the Italian front roughly in two – on the other side of these mountains, the story is much the same. The attempt to outflank the German Gustav Line through the Anzio Bridgehead bogged down, and now another frontal assault is being directed against Cassino. [It failed, and towards the end of March this sector lapsed into the ugly stalemate on the rest of the front.]

However, the Germans have another line behind Cassino which is regarded as being extremely strong and has been given the name of the Adolf Hitler Line. By the way, Gustav means nothing more than G, the German G for Gustav, just as we say G for George. The Adolph Hitler Line is anchored on Pontecorvo and is meant to hold the valley of the Liri. On the outskirts of Rome itself, the Germans have defence positions although not fully developed. All these preparations are indications that the Nazis are determined to hold [Italy] at almost any cost, not for prestige purposes alone but as an outer bastion of the Reich ...

The conditions before Cassino and on the steep rocky slopes of Monte Cassino were, if anything, worse than those suffered by Canadians along the Adriatic coast. The famous American war correspondent Ernie Pyle wrote that the GIs were knee deep in mud: they were kept in the line for so long that they lived in wet clothes for weeks, with dire consequences to their health and morale.

It was indeed a winter of discontent for the Allies in Italy, and to add to the depression and gloom, Vesuvius erupted! On 18 March molten lava began flowing down the sides of the volcano, and a couple of days later a series of violent explosions sent mushroom clouds of ashes into the stratosphere, burying the town of San Sebastiano and reburying the ruins of Pompeii, and coating the soggy landscape in the Canadian sector of the front with yellow-grey slime.

The only light in the darkness was the regrouping of the Allied ground forces in preparation for the spring offensive. The American Fifth Army had failed in repeated attempts to take Cassino, the anchor of the German winter line. General Mark Clark had frittered away division after division in these assaults, and it was felt that a much heavier attack at corps or army level was needed to dislodge the formidable Nazi defences. So the Eighth Army was to be moved from the Adriatic to a narrow sector before Cassino, while the Fifth Army was to concentrate on the western end of the Italian front and on the Anzio Beachhead, where there had been no break-out. The Eighth Army was to have the experienced British XIII Corps in front for the assault, with the I Canadian Corps in reserve. The V British Corps was to have a holding role on the Adriatic front. Much of the movement occurred in March, but the 1st Canadian Division defended the Ortona salient until 20 April, when Major-General Chris Vokes handed over to the British commander of the 10th Indian Division.

At about the same time, Lieutenant-General H.D.G. Crerar, who had had brief operational experience as the commander of I Canadian Corps, left Italy to become GOC-in-C (General Officer Commanding-in-Chief) of the First Canadian Army; his post was taken by Lieutenant-General E.L.M. Burns, the commander of the 5th Division. He, in his turn, was succeeded by Major-General B.M. 'Bert' Hoffmeister, the brilliant part-time soldier and one NPAM (Non-Permanent Active Militia) officer to become a general.

Of course we knew about the regrouping of the Allied forces in Italy, but in our reports we could only hint at 'the offensive that was bound to come in the spring,' and even talking about it was discouraged: 'Walls Have Ears' and 'Every Eyetie Is a Spy.' Since there was so little activity along the Arielli, where the Canadians were dug in, it was a good time to visit other sectors of the front. On our left, Lieutenant-General Wladislaw Anders's II Polish Corps held positions in the high Apennines. We set out in our jeep up the steep and winding roads; it was the beginning of April, the weather was at last warming up, and the scenery was gorgeous.

We spent a couple of days with the Poles in their mountain lair, and it was like a foreign visit. Most of them had been prisoners of war in the Soviet Union and had been allowed to leave in some kind of deal that Stalin made with Churchill. As I said in a letter home, 'I don't know whether they hate the Russians worse than the Germans, but the difference is very little.' They seemed like a lost army, and they reminded me of H.G. Wells's apocalyptic vision of the aftermath of a world war where armed bands fought among the ruins. 'We go on fighting for what we don't know,' an officer said – he was an aristocrat and former great landowner – 'At first, we were fighting for a little piece of country but now that has been taken from us.' I never mentioned any of this in my broadcast on the Poles, nor did the officer in the recorded interview I had with him.

About the middle of April the press camp moved from the humble abodes of San Vito across the Apennines to a comfortable, if not palatial, villa in Venafro, a town south of Cassino. Just before leaving the Adriatic sector, I had my portrait painted by Spoltori, a popular artist of pre-war days who had done portraits of the pope and Mussolini and other famous people, or so he said. His studio was in the small town of Lanciano, and evidently he had been caught there by the war, since Lanciano was virtually in the front line. (I had the portrait shipped home and it now hangs in my dining room in West Vancouver.) I think it was Bill Boss who discovered Spoltori. Bill had been a PR officer, and a very good one, before being released from the army to serve as a Canadian Press war correspondent. He was a linguist who could speak Italian fluently and got to know the country and its people much better than most of us; Boss was also a musician and conducted the Rome symphony orchestra in a concert during a lull in the Italian campaign.

With a month or more to go before the Eighth Army would be ready for the all-out attack on Cassino and the beginning of the Battle for Rome, there was plenty of time to make a side trip to the Anzio Beachhead. In a letter home I observed that the beachhead was a 'very interesting and exciting place – almost too much like a story book to be real.' Actually, Anzio was a disaster: the only Allied landing since Dieppe that had failed. When they went ashore at this seaside resort on 22 January 1944, the British and American forces caught the enemy completely by surprise, there was no opposition whatsoever. But indecisive leadership allowed Field Marshal Albert Kesselring, the German commander in Italy, to rush up troops from as far away as France and Germany and almost drive the attackers back into the sea. The Allies hung on grimly to a coastal strip no more than six miles wide: and Anzio became a Gallipoli.

The reason for this ghastly SNAFU, according to *Anzio*, Wynford Vaughan-Thomas's authoritative book on the beachhead, was divided counsel. The Americans never really believed in the Italian campaign; they had always regarded it as a sideshow, and a sideshow that got in the way of preparations for the main thrust across the channel. Furthermore, the original plans called for this 'left hook' landing at Anzio only after the Eighth Army had reached Pescara, some thirty miles up the Adriatic coast from Ortona, and the Fifth Army had got to Frosinone, halfway between Cassino and Rome. Neither of these objectives was achieved, however, and the plans for Anzio were abandoned on 22 December 1943.

It was Winston Churchill who revived them. The prime minister had come down with pneumonia on the way back from exhausting conferences at Teheran and Cairo. While recuperating in General Eisenhower's villa near the ruins of Carthage in North Africa, he began reviewing the situation in Italy, which was lapsing into a bloody stalemate. Churchill had always been in favour of an Anzio landing and was annoyed to find that the plans had been scrapped. He felt that this 'cat's claw,' as he called it, according to Vaughan-Thomas, would loosen the whole Italian front. He got the CIGS, General Sir Alan Brooke, to agree, but he had to use all his persuasive powers to bring his 'good friend' President Roosevelt on side.

However, the American Fifth Army commanders were not enthusiastic. They were given less than a month to do all the planning for the landing of two divisions at Anzio, which was quite different from the original concept of an attack by a single division. They had to rush, because all the hundreds of landing craft needed had to be returned to the United Kingdom by the end of January. And they put in charge of this combined operation a Major-General John P. Lucas, who mirrored their reluctance; according to Vaughan-Thomas, Lucas left the final planning conference muttering, 'This is going to be worse than Gallipoli.'

We made the side trip to Anzio towards the end of April, and by then the beachhead was as quiet as other sectors of the Italian front. The last Nazi attempt to drive the Allies into the sea had ended at the beginning of March, and the fighting had degenerated into the sort of trench warfare, with artillery exchanges and night patrols, that the Canadians were experiencing along the Arielli above Ortona. Only this was worse. The Germans had the whole of the beachhead under surveillance from their observation posts in the Alban Hills, and as a result everyone had to take shelter underground. The forward troops had dugouts in the ditches, or wadis, as they were called, while headquarters and hospitals and workshops were in the wine cellars that honeycombed Anzio and its sister town of Nettuno. The PR camp was in a waterfront villa, which was built down the side of a cliff, so that the lower floors, where we worked and lived, were really underground, and nobody used the upper floor except as an entrance or exit.

From the villa we could see the whole half moon of the bay and, at one end, the sandspit and the thin white wisp of a smokescreen. This was the beginning of one of three smokescreens that hung like foggy curtains around the beachhead and were supposed to dim the prying eyes of the enemy. We drove through the smokescreens to visit the Canadians, who were part of a combined American Canadian Special Service Force, which had been formed as a super commando unit to blow up the Norwegian power stations but, in the end, had been used as shock troops; in this case, it was holding the southern end of the beachhead. The

Canadians wore American uniforms and were under American command. In a broadcast I described our journey through this weird landscape:

... Before reaching the smoke screen I couldn't help wondering what good it did: the Alban Hills tower over the low line of this man-made cloud. It was a very clear day and I could distinguish every feature of these German-held hills. I've never felt so exposed on any front in this theatre of war. The only time I was reasonably sure that the enemy could not see us was when we entered the smokescreen. It was like something out of a fairy tale driving into the white cloud that billowed over the road; then we were out of its thick fog and the Alban Hills appeared closer than ever, and there was a warning sign: 'Dust Brings Shell Fire' ...

At Anzio the Germans not only held the high ground but had air superiority: the beachhead was out of the range of Allied fighter planes. Every night there was a radio show to which we all listened in the news room on a lower floor of the Public Relations villa, a floor that hugged the side of the cliff. It began when the huge, twelve-inch railway guns that the Germans had in the Alban Hills fired a salvo; the shells – they were meant to keep our anti-aircraft gunners in their shelters – sounded like an express train overhead and usually landed with a great splash in the bay. Then the ack-ack coordinator began calling out on the radio the positions of the attacking planes. There was a numbered grid of the beachhead area and the Alban Hills, and we had a copy pinned on the wall.

'Six hostiles at four-five-four-three heading due west, altitude approximately three thousand feet,' the co-ordinator said; he had a Brooklyn accent. 'Enemy force splitting up and coming down. Three hostiles on five-four-three-two and three hostiles on five-six-five-four.' The coordinator's voice became more insistent and excited. As the planes spread out into a wide v formation, he kept calling their positions, and his delivery increased to the point that he began sounding like an auctioneer. 'Red barrage fire!' he shouted over the radio, and we heard a distant rumble of the guns. The 'hostiles' were now over the outer perimeter of the beachhead. 'White barrage fire!' And the guns sounded much closer and we could see from the grid that the planes were converging on the towns. 'Anzio Nettuno barrage fire!' the coordinator yelled. The planes were directly overhead. For once we were the hunted, and we crouched close to the cliff wall. All hell broke loose. Above the thunder of the guns and the tearing roar of the aircraft engines the jolting crashes of the bombs shook our villa and sent bits of plaster skittering down.

It was a moment of terror but was over quickly, and the radio reported that the enemy planes were now off the grid and were, presumably, returning to their bases. The coordinator praised the gunners and asserted that they had scored direct hits on a couple of the 'hostiles,' but the BBC correspondent, Wynford Vaughan-Thomas, said that the coordinator always made a claim of enemy losses to boost morale.

The Anzio Beachhead was a joint Anglo-American enterprise, but the Americans were in charge. I remember attending a briefing by an American general at a corps headquarters, which was down in a dank wine cellar. What amazed me, however, was the deep underground headquarters being excavated for the Fifth Army commander, General Mark Clark. This was an extension of the cellars of the Villa Borghese,* a fine palace with pillars and parapets and classical statues on the outskirts of Anzio. I went there because Canadian engineers were being used to dig this bomb-proof shelter for the top brass. They were the only other Canadians in the beachhead, besides members of the joint American Canadian Special Service Force, and they belonged to a tunnelling company that had been used in Gibraltar. They were mostly hard-rock miners and diamond drillers from Sudbury and

*Prince Borghese, whose palace outside Anzio had been taken over as Fifth Army headquarters, was an unreconstructed Fascist and remained loyal to Mussolini; he was also a dashing and courageous, if not foolhardy, commander. He got together enough fast-motor torpedo boats to raid the Allied anchorage off Anzio on the night of 18 February 1944, but the attack was easily beaten off.

Kirkland Lake, Ontario. That there were some thirty of these Canadian sappers gives some idea of the magnitude of the job; they had done some notable work in the Mediterranean Theatre, such as building bridges and clearing harbours, and they were delighted to be working underground again.

It was like being in a mine: there were rusty stretches of a narrow-gauge railway track and tip trucks full of muck, the whole dimly lit by a couple of naked electric light bulbs. Water was dripping from the ceiling, but I was told there was no need to shore it up because the limestone was solid. A heavy explosion that loosened some pebbles from the walls startled us, but I was assured that it was just a bit of dynamiting and we need not worry about enemy bombing, since we were forty-eight feet underground. I did a report from this monstrous man-made cavern, a 'Little [GI] Joe' report about the Canadian miners; I said nothing about what this huge underground headquarters had to do with Allied strategy. It was more the sort of shelter that one would have expected at Verdun in the First World War, and it seemed to me to represent a siege mentality, not the spirit of attack.

Since the underground headquarters would not be ready for some weeks – the bare walls would have to be plastered and the ceiling waterproofed – General Clark could have occupied it for only a few days before the break-out from the beachhead in the coming Battle for Rome.

10

Battle for Rome

Venafro, Italy, 18 May 1944:
Eighth Army's concentrated attack on Cassino finally dislodges Germans. British and Canadian forces advance into Liri Valley.

To my mind, Cassino was the ultimate in war's destruction, a monument to the futility of the popularly held illusion that the war could be won by bombing, or 'Victory through Air Power,' as the title of Alexander De Seversky's seminal book put it. From a distance, it looked as though the town and the Benedictine abbey had simply become part of the surrounding rock, which had also been blasted to bits, and had melted into the mountainside. We had to go a good way up the sinister Highway No. 6, the ancient Via Casilina, which leads to Rome, to be able to distinguish the rubble and the ruins. No place of its size, just a couple of square miles, had been the target of so many air raids; it could be said, as the U.S. air force claimed, that Cassino had been wiped off the face of the earth. Yet such massive destruction was really of no military value; it left the enemy in command of Cassino and more firmly entrenched than ever before, while the Allies lost ground.

This devastation occurred before we moved across the Apennines to Venafro and rather better quarters in a marchesa's palace (the marchesa stayed on and occupied a couple of rooms in the servants' quarters). We heard all about it, however, about the 'thousand-bomber raid,' and how the New Zealanders, who had held two-thirds of Cassino, had been very wisely withdrawn to the outskirts; when the dust settled and the fighting resumed, the New Zealanders could regain only one-third of the town, while the Germans held two-thirds of it. Then there was the way that American bombers had hit the rear areas, including Venafro – fortunately missing the marchesa's palace – and Eighth Army headquarters. The British gleefully recounted how the Yanks had scored a near-hit on the commander's caravan and overturned it. By all accounts, General Sir Oliver Leese – he had succeeded Montgomery, who had gone to England for the Normandy invasion – was not pleased.

The facts, obtained through research, showed that claims made in the heat of battle, including the Battle of Britain, were exaggerated: 460 bombers, not 1,000 bombers, struck Cassino on 14 March; however, the 240 planes that had smashed the Benedictine abbey the month before should be included in the total, which would bring the number to 700 – a figure much closer to the legendary thousand. Otherwise, it was just as we were told: more than forty of the heavy bombers, the Flying Fortresses and Liberators, dropped their loads behind the lines, causing many Allied casualties, according to John Ellis's book, *Cassino – The Hollow Victory*. The American commander of the Mediterranean Allied Airforce, Lieutenant-General Ira Eaker, was said to be somewhat embarrassed.

As soon as the bombing stopped, Allied artillery poured 200,000 shells into Cassino, grinding the rubble and the ruins into powder, so that a pall of dust hung over the town. In surveying this scene of devastation, John Ellis says that the German commander, General von Senger und Etterlin, compared it to the battlefield of the Somme and quoted Hitler as saying that Cassino was 'the only battlefield of this war that represented those of the last.' How did the Germans survive this fearsome bombardment? It was hell let

loose; as one observer described it, 'We could see nothing but
smoke and dust and the bombs shook the ground as if there were
an earthquake – the men there must be going mad.' The worst
part of the bombing and shelling, according to survivors, was its
duration: it went on for some five hours. The Nazi paratroopers
were resilient, however, and while many were killed, others had
taken shelter in bunkers and caves. As soon as the barrage
stopped, they quickly returned to their strong points, which, if
anything, had been improved by the bombing, and held off the
attacking New Zealand and Indian troops. German prisoners of
war said that Cassino was worse than anything they had experienced on the Russian front.

One of the reasons the Allied attacks failed was that the air
raids had created such deep craters that the tanks could not get up
to support the infantry. The Nazi paratroopers were reinforced and
retook some of the ground, and after a week it soon became
apparent to the Allied command that the attack would have to be
given up. The troops were completely exhausted. General Sir
Harold Alexander came to the front and agreed to call off the
battle. If it was any consolation for the New Zealanders and the
Indians (the Ghurkas had suffered terribly), Alexander called the
paratroopers 'the best soldiers in the world': as Ellis quoted him:
'I do not think any other troops could have stood up to it [the
Allied bombardment and attack] perhaps except these para boys.'
On 23 March, just nine days after the 'thousand-bomber raid,' the
Allied winter offensive officially ended.

The static warfare that ensued was a frustrating time for all of
us, for none more so than Yvon Beaulne, a genial fellow of good
girth who was with army Public Relations and was the CBC's
conducting officer for much of our time in Italy. He was overcome
by the awful state of limbo that we were in, with Rome, that
shining city, still so far beyond our reach. Like a knight of old, Yvon
shaved his head and swore that he would not let his hair grow until
we reached Rome. Whether this was meant as an offensive gesture
to strike terror into the hearts of the enemy is not clear, but
Lieutenant Beaulne looked more like a benevolent Friar Tuck than

the caricature of a Hun. During the lull he spent a short time with the Polish Corps and picked up a smattering of Polish; like Bill Boss, he was a linguist. He said that the lingua franca of the Polish officers was French, however, which was the language of the nobles of the old Russian Empire and the tsarist court. (After the war, Yvon Beaulne joined External Affairs and served as ambassador to a number of countries and at the United Nations.)

Although we knew nothing about it at the time, when the I Canadian Corps moved from the Adriatic for the Eighth Army's attack on Cassino, it was engaged in an elaborate plan of deception. Dummy signals were sent out to give the illusion that the corps was in the Salerno area preparing for an amphibious assault on the port of Civitavecchia, about forty miles north of Rome. The date for the bogus landing was given as 15 May, and it was hoped that Kesselring would believe that the beginning of the Cassino offensive on 11 May was merely a diversionary attack and concentrate the bulk of his reserves along the Tyrrhenian coast above the Tiber. There had been a diversionary attack on the Garigliano before the Anzio landing. It was a carefully prepared and realistic plot, and an examination of captured German war diaries and intelligence files shows that the enemy was taken in and kept many of its reserves north of Rome. As happened before, however, Kesselring was able to react quickly, and the deception did not achieve its full objective.

Meanwhile, we went around looking for stories, totally ignorant of the way the Canadians were trying to outwit the Germans with this undercover signals operation. Furthermore, we were being kept in the dark generally because we were not allowed to visit any of the regrouped Canadian units. This was the reason we visited the Polish Corps and the Anzio Beachhead. Our search for news took us to Bari, where King Victor Emmanuel and the Italian government had fled after signing an armistice agreement with the Allies. There I met Vladimir Deijer, a Yugoslav partisan leader who was setting up a hospital in the Italian port. I also visited a Canadian hospital in the environs of Bari and was given a warm welcome by the staff. One of the surgeons said that I was very lucky, that I had arrived just in time to see an amputation. I thanked him but said that I would rather not.

At last, the Day of the Offensive: on 11 May there was a briefing at Eighth Army's advance headquarters, where we were told that the attack would begin that evening with the heaviest barrage of the war. Obviously, I had to get the sound of the opening round of gunfire, so we took the portable recording equipment in a jeep to some scrub land just below the Rapido River, also known as the Gari, that ran like a moat in front of the great fortress of Monte Cassino, past the ruined town to join up with the Liri River and become the Garigliano, which eventually emptied into the Tyrrhenian Sea. The Rapido or Gari River, with the Liri and the Garigliano, formed the water barrier along which the German Gustav Line had been built, its anchor the massif of Monte Cassino. We had selected the place to make the recording very carefully because we wanted to be in the midst of the artillery, in front of the howitzers and just behind the twenty-five-pounders. We were told that there would be 2,000 guns in the shoot. As I said in the broadcast, darkness had fallen with the opening fire of the Battle for Rome:

... The night is lit by the flashes of the guns. It's just as though hundreds of arc lights were flickering and sputtering in the valley and behind the mountains too. The white flames bring the hills out in black relief ... Sometimes it's so bright that I can see the CBC engineer, Lloyd Moore, bending over our equipment recording this ... It's an amazing and terrifying sight and yet thrilling. I don't know how to describe it properly in words, and I think it is easier for you to picture it by listening ...

This is the greatest artillery action of the Eighth Army – far greater than the famous barrage at El Alamein. There are guns in front of us – they're the ones that make the sharp cracks – and guns behind us – if you listen carefully you'll hear the whoosh of their shells going over our heads – and guns to the side of us ...

Allied strategy was not much different from what had gone

before and failed. It was a frontal assault, only this time there was a much bigger battering-ram: it consisted of the British XIII Corps with two divisions in front, at the 'sharp end,' and the whole of the Eighth Army behind them. Previously it had been at a divisional level, which was not a big enough stick to make more than a dent in the Gustav Line. I Canadian Corps was in reserve, and, once there was a breakthrough into the Liri Valley, it would be brought into action against the Germans' next defences, the Adolf Hitler Line.

The smoke of battle, a deep, swirling fog, hung like a curtain over the Rapido River in front of Cassino. It was made up partly from the ceaseless shell fire, but mostly it came from smoke cannisters and was meant to cover the sappers and pioneers who were working furiously on bridging the narrow stream so that tanks could cross. They had to build and rebuild the bridges, since the strong current and the soft, mushy banks resulted in more than one of the bridges being washed away. Another sank under the weight of a forty-ton monster and drowned. The tanks waiting to cross were so well camouflaged that I didn't notice them at thirty yards. As I reported, 'The dusty bush country on both sides of the Gari and Rapido, which are one and the same river, is full of the dead that lived only a few hours ago.' The Germans were putting up a fierce resistance, as everyone expected them to do, and the Nazi paratroopers had taken full advantage of the Allied bombing of the Benedictine abbey, which had smashed the building but had done little damage to its ten-foot-thick walls except to turn them into formidable defence positions. The smoke obscured the great massif of Monte Cassino.

Finally the British and Indian troops of the XIII Corps were able to take Cassino and open the way to the Liri Valley. They were supported by the First Canadian Army Tank Brigade, the only Canadian formation to participate in the Battle of Cassino. Owing to the gallant work of the engineers, the Canadian tanks were the first to get across the river on 12 May. The job of taking the monastery was given to the Polish Corps, and as mentioned above, it was difficult to describe the dreadful hardships on the steep, rocky slopes of Monte Cassino and the grim and bloody struggle that went on there.

The Poles had to crouch behind boulders and stones and, as they advanced, they came under concentrated fire from three sides. I was told that some of the German guns were actually shooting at them from behind. The worst part of the fighting was when the Poles gained a ridge and were within 400 yards of the monastery. The Germans had had three months since the Allied bombing to prepare their positions. They fought from the broken walls of the abbey, they fought from heavily sand-bagged machine-gun posts in its ruins, they fought with what I called 'the cold savagery of the paratroops,' they counter-attacked time and time again. But the Poles pressed on, despite the most terrible casualties, and on 18 May they entered the Benedictine monastery and planted their flag on one of its still-standing towers. The next day I climbed up that ghastly corpse-strewn mountainside and in a broadcast said:

... I have never seen such a grisly sight as I saw [that day]. There were the dead that had stormed and taken this fortress [of Monte Cassino] only yesterday. And there were the dead that had tried to take it months ago. I almost stumbled over a head that had almost mummified. The horrible thing about these battlefields above Cassino was that the men who fought there lived with the dead around them. A Polish officer pointed to a strange looking metal object that was lying on the rocky wall and said: 'a German flame thrower.' There were some terribly charred corpses nearby. The officer wanted us to look over the side. Just below us German dead were sprawled over some bunkers ...

My friend Wally Reyburn accompanied me on the climb up that blasted escarpment, which was still under enemy shell fire; in fact, the Polish officer told us not to bunch together. The litter of war, broken boxes, tin cans, bits and pieces of equipment, was scattered across the precipitous hillside. It was not the sight of the dead, the swollen, glaucous faces, the staring eyes, that turned our stomachs but the stench, a horror that I did not mention in my broadcast.

When we reached the monastery, we climbed over a broken wall and entered a deep underground crypt that had been used as a bomb shelter. We realized it had also been used by the Nazi paratroopers, because we saw some torn German uniforms, even a water bottle and a helmet. They had been discarded when the enemy withdrew, Later we learned that it was not the Poles' costly frontal attack that had forced the Germans out of the battered abbey but General Alphonse Juin's Free French forces, which had fought their way through the mountains and were threatening to cut off the enemy's line of retreat. A couple of monks were in the crypt and so were some ragged civilians; they looked drawn and tired. On one wall was a mosaic, which, if my memory is correct, included a dove of peace and an olive branch.

I tried to find the crypt when I visited the monastery of Monte Cassino in the early spring of 1962. It had been rebuilt 'where it was, as it was,' at the express wish of the abbot, and in the reconstruction the foundations of earlier buildings were unearthed and the crypt may have been filled in. There stood the great fortress abbey; from a distance it looked just as it had before it was destroyed by American bombers; but up close it seemed a bit incongruous – it was just too shining new for a fifteenth-century building. Dom Luigi, a benevolent, bespectacled monk, was our guide; he took my wife and me through the central cloister, up the processional steps to the basilica, which is as large as any cathedral. All the inlaid marble had been replaced; the beautiful altars were studded with semiprecious stones, agates and lapis lazuli and amethyst, which were found among the ruins; and the gilded ceilings and the dome of the reliquary chapel had been painted in the old style by a modern Italian artist.

Before he led us into the monastery, above whose gates was written in large letters 'PAX', Dom Luigi made it clear that the Benedictine order regarded the bombing as a 'war crime.' He gave us a booklet put out by the order, which asserted that no Germans were in the monastery before the bombing and reprinted a facsimile of a declaration to this effect, signed by the Venerable Gregorio Diamare, the abbot at the time.

Who was responsible for the destruction of one of the greatest treasures of Christendom? There was no doubt that Lieutenant-General Sir Bernard Freyberg, the commander of the New Zealand Division, wanted it done, because his troops claimed that the Germans were firing on them from the monastery. But Freyberg could not give the order. The New Zealanders were in the Fifth Army, and the Fifth Army's commander, General Mark Clark, was opposed to the bombing, according to David Hapgood's book, *Monte Cassino*. But Clark was in an awkward position: he had had little war experience and under him were British and Indian troops and now New Zealanders, who had been fighting for years in the Western Desert, in Greece, and elsewhere. And the New Zealanders were openly contemptuous of Americans, especially the officers. But that was the way that veterans behaved towards new and untried troops. I know that the 1st Canadian Division, which landed in Sicily and fought its way up Italy, resented having to take orders from the newly arrived I Canadian Corps. Here was General Clark faced not only with a great soldier but a legendary hero who had won the VC in the First World War and who had, in a way, more power than he had, for General Freyberg had the right to withdraw the New Zealand Division if he thought that it was being misused. (This was an authority that General McNaughton had wanted but had not had.)

At any rate, Clark would not agree, and so Freyberg went over his head to General Alexander, the Fifteenth Army group commander, and it was Alexander who gave the order. Thus, on 15 February 1944, some 240 heavy and medium bombers dropped more than 450 tons of high explosive and incendiaries on the Benedictine abbey. It was by far the largest force ever sent against a target as small as a building. As in the case of the town of Cassino, quite a few bombs fell far short of their mark. General Clark refused to go forward and join the officers and men, who behaved like riotous fans at a football game and cheered and shouted as the monastery went up in smoke; he stayed at his headquarters some seventeen miles from Monte Cassino, and David Hapgood says that sixteen bombs exploded only yards away from the trailer in which Clark was doing paperwork.

Dom Luigi happened to be away from the monastery that evil day. He told us that hundreds of civilians who had taken shelter there were killed (the booklet says that at least 150 died), but that all the monks who remained behind were 'under the special protection of St Benedict' and were spared. Another miracle, Dom Luigi said as he led us down into the crypts, was that the much-larger-than-life statue of St Benedict had stood upright in the central cloister, although all else had been toppled and smashed during the fury of the bombardment.

We went into a large workshop where artisans were engaged in the restoration of the choir stalls. Carved panels had been salvaged from the ruins, and one of them had a square hole cut out of it. 'That was not due to war damage,' was Dom Luigi's caustic remark. On the ground we saw a number of broken and charred cherubs which had been part of the decoration of the choir stalls. It was rather a gruesome sight, these headless, armless, wooden babies, like so many mutilated corpses. The artisans would make them whole, and on one side of the workshop were two of these choir stalls restored to all their baroque beauty. 'The governor-general of Canada has one of these cherubs on his desk,' Dom Luigi asserted. When we appeared startled and incredulous, he explained that he had meant a former governor-general of Canada, General Alexander. How did he know this? 'A Roman Catholic prelate reported to us that he had seen it on his desk, and Alexander admitted that it was from Monte Cassino,' Dom Luigi said and added, with a gentle smile, 'He has not returned this souvenir.'

When my wife and I left, Dom Luigi shook our hands warmly and bade us farewell on behalf of St Benedict. On our way out, we passed through the central cloister in front of the founder's statue and noticed that, while it may have stood there throughout the bombing when all around had fallen, it had lost its head, for there was a new one in place, all shining white marble, contrasting with the streaked, war-stained trunk.

The fall of the great bastion of Monte Cassino meant that the Germans had to abandon the Gustav Line that they had held for so many months and fall back on their next line of defence, the Hitler Line. There was a danger that they might have been outflanked, but the Wehrmacht leadership was such that they withdrew in good order, leaving rearguards to slow the Allied advance. The British and Indian troops who had wrested the ruined remains of Cassino from the Nazis were to be relieved after days of bitter fighting, and the Canadians were to take on the next phase of the battle, the attack on the Hitler Line. The I Canadian Corps had to pass through the XIII Corps, and this was a difficult manoeuvre, since there were few bridges across the Rapido and even fewer roads through the green fields of the Liri Valley. It led to horrendous traffic jams, and I could not help thinking what would have happened if we had not had complete dominance of the air. (In May 1944 the Allies had 4,000 combat planes in Italy, the Germans 450.) In a broadcast, however, I spoke in glowing terms:

... They were like rivers, these great convoys, rivers of supplies flowing toward the tidal wave of advance that was piling up against the barrier of the Hitler Line. There were literally hundreds of vehicles. The car tracks had been widened to three lanes of traffic, and the engineers had driven new roads through the wheat fields. Further along the road we came to a halt by a field of mustard that smelled sweetly after this morning's light rain. An infantry battalion was debussing from a long line of troop carriers. Later we passed the soldiers marching in single file through the wheat fields. They were Canadian infantry men and they were whistling and singing as they marched. They were new troops who had no experience of an attack yet. And everyone of us in our jeep was stirred by the happy way they were marching into battle ...

It was to be a baptism of fire for most of the 5th Canadian Division as well as Canadian Corps troops. In the euphoria of the victory at Cassino, there was talk of a breakthrough before the Germans had time to settle down in the Hitler Line, and the order was given to move forward with the 'utmost energy.' The First Canadian Army Tank Brigade and a British division advanced rapidly through the Liri Valley and reached Aquino in the dark.

The next morning, when the sun burned off the mist, the Canadians found themselves in the open within point-blank range of the Panther tank turrets that were part of the fortifications of the Hitler Line. According to the official history, three Sherman tanks were quickly knocked out, and the infantry suffered heavily from shelling and mortaring and had to retire. By the time the Ontario Regiment was able to pull back, it had lost thirteen Shermans, and every one of its remaining tanks had received at least one direct hit.

Thus, the kind of set-piece battle that the Eighth Army liked so much was inevitable. For three days – the minimum time needed to prepare for a major assault on the Hitler Line – the roads and car tracks that the engineers had driven through the wheat fields in the Liri Valley were clogged with military traffic; the gunners worked without sleep to get their artillery and ammunition into position and establish lines of fire. This was to be the first major engagement of I Canadian Corps, and, as might be expected, the corps commander, General Burns, gave the task of breaching the Hitler Line to Major General Chris Vokes and the experienced 1st Canadian Division. They were to open up a gap in the main sector through which the 5th Canadian Armoured Division was to drive, with the objective of securing a bridgehead over the Melfa River, some five miles away, and the last defence of the Hitler Line.

As I said in a broadcast, the 1st Canadian Division had been given the hard part to crack: the steel and concrete fortifications with their pillboxes, bunkers, emplacements (the Panther tank turrets had 75-millimetre guns), minefields, and barbed wire that I was told was twenty feet thick. A mighty cannonade by some 800 guns opened the assault on the Hitler Line in the early-morning hours of 23 May. This time we were set up in the attic of an old Italian farmhouse that overlooked the front; there was not much to see because of the thick haze, but we were able to record not only the sound of our own guns but also the crumps of returning German fire. When the mist lifted later in the morning, we could make out the smoking remains of some of our tanks. There were heavy casualties but the attack went well, and by first light on 24 May, 'Empire Day,' as I was to note, a three-mile segment of the Hitler Line from Pontecorvo to the outskirts of Aquino was cleared of the enemy.

Now it was the turn of Major-General Bert Hoffmeister's 5th Armoured Division, and at eight o'clock that morning a task force of 100 tanks and self-propelled guns poured through the wide gap that the 1st Division had torn in the main German defences. By ten o'clock the task force, which was supported by fighter bombers, attacked Nazi paratroopers who were attempting to set up positions in front of the Melfa River. They drove the enemy back and the advance continued. There were armoured clashes. Everything was happening so fast. The time set for reaching the Melfa was three days, but I reported that a tank regiment got there 'in a couple of hours and a crossing was made that afternoon.'

The man who performed this feat was Lieutenant E.J. Perkins, known as Perky, a small unassuming fellow, who led his reconnaissance troop of three light tanks to the steep banks of the shallow river. Somehow they were able to get across despite intense shell and mortar fire. Then Perky and his men took over a house, capturing eight German soldiers. They were alone in the face of enemy counter-attacks, and, in telling the story of Perky, I said that on two occasions he was ordered to withdraw, but he asked to stay. He did: he was awarded the DSO, a signal honour, next to the Victoria Cross, for a junior officer.

Some days later I heard on the grapevine, or the old-boy officers' network, that Jack Mahony had won the VC. I could not believe it, but I was assured that it was true. I was surprised and excited because I had met Jack Mahony: he was a stringer (a part-time correspondent) for the *Province* in New Westminster, and he had helped me on a couple of occasions when I had been sent there to report on some event. Jack was a nice guy, mild mannered, soft-spoken, who would never hurt anyone, or so he seemed to me. I could not have imagined him as a fighting officer and a leader in battle, which just shows how mistaken one can be from appearances. I was determined to get an interview with him, which I did when his unit came out of the line.

Major J.K. Mahony was a company commander with the Westminster Regiment (motorized infantry), and, as I commented at the beginning of the interview with him, 'a lot of the credit for routing the Germans beyond the Hitler Line' was due to him and his men, who stormed across the Melfa River and clung to the opposite bank for several hours until the rest of the battalion could reach them. Jack Mahony set up his headquarters in the farmhouse that Perkins had captured. The men dug in and suffered heavy losses when they attempted to clear buildings from which the enemy was firing on them. Despite painful wounds, Mahony carried on and went around encouraging his men. The climax came when three enemy tanks closed in on them and then, miraculously, turned around and were not seen again. I said in the broadcast that it was due to Major Mahony's leadership that 'his little band, although it had lost half its number stuck it out for almost thirty-six hours.' In the interview Jack Mahony praised his men for holding the bridgehead across the Melfa against all that Jerry could throw at them.

P.S.: I guess there were times when you didn't think you were going to get out of it alive, Jack?

J.M.: Yes, when I saw those three tanks charging us, I really thought our number was up. And I still can't understand why they turned back when they got within two hundred yards of us. Of course, we were letting them have it with everything we had [Mahony's men had no anti-tank guns] but the bullets were just bouncing off their armour.

P.S.: That's amazing, Jack, I thought these Nazis would be supermen as long as they had a lot of steel to protect them?

J.M.: Well, the Heinie is a pretty good fighter as long as the odds are with him, but once they see the game is up and we don't intend to quit, then they just give up. At least, that's the way we found them. I remember one German prisoner who went down on his knees in front of me begging for his life. Of course I never had any intention of shooting him, but that's the kind of supermen they are.

P.S.: Well, Jack, I suppose you had no time to do anything but direct the fighting during the daylight. But what did you do at night?

J.M.: I was trying to keep myself warm. You see I had a proper ducking crossing the Melfa and I was soaking wet. I tried to get the chill out of my bones by digging all night.

The day or so that it took to strengthen and expand the frail bridgehead that Perkins and Mahony had established across the Melfa River changed the course of the battle. The Fifth Army was breaking out of the Anzio Beachhead; actually, it started its offensive just half an hour after the I Canadian Corps began its attack on the Hitler Line, and the combined American Canadian Special Service Force, which I had visited in the beachhead, had penetrated so far that it was threatening to cut Highway No. 6, the Road to Rome, and outflank the enemy. The Germans began a systematic withdrawal, and the Allied advance turned into a pursuit. The 5th Canadian Armoured Division had passed its first test, bloodied but triumphant.

It was strangely quiet in the Liri Valley and, without the smoke of battle, one could admire its beauty. It was greener than any part of Italy that we had seen up to then, and I noted there were 'great patches of red poppies.' Yet this ideal countryside was littered with the wreckage of war: the smashed fortifications of the Hitler Line, the upended guns, the burned-out trucks; and, from the Hitler Line to the Melfa River and beyond, scores of tank carcases, many of them blackened by fire, others with their turrets knocked askew and their tracks blown off. Most of the tanks were ours, Shermans whose high silhouette made them an easier target, but there were a few of the enemy's, the low-profiled and deadly Panthers. (In May 1944 the Allies had 1,900 tanks in Italy, the

Germans 450.) The tanks of the Second Armoured Regiment, known as the Strathconas, were the first to reach the Melfa River, and I met the commander, Lieutenant-Colonel P.G. Griffin. I remember him because he was the only field officer I saw in Italy who was wearing First World War ribbons. His arm was bandaged and he looked haggard and absolutely exhausted; he had been a brilliant tactician but, in his forties, he was really too old to be in the field.

We could not keep up with the advance now as we bumped over mud roads in blinding clouds of dust. It was like the first rapturous days in Sicily again. One morning it took three hours of bucking the most fearful traffic for us to reach an armoured formation's headquarters, only to find that its forward elements were still miles ahead. There were some burned-out tanks by the headquarters, and along the road I noticed several new graves marked by rough wooden crosses. 'You can't advance without casualties,' an officer said, 'at least not against Jerry.' In the distance we could hear the sound of insistent gunfire. On the way back, Hank, the driver of our jeep, said that if the Canadians kept on advancing like this, 'you'll have to get a plane to keep up with them.'

Hank was right. The only way to cover the pursuit of the withdrawing Germans was by plane. The next day I was fortunate enough to be given a ride by a British army pilot in a small light plane that was used as an air 'O Pip,' or observation post, for the guns. From a height of a couple of thousand feet, I could look down on the battlefield and see the Germans retreating down the Road to Rome. It was a thrilling experience, but, as I said in my report, 'it didn't seem real somehow, and I had to make myself believe that the red flashes in the mountains were German guns firing, and that those little black beetles crawling down below were Canadian tanks advancing.'

The Allied forces had broken out of the Anzio Beachhead and had linked up with the main Allied forces moving up from the south. The 5th Canadian Division was being gradually relieved and moved into reserve as other fresh formations passed through them to continue the pursuit, and the same was happpening to the 1st Canadian Division. The Germans were in desperate straits. Rome was within our grasp and Lieutenant Yvon Beaulne, our conducting officer, could stop shaving his head. It was time to switch from the Eighth Army to the Fifth Army's front.

11

Pope Pius Gets on Side

Rome, 4 June 1944:
Flying columns of the Allied Fifth Army entered Rome today
and seized the bridges across the Tiber which were left intact
on Hitler's orders. Rome is now an Open City.

The entry into Rome was a tense, nerve-wracking business for
me because I found out that the CBC had been left off the
roster of broadcasters to report on the capture of the first Axis
capital. A directive from Allied Force headquarters, dated 30 May
1944, said that the Fifth Army would move a short-wave transmitter on a half-track to the outskirts of the city when it was about to
fall, and it was setting aside a half-hour of air time for the radio
correspondents. There would be 'special spots,' as the memo put it,
of two and a half minutes' duration with a fifteen-second break
between spots, but what disturbed me was that a draw had
already been made as to the order in which the networks would
make their broadcasts, and there was no mention of the CBC. When
I protested to Major Royd Beamish, the Canadian PR officer at
Allied Force headquarters, he replied that the draw had been
conducted at Fifth Army and that no one at AFHQ knew about it

until it was done. 'Fifth Army,' Beamish wrote, 'have assumed the attitude that the Rome show is their pigeon and theirs only.'

That was typical of General Mark Clark: he was determined to keep all the honour and glory of conquering Rome for the American Fifth Army, and especially for himself. Not only did he not inform AFHQ; he had not even told the army group commander, General Alexander, when he ordered his forces to swing left and drive for Rome instead of pressing forward to cut the German line of retreat, which had been the Allied strategy. It was a 'great missed opportunity,' according to the war historian Max Hastings. As a result, the Nazi Tenth Army escaped: every division, every formation, although greatly depleted, got away. Conducting the draw for air time at Fifth Army was the way that General Clark showed his disdain for the British – for besides his immediate superior, General Alexander, General Maitland 'Jumbo' Wilson had taken over from General Eisenhower at AFHQ. Major Beamish* assured me, however, that I would cover the entry into Rome and that I would get on the air, even if last.

On 3 June we left the Canadian encampment and the Eighth Army area. There were five of us in a jeep, Benoit Lafleur, Lloyd Moore, Lieutenant Yvon Beaulne, the driver, and I, together with our baggage and the portable recording equipment. We drove past the French lines to Highway No. 7, the ancient Appian Way, and

---

*Some weeks after the Allied entry into Rome, Major Royd Beamish and Sergeant George Powell of the *Maple Leaf* staff were sent on assignment to Canada. They had been selected because of their length of service overseas, four to five years, and the main purpose of their mission was to provide the troops with news from home. They divided the country between them, with Royd covering central and western Ontario and the prairie provinces, while George did the Maritimes, Quebec, eastern Ontario, British Columbia, and Yukon. They went to see every premier in order to get 'stirring' messages from them, and Powell recalled that he got a much warmer reception from BC's Premier John Hart than from Maurice Duplessis. They took part in Victory Bond drives and particularly in a great national radio show, which starred Beatrice Lillie, Frederic March and his wife, Florence Eldridge, and Canadian tenor Raoul Jobin; Finance Minister J.L. Ilsley set a precedent by appearing on this show. While he was on this assignment, Sergeant Powell was commissioned, and he emerged after a month's course at Brockville as Second Lieutenant Powell.

bowled along through the flooded Pontine Marshes to the old Anzio Beachhead area. It was fairly late by the time we reached the Fifth Army camp in Nettuno, which was the assembly area and was swarming with war correspondents. We spent the night there, and at five o'clock the next morning we were off again in a long convoy through badly battered towns, where the heaviest fighting had occurred in the break-out from the beachhead to Valmontone. There we rejoined Highway No. 6 and rolled along this road which seemed strangely quiet and peaceful, until we reached the Breda armament works on the edge of Rome. On high ground nearby the Fifth Army had set up its mobile short-wave transmitter.

An atmosphere of excitement and frenzied expectation seemed to grip everyone, including the correspondents. 'So this is Rome,' people kept saying, although the euphoria was a bit premature. An American general, according to historian John Ellis, noted at the time that command had 'gone to hell' and that 'all semblance of discipline has broken down.' German rearguards were still holding out, probably with a couple of self-propelled guns, and they were shelling the road ahead. Beny Lafleur and I had to hit the ground a couple of times when we went to have a look. But no one was paying much attention, and we saw a wedding party, the bride in her flowing white dress, the groom, and others, walking along the road as though there was no gunfire, nothing happening, finally all disappearing over the ridge. That was a fantastic sight, but I wrote in my diary that the advance had become a wild party. The Italians had brought out bottles of wine, and the assault troops, men as well as officers, joined in the drinking and dancing and celebration. A girl did a striptease and the women seemed only too eager to be taken into the sun-drenched fields. The Caesars and the Roman legionaries would have understood such an orgy. Needless to say, I never told this story in my broadcast.

We had to wait for the official communiqué announcing the Allied entry into Rome before going on the air. Then, with our copy checked and approved by the censors, who had been brought up to the front, we lined up in the order of the draw to go on the air. I was last and I described in part what I had seen:

... I watched the fighting on the outskirts of the city from a vantage point in the Pignataro suburb. Above the crash of artillery and the sharp clatter of machine gun fire I heard some heavier explosions which shook the ground where I was standing, and I saw great clouds of smoke arise above the roof tops.

... A few Romans dared to venture out into the open and they cheered our soldiers and shook their hands. Grateful women pressed glasses of wine into their hands and insisted that they drink to the new day that would bring back the glory that was Rome. The first Allied troops to enter the Italian city followed the route that the Roman legions used. They marched down Highway Six, the ancient Via Casilina. On their way, they passed the ruins of the old [Roman] viaduct and many of the great historic monuments of this city. Soldiers with whom I talked were worn out after weeks of advancing. But they were happy and proud to be the first to enter Rome. Their route was marked by German signs which the Nazis hadn't had time to remove. One of these signs which was evidently directed at the German soldiers said: 'No Looting in the City' ...

It was my first 'live' broadcast from the front, and, according to A.E. Powley in his book about the CBC coverage of the war, 'the only time it happened in our battlefield reporting.' I felt that I was talking into a barrel, but I heard later that I was one of the few who got through without too much disruptive static. It was a triumphal occasion, this entry into Rome, and a war correspondent could be excused for sounding like a booster. However, I did not go as far as Gordon Fraser of NBC, who preceded me and ended his piece by saying, 'And this correspondent has his helmet off to the men who made it possible, the foot soldier, the infantry man who hasn't stopped slugging since the jump-off, May the eleventh.'

The German rearguards had withdrawn, and on the night of 4 June 1944 Beny and I had dinner at the Grand Hotel, and I remember the first course was prosciutto (thinly sliced Parma ham) and melon. It was such a delight after a diet of compo rations that were mainly canned stew and bully beef. The main dining-room was full of American troops and there were some beautifully dressed women. A band played. I got a room in the hotel, and for the first time in months I slept between sheets on a proper bed. It was marvellous and I had a splendid rest.

Sholto Watt had an even better room at the Excelsior Hotel; it was luxuriously furnished with golden covers and curtains and a thick carpet that was the same ivory color as the walls. But what impressed Sholto was that when he pressed the bell above his bed, a waiter appeared and brought him breakfast. 'That really was extraordinary, don't you think?' Sholto asked. In a grand gesture of noblesse oblige, Sholto gave his safari bed to our conducting officer, Yvon Beaulne. He must have regretted doing so, because we were soon kicked out of our fine living quarters, since the great hotels were taken over for officers' rest camps (so called) and for the Allied military government.

The next day we were up early to record the triumphal entry of the Allied forces into Rome. Since 4 June was a Sunday, General Clark had felt that it would be more appropriate for the big parade to take place the following day. The German rearguards might have had something to do with his decision. It was a spectacular show of might, with thousands of troops and long lines of guns and tanks, and the Roman crowds loved it. I caught a glimpse of General Clark standing in a jeep, surrounded by army cameramen, obviously revelling in all the adulation. I thought that with his suntanned angular features and his large nose he looked like a Caesar, although he was much taller. An American Caesar. When we played back the recording of the march past, we heard, above the sound of all the cheering and yelling, a small boy's voice piping up, 'Viva Mussolini.'

While most of the troops in the Fifth Army's parade through Rome were American, there were some Canadians, although they wore American uniforms. They belonged to the combined American Canadian Special Service Force, and a battle group from this SS force had been among the flying columns that seized the bridges over the Tiber. (As might be expected, Canadians of I Canadian Corps were disappointed that they were not included in the triumphal entry into Rome.) Although attention was concentrated on the Allied march past, I noted in my diary that armed civilians broke into Fascist stores, and that young Italians were riding around the city in cars flying red flags. Also, that an American sergeant got onto the balcony of the Palazzo Venizia, from which Mussolini used to harangue the populace, and spoke. There was no record of what he said.

Besides the celebration of the Allied victory, the first rapturous impression of Rome was that it was whole and undamaged. At least that was true of the main part of the city; the outer suburbs, where the factories and the railways were, had been bombed. We had got so used to destruction on the Road to Rome that it was wonderful to see all these clean buildings without any mark on them, without so much as a bullet hole; on that first day, the open unsullied city was more thrilling than all its monuments and treasures.

Rome, Tuesday, 6 June 1944, 11 a.m.:
American, British and Canadian troops land in force on the Normandy coast between Cherbourg and Le Havre. Thousands of ships and planes involved in the greatest combined operation.

A couple of friends and I were strolling along the Via Veneto, so bright and shining in the morning sun, when we saw some GIs gathered around a parked U.S. army half-track; its radio was blaring out the news of D-Day. It would be an exaggeration to say that veteran war correspondents broke down and cried like babies, but we realized that we had lost the greatest story so far in the war, the capture of the first Axis capital – it had lasted little more than a day. No one was going to be interested in what the Canadians were doing in Italy now, and, in any case, they were out of the line and resting somewhere to the south. Ah, to hell with it, we would take a holiday, and what better place to take a holiday than in Rome.

For some correspondents, 'the greatest story of the war so far,' the capture of the first Axis capital, did not last for even a day. Gordon Hutton, one of our best conducting officers in Italy, told the sad story of what happened to Sholto Watt and Paul Morton. He had escorted them into Rome on the evening of the day it fell, 4 June 1944, and Gordon, who retired to Saltspring Island, recalled that they were 'beside themselves with excitement: at long last, here was an opportunity to file a cornucopia of copy heralding the capture of the first major capital city by the Allies. Sure-fire, front page, Extra! Extra! stuff – and no mistake!' The two newspaper correspondents went to work with a will and wrote glowing accounts of the way the Romans welcomed the Allied troops; their reports were datelined 'June 6, 1944.'

Meanwhile Yvon Beaulne was having trouble; he had requisitioned a fine villa for the Canadian army Public Relations, the Villa Jacomeni, but now was faced with a potential riot. Apparently, the villa had been a Fascist headquarters, and a crowd, which included some partisans with their distinctive red kerchiefs, gathered outside and threatened to set fire to the building. He agreed to meet a couple of partisans who took him up to a room on the third floor and showed him alleged instruments of torture. The partisans were out to get the three Jacomeni brothers who were living in the villa and looking after the place, but Yvon, being a kind-hearted fellow, arranged with the Vatican to have them driven to Naples. In the end, he had to give up the villa; he got another one that was not as grand but was closer to the centre of the city.

On 9 June, according to my diary, only a few days after we entered Rome, Pope Pius XII received the Allied war correspondents. Eugenio Pacelli, who was elected pope in the spring of 1939, came from an aristocratic family; as a cardinal he had been a diplomat and evidently believed that the church had to accommodate itself to the winning side. He got along so well with Hitler at one time that a German officer had made a play on words by saying: 'Now the Pope is nearer to Himmler than to Himmel (heaven).' Pius XII was severely criticized for not speaking out against the way the Nazis were rounding up the Jews in Italy.

Quite clearly, the purpose of this audience was to make known to the world that the pope had changed sides and was now supporting the Allies.

In retrospect, it was an amazing scene in the Consistory Hall of the Vatican, a long room the ceiling of which was decorated with the first gold ingots brought from the New World. We were lined up around three sides of the hall because His Holiness was to meet each of us individually, and I must say we were rather a scruffy crowd in our battledress and fatigues. The greatest lack of dignity displayed, however, was the attire of the few women correspondents: they wore army issue blouses and slacks and did not bother to cover their heads. One of them, a large lady with the nickname of 'Pee Wee,' seemed to be bulging out of her clothes, but, when he saw her, the Pope, a thin, ascetic man, did not wince. For the first time, news cameramen were allowed into the sacred precincts of the Vatican, and these war cameramen were a tough, undisciplined lot. They scrambled to get the best shots, some of them kneeling, others even lying on the floor, and there were cries of 'Hold it, Your Holiness.'

As the pope moved around the hall, speaking to each of us individually, the cameramen followed him, crowding and jostling, with flash bulbs popping. Never once were they motioned away. The pontiff was accompanied by a couple of acolytes who handed out rosaries and postcard-sized colour pictures of Pius XII. I noticed that one particularly aggressive Jewish cameraman got into line twice and got a couple of rosaries. 'Wit' them rosaries,' he announced, 'I can lay any RC babe in New York.' At the end of the audience the pope gave us his blessing, and when he raised his arms, there was an arc of bursting flash bulbs. Although I did not go into as much graphic detail in my *Maclean's* magazine article 'So This Is Rome' (15 July 1944), I did say, 'I thought the Pope had shown the greatest possible restraint and dignity under the circumstances.'

As might be expected, the Catholic correspondents were indignant at the way the pope was treated. A British correspondent, Tony Beckwith, called it 'The Rape of Rome.' 'It was disgusting,' an American correspondent said, 'I was never so embarrassed or ashamed at the conduct of my fellow workers before.' Someone declared it 'quite grotesque,' which was probably the best description of the papal reception. My friend Wynford Vaughan-Thomas, who was a great storyteller, asserted that at the time of the audience a Scottish pipe band was playing in the piazza opposite St Peter's and the Vatican, and he quoted the pipe major as saying, 'Hoot mon, we're going to blow yon Popey a tune.'

Some time later, Beny Lafleur told me that he had been in touch with a Monsignor McGuigan, an Irish priest with the Curia, and there was a possibility that the pope would speak to Canada over the CBC. It would be a short message, but the first time that His Holiness would make a broadcast over any other facility than Vatican Radio. I urged Beny to redouble his efforts and said that he should point out to the monsignor that there were two languages in Canada and that, therefore, the pope should send two messages, one in French and the other in English.

Once the final arrangements were made, I suggested to Beny that we should have a photograph taken of Pius XII speaking into the CBC microphone. We agreed that our bosses, Dan McArthur et al., would expect nothing less, but after all the turmoil at the audience, no Canadian army cameraman, nor any other outside cameraman, would be allowed to photograph the pope. (In fact, neither Beny nor I was allowed in the Vatican when the pope delivered his radio message. I am not sure how the microphone was set up, but Joe Beauregard had run a wire down to the CBC van, which was parked immediately below the window of the second-floor room where His Holiness was to make the broadcast. We sat in the van listening while Joe recorded. I remember thinking that Pius XII's English was difficult to understand.) But how were we going to get that picture of the pope speaking into the CBC mike? Then we discovered that there was an official papal photographer.

We went in search of him, and I had visions of his being a high-ranking cleric, a monsignor at the very least, perhaps a bishop or even a cardinal. However, the papal photographer turned out to be a businessman who had the finest camera shop in Rome. I told him what we wanted; I said that the CBC microphone must be front and centre, and he expected there would be no difficulty in his taking such a picture. 'In any case,' he said, and he was obviously a smart businessman in his neat pin-striped blue suit, 'if there were any objection, I have a lot of portraits of His Holiness and I could select a suitable one and superimpose a photograph of the CBC microphone.' I said that I would prefer the real thing, but I was confident now that we would get the picture. (The photograph of Pope Pius XII speaking into a CBC microphone had pride of place in Dr Frigon's office during his tenure as general manager.)

The pope's broadcast was Benoit Lafleur's initiative and, in due course, he received the bill for the picture which, if I remember correctly, was for the lira equivalent of $100, a lot of money in those days. Poor Beny was greatly agitated; he had already been in trouble for running up a cable toll of $70 on a single service message from Algiers. (This was when he was to be expelled from the Mediterranean Theatre; the CBC had five correspondents there at the time of the Sicilian campaign, Ouimet, Halton, Cowan, Lafleur, and me, and five was too many, so Beny was to be returned to London. The ignominy of this was too much, and he poured out his feelings in a lengthy cable sent at full rate to Canada. Fortunately, he was able to stay by wangling an accreditation with the French force about to invade Corsica, and spun out that assignment long enough to be on hand to replace Ouimet in Italy.) The CBC never forgot that $70 cable and would make a snide reference to it whenever there was an austerity campaign, which was quite often. For the fourth or fifth time, Bert Powley wired me 'to impress on all staff to keep cable costs down.' My reply in telegraphese was: 'UNSENT ANY LONG CABLES ETLAFLEUR SO HURT PARCONTINUED REFERENCE ALGIERS MESSAGE WILLING REIMBURSE CBC STOP EXNOW ECONOMY FIRST CUMUS.' That put a stop to the admonitions, and Powley even became solicitous about our welfare.

When Beny showed me the photographer's bill, he looked

downcast, but I said there was no need to worry – just enclose it with the picture, a fine glossy print, with the CBC mike and Pius XII in sharp focus, and send it to the corporation. That was the last we heard of it, except for a strange request for the microphone that the pope had used in his broadcast. I wondered whether they were going to set up a shrine in the Montreal headquarters, or was the microphone to become a holy relic? The first radio relic? However, there was a problem in meeting this request. We had about half a dozen mikes in the van, they were handsome mikes, leftovers from the 1939 royal tour, and they all looked alike. There was no way of telling which one the pope had used. At any rate, Lloyd Moore had to find it; I was not a witness to how he did this, but Lloyd told me that he had murmured some incantations, such as eeny, meeny, miney, moe, picked one that was not working well, and sent it off to Canada.

For days the Allied forces continued to roll through the centre of Rome. I noted in my diary on 8 June that there was heavy military traffic; troops overflowed the sidewalks and Brits began to appear in numbers. On 10 June a column of tanks rumbled past the Hotel Internazionale where I was staying, having been turfed out of the Grand. Not all the troops passed through the city; some of them stayed, and there were military camps around the Baths of Caracalla and in the Circus Maximus, with pup tents and barbed wire and sentries marching back and forth. The American II Corps had hung a huge banner at one end of the Colosseum with the razzmatazz slogan:

Follow the Blue To Speedy Two,
Rome, Berlin, and Tokyo Too.

It was as if the Yanks were going to have a ball game in the Colosseum, and no doubt would have had one if the ancient stadium had had a level playing field instead of excavations of the underground stables. The banner did not please some Romans, however, who regarded it as boorish and a defilement of this historic monument. 'Europe is being overrun by the barbarians from the East and the West,' was Akos Tolnay's dry comment; he was a Hungarian journalist of the old school. The first joyous excitement and relief over the Allied victory had dissipated. We were now being told that the Germans had respected the Open City 'scrupulously' and had 'behaved exemplarily though coldly toward the Romans.' There was a reaction against the arrogant attitude of the Americans and of the Allied military government. U.S. military police now guarded the great hotels and refused to allow anyone to enter without a special pass. 'Nazi troops would give lifts to poor people,' Tolnay said, 'but your troops will give lifts to no one. Some Italian partisans came to see me – I tried to turn them away – they said that they had to get to Naples. What should they do? I suggested that they might do best by approaching the American Negro troops. Later these partisans told me that they had done this, but the Negro drivers wanted six hundred lira to give them a lift to Naples.'

Akos Tolnay could be described as a member of the International Set: he had been in Rome for years before the war and had no intention of leaving. George Popoff was another: he was a Bulgarian journalist working as a Swiss correspondent. I remember a party in Popoff's roof-top apartment with its wide terrace where there were tubs of sweet-smelling jasmine and oleander and from which there was a spectacular view of Rome and the Tiber River. Sholto Watt was there, curled up in a deck-chair, and so were a few other guests (Sholto had taken up residence in the apartment after being kicked out of various hotels.) We had a lot of fun recounting our experiences, drinking wine, and eating the delectable dishes that George's cook had concocted out of bully beef.

Then there was Antoinette, a decorative member of the International Set. I met her through Paul Morton, who was a correspondent for the *Toronto Star*. I got to know Paul quite well when we were waiting around in Venafro for the Battle for Rome to begin; he was a slim, handsome fellow who was considered a bit erratic; he could be moody and, on occasion, sullen and withdrawn. But mostly, he was charming and articulate and I found him to be a good companion. The odd time we talked far into the night. Paul was very anti-establishment, and, while I went along with him and most of us had left-wing sympathies then, he held much more extreme views than any of us. I remember going with Paul to an ENSA concert for the troops in Venafro, and when the national anthem was played, Paul refused to stand up. I thought that this was foolhardy and that, if it was reported, he could have been dis-accredited.

I went out with Paul Morton a couple of times in Rome, once when he had got hold of a small, requisitioned Fiat and we drove to the beaches at the mouth of the Tiber and had a fine lunch in what looked like a resort hotel – the long arm of the military had not yet reached out to convert this into an officers' rest camp. The other time was at a party in a villa that was said to be owned by Manfredi, the contractor who built the Hitler Line; he was still in business, according to Morton, who said the Allies never arrested Fascists, only Communists. There were mostly British officers, including a couple of air marshals, at this party; among the women were an Italian film star, or so she was introduced, and Antoinette de Lisle, who was widely known as the mistress or former mistress of Crown Prince Bertil of Sweden. Antoinette, or Tony, as she was known, had a beak-like nose and was not so much beautiful as elegant. Paul was living with her in this villa of Manfredi's – he was fortunate enough to have met Tony before he was chucked out of the Excelsior Hotel. There was plenty to drink, but one of the officers said that they did not want a repeat of the scandal that had occurred at the last party when a Guards officer fell off the balcony. 'So blotto, ole boy, that he didn't break a bone.' Paul, who did not hold his liquor very well, became disgusted with the party and started filling glasses with Javel water. But, as I wrote in my diary, Tony prevented anyone from being poisoned. After Paul Morton left Antoinette, she took up with General Mark Clark, which showed what a democratic courtesan she was.

It was not difficult to meet women in liberated Rome; it was difficult *not* to meet them. At a cocktail party given by Akos Tolnay I met Fiora, who invited me to a golf club on the outskirts of the city. It was a lovely, warm evening, and when we reached the club we found a party sitting at a long table on the terrace. There must have been forty or fifty people, young Allied officers and Italian girls in their summer frocks. A light supper was served and afterwards there was dancing in the clubhouse, and I found out that the girls were mostly young wives, members of the Roman equivalent of the Junior League. In fact, I was told that their association or group had organized this party. Maybe they felt that it was their patriotic duty, now that Italy was a co-belligerent; if so, it was a good excuse to meet desirable young men.

But what surprised me was that these young matrons entertained us in their homes, with their husbands often present. And at these parties they were quite open about going out with the Allied officers and making trysts and forming liaisons. Their husbands must have known. This situation was a bit confusing and embarrassing for the clean-cut young Canadians and Americans, who had been brought up to think it was wrong to have an affair with a married woman, especially if the husband knew. But sex overcame their moral scruples.

Paola, whom I met at the golf club, came from a wealthy family and had a magnficent apartment. Although she was only twenty-nine years old, she had had four children, and she felt that she had fulfilled her marriage vows and should be free to have fun. In this she was no different from many Roman wives; their husbands had mistresses, and they should have lovers. But Paola had a problem. 'My husband, I don't love,' she told me, 'but he loves me – he's stupid.'

Picnics were arranged on the banks of the Tiber, to which the girls brought basket lunches and bottles of wine, and dances in various villas and some of the hotels. There were no shortages for the rich in Rome. Paola had a party in her flat, and I noted that there were fifty guests. Her husband was there and so were other husbands, skulking around in the shadows, and I wrote in my diary that they were a 'pathetic sight, the Italian husbands at these parties.' They were largely shunned or ignored. The Italian husbands were the victims of conquest while their wives were enjoying being the prizes.

Needless to say, I was soon kicked out of the Hotel Internazionale, which was taken over by the RAF PR. I wrote to Bert Powley that I needed a rest and complained about 'these base wallahs requisitioning every place we try to rest our head and chucking us from bed to bed,' and he agreed to my taking a holiday, as long as I was available to go to the front if anything happened. So I rented a small apartment at the foot of the Spanish Steps: it was close enough to the Albergo Citta, the British army PR hotel, that I could take my meals there. The British were so much more civilized in the way they ran their messes; dinner was at eight and it was well served by candlelight. With the Americans, if it was not steak, it was chow and cafeteria style. The Canadians were in between.

It was a pleasant place, the Citta or Hotel de la Ville as it was usually called, and was easy to find, situated as it was at the top of the Spanish Steps. Among the friends who visited me at the hotel was Captain Lloyd McKenzie. He had been with me when I returned to Italy on that creaking old tub the *Almazora*, and, according to my diary, we had had long chats about the good old days in Victoria and other important subjects. Now, here he was in his Lanark and Renfrew Scottish uniform, looking every inch a Highland officer, striding into the Hotel de la Ville. We went into the hotel's very English bar and were having a drink when an American correspondent with whom I was acquainted – I think he was from the Chicago *Tribune* – came up to us. I introduced him to 'Captain Lloyd McKenzie,' and I have the word of Lloyd for what happened next. The American correspondent appeared awestricken. 'Are you really Lord McKenzie?' he asked. According to Lloyd, whose veracity could not be questioned, since he became an eminent judge on the Supreme Court of British Columbia, I said, 'Yes, he is, and he's the Duke of Ucluelet.'

The Americanization of Rome proceeded apace with Irving Berlin's *This Is the Army* playing in the Opera House. Of course, Canadians were always being mixed up with either the Americans or the British, but we had our cultural moment when Bill Boss conducted the Rome symphony orchestra. In the spirit of co-belligerency, the orchestra director, whose name, unfortunate to Anglo-Saxon ears, was Nino Stincho, wanted a musician from each of the Allied forces to put on a concert. Since Bill Boss had formed and conducted an orchestra in Ottawa, he was asked, and he readily agreed. He chose as his main work Tchaikovsky's Fourth Symphony, and Captain Yvon Beaulne – not only had he become hirsute again but he had been promoted – said that Bill spent a couple of weeks preparing. The concert was a great success, the Opera House was packed, and Bill Boss, looking the very model of a maestro with the red beard that he had cultivated since leaving the army and becoming a war correspondent, ended it with his own rousing arrangement of 'O Canada.' (Boss also conducted a leading Dutch orchestra, the Radio Hilversum orchestra, in August 1945. This time his main work was Tchaikovsky's 'Marche Slav.')

Although the Canadian corps was resting and refitting in the Volturno Valley, which was closer to Naples than anywhere else, we did see a lot of Canadian troops in Rome. They were granted short periods of leave in the Italian capital and were provided with transportation and accommodation. A Canada Club was opened on the Via Nazionale, and, according to the official history, sufficient living quarters were requisitioned for 150 officers and 1,000 men. Since the Canadians were to be in reserve until the end of July, there was not much point in my going to the front, although I did make several sorties.

On 21 June I left Rome for Perugia, but I was back on 23 June without anything noted in my diary. On 8 July it took five hours to drive to the Eighth Army press camp north of Lake Trasimene for General Sir Oliver Leese's conference, to be held the following day. General Leese was a large, slightly stooped, horse-faced man who was in striking contrast to his predecessor and had none of Monty's popular appeal: the Eighth Army commander praised the fighting quality of the Canadian troops but could not hide his contempt for the Canadian command. It developed that, at the time, General Leese, with General Alexander's concurrence, was proposing to break up the I Canadian Corps and put the 1st Division and the 5th Armoured Division under the command of a

British corps. It took some persuasion on the part of the Canadian brass to get him to relent, and this was the reason the I Canadian Corps was kept in reserve for such a long period of almost two months. On that trip I visited the Army Tank Brigade, which was the only Canadian formation in the line.

It was a fateful day, 20 July, to leave for the Fifth Army front, and I noted in my diary, 'Hitler bombed!' The radio was full of it. I teamed up with my friend, Wynford Vaughan-Thomas, to visit Leghorn. On the way back, our party stopped at an outdoor cafe, and I remember we talked about the way that the word 'liberate' had been cynically twisted to 'mean anything but.' It had become 'a synonym,' I wrote, 'for screw or fuck, or rob or steal.' One spoke of 'liberating' a typewriter or a bottle of vino. Vaughan-Thomas was most amusing about what he called the 'Four Phases of Liberation.' The first phase, he said – and the way he spoke made it seem as if there were an exclamation mark after every sentence – the first phase was when the assault troops took a town; they had no time for anything but pursuing the enemy. The second phase was when the Italians came out of their cellars to cheer the Allied soldiers and were liberated of watches, rings, and jewellery. The third phase was when the Allied military government arrived; they put the Fascists back in power, took over the main buildings, and finally and fully liberated the town. The fourth phase was well behind the lines, Vaughan-Thomas said with a grin, where the 'Eyeties, whom we had liberated, were busy liberating the liberators.'

There were other sorties, and one of the most memorable was when I followed King George VI on his tour of the front. His Majesty was travelling incognito as 'General Collingwood,' which fooled nobody and was not really meant to hide his identity. The purpose of his assuming the role of a commoner was to get him out of a sticky political situation: if he had come to Italy as the monarch, the rules of protocol were such that he would have had to meet King Victor Emmanuel, whose throne was tottering. Just before I left for the royal tour, Akos Tolnay told me that the political situation in Rome was tense and that the young people were flocking to join the Socialist and Communist parties. If it were not for the Allied Control Commission holding the lid down, as Akos put it, the king would have been out. (Victor Emmanuel hung on until May 1946, when he abdicated in favour of his son, Umberto. However, a national referendum had been taken rejecting the monarchy; Umberto left a month later and Italy became a republic.)

Once more to Perugia, where we trailed along behind the royal cavalcade, which drove for miles through lines of troops waving and cheering in the brilliant sunshine. I wrote in my diary that King George was taken to an advance position where enemy mortar shells were falling within 1,000 yards, so he could see an attack on a hill village. The next day, 26 July, it was the same, careering along behind the staff cars, and I made a note that a royal visit could slow down an advance, since the route along which we travelled was closed to traffic. I was told that a brigadier at the head of a column of 300 vehicles, which were going to exploit a possible breakthrough, was stopped by military police, while a 'badly needed' ammunition train was held up for hours. On 31 July the king visited the Canadians and invested Major Jack Mahony with the Victoria Cross.

When I got back to Rome, I found the Albergo Citta and other Public Relations hangouts rife with rumours of a big, new combined operation.

12

To Cannes and the Vercors

Off Saint Tropez, 15 August 1944:
The Allies open a new front against the Germans with American and French forces landing at beaches in southern France between Cannes and Toulon. They meet little resistance.

The hot, lazy days at the beginning of August in Rome were enlivened by the conferences and briefings on the coming combined operation. There was to be another landing, and, as might be expected, the military were not saying where it would be, and there were a number of possibilities. The correspondents speculated about another 'end run' up the Italian coast, either on the west side around Genoa or on the east side above Rimini; or the invasion of Yugoslavia or Greece or southern France, although the latter seemed the least likely. At any rate, we were going to get away from the dreary slogging match on the Italian front in which no one seemed interested, even when a city like Florence was taken. There was a great scramble for places, and I wrote in my diary that 'I succeeded in getting on a destroyer with a wire recorder.' I also noted that Bob Vermillion of the United Press was going in with the paratroops.

On 5 August we left for Naples on a Mitchell bomber, not one of my favorite planes; I would have much preferred a Dakota. We were flying in 'soup,' and when I remarked to one of the crew about the clouds, he said, 'Yeah, and there are a lot of rocks in them clouds – we'd better get her higher up.' In Naples, the Canadians were lumped together with the British in the Serena Hotel, which was definitely third rate, while the Terminus, where the American correspondents were put up, was not exactly high class, but was better. I shared a room at the Serena with Wynford Vaughan-Thomas of the BBC. That night, we went to a symphony concert conducted by Sir John Barbirolli in the San Carlo Opera House. It was a breathtaking sight, the great theatre with its rows of plush seats and gilded galleries rising to the gods; one could imagine being back at a pre-war show except that the audience was mostly in uniform.

The next day we were driven out to Allied Force headquarters in Caserta for what I called a 'fatuous' press conference. General Maitland Wilson was there, all 300 pounds of him, and he spent most of the time apologizing for the Anzio landing, which was ancient history. 'Jumbo' asserted that they would not make the same mistakes with the coming combined operation and hinted that the objective was southern France. That discription was a farce, because, while we were supposed to keep it a deep, dark secret, the Italians knew where we were going and were openly talking about it. The Bay of Naples was full of warships, and there were signs on the Via Roma wishing the Allies 'Bon Voyage' and a hoarding above one store cried out: 'Achetez Vos Souvenirs Ici Avant Que Vous Allez à Paris.'

There was another conference that I put down as 'almost equally useless,' but slowly things to come were taking shape. I found that my companion on the destroyer was to be Si Korman of the Mutual network, and I figured that the wire recorder that I was told would be on the destroyer must be his. Korman and I checked in at U.S. navy headquarters, known as Navy House, and were told to come back the next day. I met Vaughan-Thomas at the officers' shop where we joined Eric Sevareid of CBS – I spelled his name 'Severard' in my diary – who had a car. We drove down the Via Roma to a restaurant, where we filled up on pasta and vino and then headed to the beach for a swim. Eric, a tall, dark fellow, wondered what we would do for excitement after the war was over. A beautiful Neapolitan girl in a revealing black bathing suit sidled past us, and Sevareid, who looked at her with the inquiring eye of a scientist, said that he supposed that women and sex would replace war.

When Korman and I reported to Navy House, on 8 August we were told to get down to the docks that afternoon with our bags. But no ship came to pick us up. Another SNAFU. Since I had checked out of the Serena and I knew that I was going on an American destroyer, I switched to the Terminus Hotel. The next day, the U.S. navy PR assured us that 'everything will be laid on for tomorrow.' There was a great crowd at the British Navy Club, which had the reputation of having the best bar in Naples, and almost all the war correspondents were there, including Marsland Gander of the *Daily Telegraph*, London, and Reynolds Packard of United Press.

Finally we were on our way. We left Naples at 9:30 a.m. on 10 August in a Ventura naval bomber and arrived in Taranto at 10:40 a.m. A whaleboat took us to the *USS Hambleton*, and, according to my diary, we reached the destroyer in time for lunch. The first thing that the captain said when he turned over his cabin to us – he would be staying in his sea cabin – was: 'Have you any liquor? If you have, please hand it over.' Neither Si Korman nor I had brought a bottle with us since we knew that U.S. navy ships were dry. Still we did not like his attitude; perhaps it was more than this that made me write down that he was 'full of the fear of God – it sounds as though he is going to his judgment day.' There was a movie that evening on the canvas-covered afterdeck: *It Aint Hay*, with Abbott and Costello.

At two o'clock the next afternoon we set sail from Taranto. The sun beat down, and it was sweltering hot in the wardroom, and I noted that the sea water at the intake valve was 78°F. We were making a wide sweep around not only the toe of Italy but also

Sicily. The weather was warm and wonderful, and, lying on the deck getting a tan, we might have imagined ourselves on a holiday cruise if it had not been for the nagging uncertainty about our destination. There was never-ending talk about the landing, most of it gloomy. I was told that the wire-recording equipment that I was to use was on the flying bridge, which was the most dangerous position, but an officer said, 'no place is safe on a can [the navy's nickname for a destroyer].' A lieutenant expressed the considered opinion that 'a can only lasts three minutes in battle,' and a sailor said, 'a lot of us won't get back [to the United States].' It was depressing and I wondered if they were trying to frighten me or whether they were just greenhorns.

On the third day out we passed by Cape Bon in Africa, just as we had done on the way to the invasion of Sicily, which was more than a year ago, only then it was from the opposite direction. Just as it was in the past, this was the assembly area, and out of the blue Mediterranean appeared two huge American battleships, the *Texas* and the *Arkansas*, and many more warships. The *Hambleton* was one of eighteen destroyers that formed a V-shaped screen around the battleships and the British and French cruisers that escorted them. This was the classical 'battle squadron,' with the capital ships in the centre and a protective screen of destroyers around them.

It was a sight that would have warmed any navy man's heart, but I was sailing on what must have been the last battle squadron, because the *Texas* and the *Arkansas* were overage and due for the scrapyard and battleships were really out of date. Furthermore, this battle squadron was not going to meet an enemy fleet but had the more prosaic task of being the bombardment group for the beaches of Saint Raphael and Saint Tropez on the French Riviera. Still, when we headed north, the covers were taken off the guns. And there was a brief flurry of action: all the vast armament aboard the *Texas* and the *Arkansas* blasted away, even the *Hambleton* took a pot shot, at what, I could not see. It must have been a single plane, probably an enemy reconnaissance plane, maybe one of ours, and it very wisely and very quickly fled.

On 15 August, the day of the landing in southern France, we were up at 4:00 a.m. and were served the U.S. navy's traditional battle breakfast of steak and eggs. Battle stations at 5:00 a.m., and I climbed up to the flying bridge to test the wire recorder. It was an unwieldy contraption. I knew that the battleships would fire from fifteen miles offshore and the cruisers from a bit closer, but I imagined that the destroyers would go in at full speed, fire a broadside, then wheel around and return to repeat the same manoeuvre. Instead, we were just gliding in at no knots, no speed, through the early-morning haze. It was disconcerting. At 6:30 a.m. we made out the gray outline of the coast of southern France, and at 6:50 a.m. the bombardment began.

I was just behind the destroyer's forward gun, and the flying bridge whipped back and forth with every salvo. I recorded the gunfire, but the wire equipment had no fidelity, and it sounded like pellets dropping on a table. I tried to describe the scene, but it was difficult ad-libbing on the shuddering, shaking flying bridge; I stumbled and made a couple of mistakes and there was no way of editing, so I gave up. Si had no better luck. The wire recorder was useless as far as I was concerned.

Some tracer bullets came back at us, but that was the only enemy reaction, and it soon stopped. Then a rocket ship slid past and with a whoosh, whoosh, and rolling thunder let its rockets go onto the beach. After an hour the naval bombardment ceased, and the troops landed. There did not seem to be any opposition. At three o'clock in the afternoon I thumbed a lift ashore, but with no transportation, there was no way of following the troops. So I returned to the destroyer.

Later, when further details were released, we learned that at Saint Tropez we were where the U.S. 3rd Division went ashore. Further east around Saint Raphael were the landing beaches of the other American divisions, the 36th and 45th. They constituted the U.S. VI Corps and were part of Lieutenant-General Alexander Patch's American Seventh Army, which included a French corps that was to be the follow-up force. Other elements involved in the assault were French commandos who landed with the Americans, the American Canadian Special Service Force, as well as some 9,000 para and glider troops of a combined British-American Airborne Task Force. The French corps, which consisted mainly of French troops who had fought in Italy, was to drive along the coast toward Toulon and Marseilles, while the Americans pushed inland. Altogether 100,000 Allied troops and 11,000 vehicles were landed on 15 August with minimum losses; they were backed up by overwhelming naval and air support.

(For security reasons, the original code name for the invasion of southern France was changed from 'Anvil' to 'Dragoon.' 'Anvil' was to have coincided with 'Overlord,' the great cross-channel assault on Fortress Europe, but the slowness of the Allied advance in Italy meant that it had to be postponed. However, 'Dragoon' never caught on, and 'Anvil' continued to be used as the name for this combined operation, even by historians.)

The day after the bombardment, Korman and I left the *Hambleton* for the headquarters ship, where most of the correspondents were, and they were in an uproar. Apparently, the plane that was to have taken their copy back to Rome the day before could not land because the pilot had spent too much time showing Rita Hume of INS (Hearst's International News Service) the sights of the combined operation. The correspondents, particularly the agency men, were furious; they accused her of 'lifting her skirt' and using all kinds of womanly wiles to keep the pilot flying until it was too late to land. Some of their wrath fell on me because I had taken Rita to a British PR dance at the Hotel de la Ville a few days earlier. It was the first time I experienced guilt by association. I got away at noon on a French amphibian which took me to Ajaccio in Corsica, where I caught a B-25 bomber that landed in Rome at 3:30 p.m. I was on the air at eight o'clock that night:

... It's doubtful if there has ever been a combined operation as successful as the landing in Southern France. Certainly never before has so
much territory been taken in such a short time in an amphibious
invasion. More than five hundred square miles of beautiful, sunny
southern Provence are in our hands. The Riviera beachhead is not a

beachhead any more as it is at least twenty-five miles deep. It is quite likely to be considerably more than that, more than five hundred square miles, as the official information we've been given here appears to be some hours old ... The communiqué says that our casualties have been extremely light, they're actually incredibly light, almost what you would expect in a big exercise not an operation. Three hundred killed, taken prisoner or missing up to noon yesterday ... I know how astonished I was at the lack of opposition on D Day. If the Germans had had only a few guns, a few determined artillerymen, well, let's say, it would have been rather unpleasant for us in the destroyer ... It seemed to me even on the first day that the Germans didn't intend to put up a stubborn defence on the coast. They couldn't because it was too long and they didn't have enough men. They expected to hold us after we had landed and shown our hand. However, we've been too quick for them. Their first line of defence has gone. This invasion will not halt even temporarily as in Normandy ...

Although in a minor role, Canadians were involved in this combined operation. Two Canadian warships were in the invasion armada, *HMCS Prince Henry* and *HMCS Prince David*. Canadians, of course, were in the combined American Canadian Special Service Force and the *Prince Henry* was one of half a dozen ships that took the Special Service Force ashore. As I said in my broadcast, the Germans did not have enough men to defend southern France; actually they had only eight divisions and had to resort to subterfuges. I spoke to a couple of Canadian naval officers who took part in the invasion, Lieutenant Gib Milne and Sub-Lieutenant Scott Young; they said that one so-called enemy battery was nothing but 'a camouflage of sticks and stove pipes.'

However, my instant analysis of German strategy proved not to be quite right. They were not going to try to hold us as they had done in Normandy; they had no fixed line of defence, but they had left garrisons behind, especially in Toulon and Marseilles. I was to find this out when, a couple of days later, I returned to southern France with the main party of correspondents. We landed at Saint Tropez and were trucked to the PR camp near Brignoles. There, I was assigned a British conducting officer, Captain Best – I think his first name was Don, but I always addressed him by his surname, which was the English way in those days. It was 'Captain Best' or 'Best, you bastard.' Best was a solidly built fellow who had been a commando but had been wounded, and so he had been seconded to army Public Relations. I was glad to have a real soldier as my guide and companion in southern France, because there was really no front line.

We made for Toulon, where the Germans were still holding out, more than a week after the landing. Although the French were closing in and had taken most of the heights surrounding the great naval base, the battle was still raging. On the way there, we passed a column of German prisoners, unkempt and dirty but tough-looking troops. When we turned off the highway and were bumping along a stony mountain road, we had to pull over to one side to allow half a dozen truckloads of prisoners to pass. Some of them were badly burned, their faces red and scorched, and I learned that they had been captured during the fierce fighting for the powder factory on the outskirts of Toulon; the powder had caught fire and the factory became a charnel house.

From the French forward positions on the top of the 2,000-foot ridge, we could see the whole of the naval base laid out like a map below us. It was an extraordinary sight. Nearby, French mountain guns with their barrels at a high angle were hammering the town. Smoke drifted across the port and the harbour where the black shapes of warships could be discovered, one of them the French battleship *Strasbourg*, which the Germans had turned into a floating fortress. The big guns of the *Strasbourg* were firing back, and naval guns made a different sound from field artillery. It was a hard struggle, and the Germans were putting up the same fanatical resistance that they had at Cassino. 'Evidently, we built Toulon too well,' a French officer said but added, 'we're slowly squeezing the Boche out.'

Best and I next headed to Marseilles, which was not so far from Toulon. But after we had gone a few miles, there were no more Allied troops, no more military traffic, nothing. It was an eerie feeling driving along this empty road in the half-light of dusk: it looked as though there had been a fire-fight, because there were leaves and broken branches in our path. Let's not take a wrong turning, I said, but Best kept going and I had confidence in him. By the time we reached Marseilles, it was dark, and the first thing I noticed was that the electricity was on. Shafts of light filtered through the shuttered windows. The bars and cafés were open; we stopped for a drink and were greeted by scores of men and women and partisans or patriots, as they were called, with rifles on their backs, who wanted to shake our hands. All the time, as I said in a broadcast, shells were whizzing overhead:

... The silence of those dark, deserted boulevards would be broken by rifle and machine gun fire and the crash of artillery. Yet, as I say, the lights were on ... The road [in Marseilles] was deserted but when we reached a large square, we almost bumped into some French tanks. We had made our way to the square down a dark, tree-lined boulevard which I later learned was the Boulevard de Madeleine – the Boulevard de Madeleine leads into the Cannebière, the main street of Marseilles. We had just entered the Cannebière when some civilians came running out of a doorway and signalled us to stop. They said: 'There's fighting going on just two hundred yards down the street.' Just then we heard the rattle of machine gun fire. We turned around and headed back to the square – the tanks were crunching on to the pavement, harboring down for the night ... The guns opened up again and some red tracer passed overhead ...

A French officer offered to take us to see the colonel commanding the armoured regiment; we crossed the square and went down a dark boulevard to a large building around which were parked some more tanks. Inside, and upstairs, we were shown into a brightly lit and luxuriously furnished apartment; the colonel and some of his officers had just finished dinner. The host, a fat, florid Marseillaise who was probably a collaborator, rushed over to greet us and ordered drinks. There was a map of the city on a drawing-room table, and the colonel said that the Germans were mainly in the old port area. He pointed to the map and said there was a fortress gun there and it was firing up the Cannebière. In fact, through the shuttered windows we could hear the sound of an explosion. At that moment a French partisan, ragged, dirty, entered the apartment with an important message. As we left, the colonel said that they would finish off the Boche in the morning, which they did.

It was even more weird and wonderful at Cannes. The main body of American troops had pushed inland up the roads to Grenoble and Lyon, and the Canadian American Special Service Force had bypassed the resort as it swept along the coast towards the Italian frontier. The German rearguard had pulled out, but before leaving, it had blown the only bridge near the shore. Nobody had bothered to repair it – Cannes was obviously of no strategic value – until just before we arrived, when heavy planks had been placed across the gap. We drove gingerly over the rickety structure and made for one of the great hotels, the Martinez, on the Promenade, where we were welcomed with a bottle of whisky. Apparently we were the first Allies to enter Cannes, although we were followed closely by other correspondents.

The hotel manager, an excessively affable chap, said that we must stay and showed us to our rooms; he insisted on my having what looked like the bridal suite. He also wanted us to meet the hotel's oldest and most famous guest, John Harmsworth, an American tycoon who was said to have given the Harmsworth Trophy for flying. We took the elevator up to the penthouse suite where Harmsworth had spent the war years. I noticed that on the grand piano in the flat's spacious drawing room there were silver-framed portraits of all the wrong people, Reichsmarshal Goering, King Leopold of the Belgians, Marshal Petain, General Franco. A nurse wheeled Harmsworth in to meet us; he had suffered a stroke that had affected his speech, and only his nurse could understand what he was trying to say. After the introductions and mixing us up with Americans, the old man made some slurred sounds, which the nurse translated. 'Mr Harmsworth,' she said, 'would like to know what has happened to Charles Lindbergh.'

Downstairs at lunch, sitting at the table next to us was a group of men whose workmen's clothes seemed out of place in the Martinez's elegant dining-room. They turned out to be Communists, and from the whispered remarks of the waiters and other diners we learned that these men were running Cannes. It seemed crazy, but this resort of the idle rich, where Harmsworth and people like him could live in comfort and luxury during the war, had been taken over by the Resistance or the Communist part of the Resistance, known as the Franc Tireur et Partisan Français. Maybe it was just retribution! When we came into Cannes we had noticed a number of cars bearing the letters FTPF; there were more of them than those with the letters FFI (Forces Françaises de l'Intérieur), the main Resistance organization.

At any rate, one of the Communists, a broad-shouldered man with a weatherbeaten face and a pistol in a holster at his hip, offered to show us around. He took us to the city hall, where I met a Dutch couple who had been denounced as collaborators. I was embarrassed as the tall, thin woman with a mass of greying hair appealed to me to get them released; I remember she said that she was suffering from menopause, although what this had to do with the charge of collaboration I could not understand. In any case, there was nothing that I could do. The Dutch couple, who appeared well dressed, were probably among the wealthy patrons of Cannes, all of whom must have entertained the Germans at some time or other; perhaps these two had gone too far, although they might have been the victims of a vengeful servant or neighbour, as so many were.

Then, there was the shaving of the heads of French girls who had gone out with the Germans – a punishment that I found revolting and despicable. I saw this happen more than once during our tour of southern France, but perhaps not in Cannes.

Captain Best had gone off somewhere, leaving me alone to be given this Communist tour of the city hall, but we had agreed that he would pick me up at three o'clock in the afternoon at a certain street corner. I was there five minutes early and waited; half an hour went by, then three-quarters of an hour, and I was getting more and more angry. Finally the jeep and he arrived. 'Best, you bastard,' I shouted. 'Where the hell have you been?' But Best looked beatific. 'You've been asking me to get a car,' he said. 'Well, I've got a Citroën.' I could hardly remain angry, since I had said to Best that I was tired of being bumped around in a jeep and that we should have a civilian car. I had seen some of the correspondents driving around in Citroëns. Why couldn't we have one?

I have forgotten how Best found the car, which belonged to a collaborator and had been seized by the Franc Tireur. Perhaps he had been tipped off by the Communist who took us to the city hall. The Citroën was being fixed and he would be picking it up shortly. It turned out to be a handsome black limousine. We solved the problem of gasoline by siphoning fuel from a large American station-wagon that was parked outside the Martinez. Best also took the reserve jerrican of gas from the jeep and stowed it in the back seat.

At dinner that night the Communists were at their regular table, but near us were some American officers who, we figured, must be from the station-wagon; they were all spit-and-polish and too well dressed to be anyone else but 'base wallahs,' and we felt pleased about siphoning off their gasoline. We did not pay much attention to them, however, when we heard from fellow diners the extraordinary and horrifying news that the hotel expected us to pay for our rooms and meals; one of the correspondents had been told as much, and the Martinez was a very expensive place. There was general indignation. Why, that slimy, son-of-a-bitch of a hotel manager! He must have been a bloody collaborator! We were not used to paying; we had not paid for hotel accommodation when Rome was liberated; and we were not going to pay here. In any case, we had no francs.

There was only one thing to do, and that was to leave before anyone could find out. Shortly after five o'clock the next morning, I packed my duffel bag, left the magnificent suite, and crept quietly out of the hotel. Captain Best had given orders to the driver to return the jeep to army Public Relations, which was, presumably, still in Brignoles. We took off in the Citroën and waved to the other correspondents who were also escaping from the Martinez at the same time. It was a great lark.

While in Cannes I had made arrangements to visit the legendary Vercors, a wild, forested plateau southwest of Grenoble where the Maquis, which was a name taken by the Resistance fighters, had held out against repeated German attacks. The Vercors had come to have the same immortal meaning for the French in the Second World War as Verdun had had in the First World War.

We made for the road to Grenoble, along which the American army had gone. There was not much traffic, and Best, who had been a racing driver, kept the Citroën purring along at a good speed. What comfort compared with the jeep! Whenever we saw a Citroën limousine like ours in the ditch – and there were a few, which must have meant that there had only recently been some fighting along the road – we would stop and take the spare tire. It was a necessary precaution, because our tires were old and worn, and soon the back seat was piled high with spare tires.

We found the village where we were to meet our contact, Captain Gallitzine, a French officer who was wearing an English uniform and was known as Captain Bennett or the Weatherman. There were a couple of heavily armed men with him. Captain Bennett said they would take us in their vehicle. I wrote in my diary that the Maquis were worried that I had no gun and did not know how to handle one. We turned off the main road and drove past the last, lonely American outpost, a G.I. leaning against the side of the ditch, and climbed up to a plateau where there was a fan-shaped rocky outcrop known as the 'Three Virgins.' This was where the Maquis had fought their greatest battle, Captain Bennett told us. It lasted for six weeks and ended when the Allies landed in southern France.

The Vercors began as a Resistance redoubt back in 1942, when French youths escaping from Nazi forced labour took refuge in the great forest that covered much of its 350 square miles. But the battle was due to an incredible communications SNAFU. The Maquis, who kept in close touch with the Free French in Algiers and London, apparently thought that an Allied airborne division was going to land in the Vercors and that General De Gaulle himself might come. This was part of the D-Day operation, or so they believed, but it was a ghastly misunderstanding. At the beginning of June 1944 some 4,000 Maquis proclaimed the 'Free Republic of the Vercors' and hacked out an airstrip. They festooned the electric pylons with branches so they could act as markers. But in the middle of June the Germans, not the Allies, arrived. The Maquis held on while clamouring for help. At the end of June the American OSS (Office of Strategic Services) parachuted a team of agents into the Vercors; they tried to persuade the Maquis leaders to avoid battle and return to more useful guerrilla tactics. But they were too late.

On 14 July, Bastille Day, a large quantity of supplies was dropped by the U.S. air force: there were small arms and ammunition but no heavy equipment. By now the Germans had 15–20,000 troops in action, but the Maquis still clung to the cliff tops. Then German gliders landed on the airstrip – 'For some reason,' Captain Bennett recalled, 'we thought they were Canadians' – and SS troops leapt from the gliders to attack the Maquis from the rear. Finally the Maquis commander gave the order to disperse: they had lost 750 men. The Germans behaved brutally: they took no prisoners, killed the wounded, and laid waste to a number of villages. The Nazis drove the Maquis back past Villard de Lans to the shelter of the great forest, Bennett said, but there they stood and tied up a whole German division that should have been used against the Allied landing in southern France.

We drove to Villard de Lans, a ski town, and stopped at the hotel, which had been badly shot up. There we had lunch in a sunlit clearing with the Resistance leaders: René, the Maquis commander, a former sailor, thick chested and soft-spoken with almost a lisp, who, I noted, looked like a pirate and was credited with killing 100 Germans; Jean, a large former truck driver with two prominent gold teeth, who was in charge of transport; and Pierre, a small man with a Hitler moustache who ran the Maquis communications – I should have asked him how the SNAFU came about and whether he was responsible. It was a memorable lunch and I recorded the menu in my diary: hors d'oeuvres of fresh tomatoes and little sausages, real butter, cheese and tomato soufflé, filet mignon, Roquefort cheese, and wine, both white and red, both excellent. There was a sort of diplomatic formality about the lunch, as though they were receiving a foreign delegation; Captain Best and I must have been the first outsiders to visit the Vercors. Toasts were drunk: 'Vive la Résistance!' 'Vive la France!'

The mayor of one of the villages, in his tricolour sash of office, joined us, and so did monsieur le curé, wearing a double-barred cross of Lorraine. They wanted to show us the forest where the Maquis had held out, so we all went on a tour, through the village of La Chappelle, which was almost totally destroyed, and the village of Vassieux, which was also in ruins – the Germans, the curé said, had burned many houses with the villagers locked inside. They were just now cleaning up, and amid the rubble we saw coffins with crosses leaning against them. Then we came upon the airstrip, like a ploughed field in the middle of the woods, with wrecked gliders strewn about and the same garbage and debris of war that I had seen at Cassino and on the Hitler Line. The Maquis had fortified the forest with earthworks and in front of them rolls of barbed wire and minefields, the edges of which were now marked with white tapes and had warning signs. 'The Fourth Republic began here,' the mayor said proudly.

It was late in the afternoon when we left the Vercors. I had been broadcasting over a U.S. portable radio transmitter when we were on the coast, but it had moved far inland and I decided that I had to get back to Rome. The campaign in southern France was over. The U.S. Seventh Army was beyond Lyons now and was in contact with General George Patton's U.S. Third Army, and the French corps had been greatly reinforced – many of the Maquis from the Vercors had joined – and had become the First French Army under General de Lattre de Tassigny. After securing Toulon and Marseilles, the First French Army drove inland and took up positions beside the U.S. Seventh Army; it became the right flank of the seven Allied armies massing on the borders of Germany, while the First Canadian Army was on the left flank.

So we made for the PR camp, which had moved to Voiron above Grenoble. There I met Winston Burdett of CBS, who had to return to the Italian front, and the next day we were jeeped down to the coast, to an airfield at Salon, where we were able to arrange for a bomber flight to Rome.

Captain Best drove farther north. The Citroën had performed well for us but it was beginning to disintegrate, and by the time he reached the British Second Army he had used up all the spare tires in the back seat. In a grand gesture, he gave the car away before going on leave to London.

13

Crossing the Rubicon

Rome, 2 September 1944:
Canadian forces with the British Eighth Army have broken the
Gothic Line, the German defences across the top of the Italian
boot.

As sometimes happened, this radio report, which I heard about
when I returned to Rome, gave the wrong impression: it
implied that the Allies had won a decisive victory and that there
was nothing now to stop them from sweeping into the Po Valley
and rolling up the Italian front. It would have been more accurate
to have said that I Canadian Corps had broken *into* the Gothic
Line, because the German defences that stretched from Spezia and
Pisa on the west coast in a great arc to Pesaro and Rimini on the
Adriatic Sea were some twenty miles deep in places. Although the
Nazis had not had time to complete the Gothic Line, it was
nevertheless a formidable barrier, with thousands of machine-gun
posts and hundreds of gun positions, protected by vast minefields
and miles of anti-tank ditches. Some of the bloodiest battles
occurred within its environs, and I was to describe San Martino in
one of my broadcasts as a little Cassino. The Allies were not to

cross the Po Valley for some months, and by that time I had left the Mediterranean Theatre. Yet this bulletin, which I was told about but did not hear, made me anxious to get moving and not miss a big story.

It was back to the real war after enjoying a fine old 'picnic': that was the way I described the campaign in southern France in a letter to my mother and father, dated 29 August. I wrote about our 'dashing wildly around,' and I must have said that we had got to someplace 'almost in the Alps' and given its name, but that had been cut out by the censor. I said that we stayed often in hotels in Cannes and at Brignoles, 'and now in the' ... and there was another scissored gap. They did let me say that it hardly seemed like war in southern France, with the electric lights on in the cities and running water in the hotels, but this letter had the most cut out of it of any of my letters home. I told my parents that the 'FFI [French Forces of the Interior] have almost every town under control when we enter it,' and that the Allied troops are 'like men who came to do a job only to find the job has been done.'

The flight to Ancona was washed out the first day, but on 4 September I was able to get away and reached the Adriatic port at noon. A kind Polish public relations officer entertained me to lunch and then drove me in his jeep to Eighth Army headquarters, where I bummed a lift to the Canadian PR camp at Cattolica. 'The war has made me a marvellous hitch hiker,' I said in another letter home. Public Relations occupied a villa in this town, which was close to the sea, and I was put in a second-floor bedroom, but I got no sleep that first night because of the shell fire and the air raids. We were very far forward, a little more than a mile from the front. I remember a great sheet of flame outside the window and being almost blown out of my safari-bed by a bomb that must have landed only a few yards from the house. It was a rude awakening to the miseries of the Italian front after the pleasures of southern France.

Just as they had done at the Hitler Line, the Canadians had crashed through the hard outer edge of the Gothic Line, the concrete and steel wall, in a little more than a couple of days of fierce fighting, but there was no open road after that. The Germans had pulled back, as they had done before, and were to contest every ridge and every river, every natural feature, and they had better-fortified terrain to defend around Rimini than they had had in the Liri Valley. Once more hopes were dashed and there was disappointment. 'What was to have been a headlong pursuit,' the official Canadian history said, 'turned into a bitter, creeping battle which lasted eighteen days.'

It was not till 13 September that the next big push occurred and that was against the Germans entrenched on the so-called Coriano Ridge, named after the town on a hilltop. This was another set-piece action, and we had to get the jeep and the recording equipment in place on the day before because the attack was to begin at one o'clock in the morning. Precisely at that time, the inky black landscape was lit by the fire of 700 guns that were massed all around us, and we got one of the best actualities of a battle. It was a shattering barrage and left the enemy stunned; the Cape Breton Highlanders – this was a 5th Division show – drove past Coriano but then ran into mines, which must have been a dreadful experience in the darkness. And, as so often happened, the Germans quickly recovered and began shelling the advancing Canadians.

There were minefields around the town and the enemy tanks had positioned themselves in houses that they had knocked down and turned into strongholds. For the first time I saw 'Sherman-dozers,' Sherman tanks fitted with bulldozer blades, gouging out a path for the tanks up the ridge. It was a bloody struggle, which went on for a couple of days, but by nightfall on 14 September the last German machine-gunners and snipers had withdrawn, and Coriano was firmly in the hands of the Canadians. Later I learned that at about this time the Fifth Army, which was on the left of the Eighth Army, was to attack the Gothic Line, so that the I Canadian Corps had penetrated only that portion of the German defence system that was beside the Adriatic.

After Coriano there was the Fortunato feature and other ridges to be taken from a determined enemy who had the advantage of well-surveyed and prepared positions. It was the 1st Division's turn, and the West Novas were hard pressed but took San Lorenzo; the 'Vindoos,' the Royal Twenty-Second, drove into San Martino, but, owing to a signals mix-up, Nazi paratroopers retook the knoll and the village. In the days of fierce fighting the Seaforths suffered heavy losses before the Canadians were able to secure San Martino. The enemy, according to the official Canadian history, had shown great determination and skill in resisting the Allied advance, 'and had counter-attacked with the utmost persistence – one village was reported to have changed hands ten times.' There were many the rivers to cross, the Melo, the Marano, the Ausa, the Marecchia, the Salto, to name but a few. And the Uso, which had a particular significance, as I pointed out in a broadcast:

... I'm on top of a tower in the Lombardy plain, a tower that serves as an observation post. From it I can see the clump of woods where the Canadians are crossing the Rubicon. The river is hidden there but further on it appears and its winding waters shine beautifully in the afternoon haze. There's a break in the coast line and in the summer houses along the sea shore, where it empties into the Adriatic. The smoke of battle rises from the muddy banks of the Rubicon, and black, angry clouds burst with thunderclaps over the woods where the Canadians are making the crossing. The Germans aren't falling back as we expected them to do once we had broken through on to the Lombardy plain. They are fighting for every stream as they have done for every hill, and they are fighting for the Rubicon. Like strange, inhuman automatons, these Germans are carrying out the orders of Kesselring and Hitler to resist to the last man and to the last bullet.

Our infantrymen are still carrying the brunt of battle. After struggling up those dreadful slopes before Rimini, they expected to ride in trucks behind the tanks as they swept the river flat country of the Po Valley. Instead, they are going forward, they are attacking the enemy, they are making the bridgehead, while the tanks sit under the trees waiting for the engineers to bridge the Rubicon ... The smoke almost hides the clump of woods and there is a fearful crashing sound as the Germans plaster the [river crossing], but the Canadian sappers go on working. Six planes follow each other across the sky and dive further upstream – a billowing cloud of smoke rises in the distance and then there are two sharp flashes. They must have hit something. The smoke rises fed by furious fires and adds to the battle haze. But we can still see the river ...

The Uso is the modern name for the Rubicon, although there are other rivers, the Fiumicino and the Marecchia, that also claim this distinction; however, it is generally accepted that the Uso, a muddy and sluggish creek, is the ancient Rubicon that divided Roman Italy from Cisalpine Gaul. Caesar crossed the Rubicon to march on Rome, and while I said in my broadcast that there was no analogy between his legions fording this stream and our own troops, I could not resist saying that 'the Canadians are crossing the Rubicon to march on Berlin.' It would be a slow march, even slower than I had ever reckoned. I Canadian Corps came to a temporary halt at the Fiumicino River, which in places was only a mile north of the Uso. The rains had come and would turn the Allied advance into a crawl.

Before reaching the Rubicon, the Eighth Army had overrun Rimini, the anchor of the German defences on the Adriatic. The Nazi paratroopers had withdrawn after blowing most of the bridges, and the Greek Mountain Brigade, which was temporarily under Canadian command, was the first to reach the main square and raised the Greek flag above the ruins of the city hall. I knew that the best time to get into a captured town was immediately after it was taken and before the enemy had time to regroup and shell it. So we set off in the jeep and drove along an empty road towards the dark, smoking outline of Rimini. There were the same bits of rubble, the same leaves and broken branches, that I had seen on the way to Marseilles, as well as burned-out tanks, the wreckage of trucks and carts, and broken telephone poles with crazy festoons of wires. There was also the eerie, ominous silence of a battle just ended. The Greeks were delighted to see us; I interviewed the colonel who wanted to know if I had a Canadian flag (red ensign) to hang beside the Greek flag, but I could not oblige him.

Aside from the dash into Rimini, I found that covering the Italian front had turned into a hellish bind. I said in a letter home that I was becoming stale: 'I've seen it all before and I'm finding it difficult to be fresh in my approach to almost anything.' The fact that the Italian front was not getting much attention in the news only added to my feeling of tiredness and frustration. 'The outside world,' I wrote in a letter dated 13 September, 'is not interested in whether we take a ridge when the Allies are entering Germany, Churchill and Roosevelt are meeting again, and the Russians are pushing into Yugoslavia, Hungary and Czechoslovakia.' Although this was a personal comment, I was really expressing the view of the Canadian troops. I listened to their grumbling at the front. Their morale was low, they felt they had been bypassed by the action in France and were left out of any recognition, any glory; they knew that nothing they did, no matter how bravely or brilliantly they fought, would make any difference to the outcome of the war. Lady Astor, who made a practice of being outrageous, is credited with naming them 'the D-Day Dodgers' (D-Day had come to mean the Normandy landing). Just as British troops in the First World War called themselves 'the Old Contemptibles,' thus turning the Kaiser's scornful reference to them into a title of honour, so the Canadian soldiers in Italy, almost half the Canadian army, called themselves 'the D-Day Dodgers.' There was a bitter little ditty that they sang, to the tune of Lili Marlene:

We are the D-Day Dodgers, out in Italy,
Always on the vino, always on the spree.
Eighth Army skivers and their tanks,
We go to war in ties and slacks,
We are the D-Day Dodgers in sunny Italy.'

Chorus

We are the D-Day Dodgers, way out in Italy,
We're always tight, we cannot fight.
What bloody use are we?

Yet the fighting in Italy was probably the hardest of anywhere in Europe. This was borne out by the heavy casualty figures, more than 14,000 for the Eighth Army alone in a very short time. Canadian losses were heavier than for any period of equal length during the whole of the Italian campaign. 'From August 25 to September 22,' as the official history, *The Canadians in Italy*, recorded, 'the First Division suffered 2,511 battle casualties, 626 of them fatal. An additional 1,005 were evacuated because of illness. Up to the time of its withdrawal from action on September 19, the Fifth Armored Division lost 1,385 officers and men, including 390 killed.' Thus, I Canadian Corps lost some 4,000 men, of whom more than 1,000 were killed, in less than a month. For what? For a few hilltop villages and Rimini, which was not much of a port and had been badly smashed by the Allied air forces.

What was the purpose of all this slaughter? What was the Allied strategy? Was it to strike at Austria and southern Germany across the greatest natural barrier in the world, the Alps? Not even our generals could be that stupid! Then it must have been to cross the Po and clear the Germans out of Italy. But was that really necessary? We had already won the war in Italy and Rome was in our hands; the Italians had given up. If it was to tie down the Wehrmacht and prevent Kesselring's two armies and twenty or so depleted divisions from reinforcing Hitler's battered forces on the Western Front, then there was no need to fight for every creek. Static warfare would have sufficed.

As for the other side: 'These Germans are just incredible,' I said in a letter to my mother and father, written in the middle of September. 'They must know they're beaten, but they go on fighting. And what seems strange to us is the waste of energy on their part. They could hold the Brenner Pass with a quarter of their strength here.' It was said that one reason the Germans clung to their defences in the Gothic Line was to keep the Po Valley open to allow their comrades in the Balkans to escape. But that was suspect reasoning, because the Germans withdrew up the Danube Valley and were not worried about any incursions from Trieste or farther west.

In retrospect, Allied strategy, the plans of the American and British high commands, seemed uncoordinated and at the same time rigid: at best, it was an amalgam to meet the insistent claims of important elements within the alliance, the British with Churchill's 'cat's claw' at Anzio, and the French with the delayed invasion of southern France; at worst, it was an expression of the military mind-set, that in a war one should attack even if there was no real objective. Nazi strategy was twisted out of reality by Hitler's demands that his troops should not give up an inch of territory, and thus they could not pull back far enough to properly prepared positions and, finally, to the easily defensible Brenner Pass. It was a strategy of desperation, of hanging on at all costs, against overwhelming odds, but the Germans had one advantage, that of good generalship.

That was the war at the highest level. But what about the war at the lowliest level, the fellows who had to carry out 'Husky' and 'Anvil' and 'Overlord,' the great schemes that had been drawn up in London and Washington? These were the assault troops, the front-line soldiers, the PBI – the 'Poor Bloody Infantry' – and there were only a few of them compared with the mass of the armed forces. I remember in Sicily, when the 1st Canadian Division was advancing through the dry, dusty foothills of Mount Etna, it would have one of its three brigades forward, and that brigade would have one of its three battalions forward, and that battalion would have one company forward, and that company would have one platoon forward – until all alone up front was 'Little Joe,' his rifle at the ready, glancing nervously from side to side, scared but thrilled that he was the spearpoint of the whole Eighth Army. This is not such an exaggeration, and it does show that an army in battle is like a broad wedge with the infantry at the sharp end.

As might be expected, morale was at its highest during the Sicilian campaign, and it continued high through the bitter street fighting at Ortona and the fierce battles on the Hitler Line: the eyes of the world were on the Fifth and Eighth armies as they were engaged in the greatest Allied offensive, which would lead to the capture of the first Axis capital, Rome. But what about the grim struggle in the Gothic Line around Rimini, where there appeared to be no real reason for attacking and no clear objective, and at the same time no one paid much attention?

I wondered what made Johnny Canuck fight. We all knew what he was fighting against, but what was he fighting for? I wrote a piece for *Maclean's* magazine entitled 'What Soldiers Think,' well before the inconsequential but bloody battles for the ridges and rivers of the Gothic Line, and it was published on 15 June 1944. Upon rereading it almost a half-century later, it seems to be rather bland, but I doubt if I could have written anything of greater depth or significance at the time.

I did find that the average fellow was shy of stating any moral principles, however, especially if he was up against it and enemy shell fire was shaking his billet; he would make a wisecrack that usually fell flat or just shake his head glumly. There were two or three who said that they were fighting to make their homes safe from Nazi attack, which was not so far-fetched, since they were referring to England. Most of the Canadians in Italy had been overseas so long that they had lost touch with things Canadian; they did not know the latest dance tune, the 'Hit of the Week,' but, worst of all, they did not know what was happening in hockey, and they had come to regard 'Blighty' as home. The number married to English girls would reach 50,000 by the time the war was over; four to five years was far too long to be separated from family and friends in Canada, and the inevitable divorces and desertions ensued, with all their unhappy consequences.

As I said in *Maclean's*, mail was of primary importance for the Canadian soldier in Italy; 'his morale depends to a large extent upon the regular flow of letters from his loved ones.' Generally speaking, the delivery was unconscionably slow and irregular. We were still getting Christmas parcels in March. One officer complained that having gone without mail for weeks, he received more than 100 letters at one time, including one from a friend who had been killed the month before.

There was no doubt that the front-line soldiers were the unsung heroes of the war. They were obviously at the greatest risk of any of our troops, but there were others who faced similar risks, such as the rear gunners in the bombing planes. However, if and when these airmen returned from a mission, they slept in beds and lived in comfort, whereas the poor bloody infantrymen had to put up with all the horrors and discomforts of ground fighting for days on end and had to sleep in slit trenches that could be half full of water. What made these soldiers fight when the fighting had so little meaning and was largely ignored, as happened in the Gothic Line? It worried me that I was never able to answer that question. None of us war correspondents was to spend enough time with the front-line soldiers, since we had to cover the battle as a whole – which was a valid enough excuse. There was one exception: Ernie Pyle, who was obsessed with the fate of the GI and became the spokesman for the 'grunt,' the American infantryman.

Ernie Pyle became the most famous of the American war correspondents through his descriptions of the harsh and brutal conditions of the front-line soldiers. He felt so deeply for these young men that his popularity when he returned to the United States, the plaudits he received, made him feel, as he said, like 'a deserter and a heel.' Pyle was certainly no propagandist; he said that war had 'become a flat, black depression without highlights, a revulsion of the mind and an exhaustion of the spirit.' He knew that it was neither God nor Flag nor Mother that impelled the soldier to risk and even lose his life; he did it for the fellow next to him: 'he couldn't let him down.' Pyle wrote of the 'powerful fraternalism in the ghastly brotherhood of war.' There they go, he said, 'ready to fight for, ready to fight for, well, at least, ready to fight for each other.'

On the way to the Rubicon, the Canadians happened to liberate San Marino, which claims the distinction of being the smallest republic in the world; its territory, much of it steep cliffs and craggy rocks, covers thirty-eight square miles. It was really just another Italian hilltop town, but because it had somehow maintained its independence, it was full of refugees from the Rimini area. I visited San Marino and met one of the two captain regents who ran the place and was presented with a small booklet of stamps – the republic's main revenue comes from postage stamps. On the inside of the booklet was written: '*Conversacioni souvencreveri wil i correspondenti Canadesi 22-9-1944   Au T. Lonfrecini Suesloes del Gouverno.*' (In memory of a conversation with a Canadian correspondent, 22 September 1944 – signed by one of the captain regents, T. Lonfrecini Suesloes.) The booklet contained some two dozen of the beautiful stamps for which San Marino was famous: they were a commemorative set to mark the twentieth anniversary of Fascism! For our benefit, however, this fact had been blacked out – but not so well that one could not read: 'Ventennale Dei Fasci 1922   1942.'

There was another tourist attraction that fell to the Canadians: the great castle of Gradara, the site of the tragic thirteenth-century love story of Francesca da Rimini that Dante and Tchaikovsky had immortalized. The beautiful Francesca was betrothed to one of the ruling Malatestas, Giovanni, an ugly brute, and fell in love and ran away with his handsome brother, Paolo, to Gradara. Giovanni found them there and had them murdered. That was the story, but it was told with such modern allusions by a sergeant, a former schoolteacher, that it enthralled the hundreds of Canadian soldiers who visited the castle while the advance was held up by the rain.

It was an autumn of discontent on the Italian front, a prelude to the bitter winter of frustration and disappointment for the western Allies. The Canadian forces were bogged down, and the desolate and dreary conditions seemed to be highlighted by the return of my friend Wally Reyburn; he had just been on leave to Canada and was full of the great times he had had at home. 'Wally painted a very enticing picture of Canada,' I wrote in a letter to my parents. 'He said there was no liquor rationing now and everyone has lots of money.'

Just when we felt that we were forgotten, who should turn up but Martha Gellhorn, the third wife of Ernest Hemingway and herself a prominent writer and journalist. Why should she visit the Italian front and of all sectors, ours? Apparently she had been commissioned to write an article on the Canadians for an American magazine. There was much moaning and grumbling by the PR, since they had to provide her not only with separate accommodation but also with a separate latrine.

Another visitor was the defence minister, Colonel J.L. Ralston; he spent a couple of days touring the front at the end of September. Later, we learned that he had come out specifically to look into the question of Canadian reinforcements. He was told that if I Canadian Corps continued to be actively engaged in fighting, as it was, then in ten days' time 'all general duty infantry reinforcements would have been committed and there would be no reserves.' The minister was also informed, however, that while Canadian battalions were slightly below authorized war establishment levels, they were stronger than their British counterparts, which had been reduced to a three-company basis (from four companies). Yet Ralston's visit led directly to the conscription crisis that was to throw Ottawa into turmoil towards the end of the year.

The defence minister must have heard of the way that Lieutenant-General E.L.M. 'Tommy' Burns's command of I Canadian Corps had been undermined by the demand of the Eighth Army commander, General Sir Oliver Leese, that Burns be fired and the Canadian corps be broken up, and that the 1st and 5th Canadian divisions be placed under the command of a British corps. As might be expected, the Canadians would not agree to this imperialist scheme, but it did have a damaging effect on General Burns's authority. Colonel Ralston was not much interested; after all, he had accepted the advice of the British in the case of General McNaughton, and he had a much greater worry now in the lack of reinforcements. He must have realized that the breaking up of the Canadian army was a grave political error, that if the 1st Canadian Division had been returned to the United Kingdom after the Sicilian campaign, as originally planned, there would not have been such heavy casualties and he would not have had to face a conscription crisis now.

General Burns was to go on to much greater fame as the first commander of the United Nations Emergency Force, while General Sir Oliver Leese simply faded away after the war. The restructuring of the Canadian forces in Italy that General Leese wanted might have received more attention if the Eighth Army commander had shown greater ability as a leader. His performance was criticized by military historians, however, as was that of General Mark Clark, the Fifth Army commander: their 'operations were consistently marred by a lack of strategic vision and slipshod staff work,' according to John Ellis, author of *Cassino – The Hollow Victory*. They relied on frontal attacks, which too often failed and could never encircle the enemy. Yet General Burns was partly to blame for his own dilemma: he had had a distinguished career and was a capable commanding officer, but he could not seem to mix with officers or men. He was an 'introvert among extroverts,' according to Major-General Chris Vokes, the flamboyant commander of the 1st Canadian Division.

As corps commander, General Burns had the code name of 'Sun Ray,' and since he seldom spoke except to issue orders and hardly ever smiled, he was known as 'Smiling Sun Ray'; he was also called 'Laughing Boy.' General Sir Oliver Leese left the Eighth Army for an appointment in Southeast Asia at the end of September; he was succeeded by General Sir Richard McCreery. If Burns hoped that there would be better relations with the new commander, he was disappointed. He decided that it was time to go, and on 5 November gave up his command of I Canadian Corps. (This was some time after I had left the Italian front.) General Vokes took over temporary command of the corps, but on 16 November Lieutenant-General Charles Foulkes was appointed GOC, much to General Vokes's chagrin – in fact, he wondered whether there had not been a horrible mix-up at headquarters of the names Foulkes and Vokes.

At last I was to be relieved and was to return to London and to Canada. On 9 October 1944, I left the Italian front for Rome. I was 'suffering from a terrific hangover,' according to my diary, 'due to the farewell party on the night before.' It was an eight-hour drive in a jeep that seemed to have no springs, and I was 'thankful' that we did not stop for lunch. The next evening Bill Herbert, who was to relieve me, arrived in Rome; he was the old buddy from Victoria and Vancouver days, and I had heard that he had recently become a CBC war correspondent. Paul Barrette from the French side was with him; Paul was to replace Benoit Lafleur, who had left some time before I did.

While in Rome, I stayed at the Villa Iaccarino, the Canadian PR mess, and I heard about how Paul Morton had gone on a shooting spree. Major Doug MacFarlane, the managing editor of the Canadian army's newspaper, the *Maple Leaf*,* was in the mess at the time; he said that it was not a party so much as a bunch of the boys sitting around drinking and 'telling lies,' when Morton suddenly pulled an automatic out of his pocket and started shooting. He didn't aim at anyone, Doug said, he just fired at the ceiling – 'I think he wanted to draw attention to himself.' Paul had been taking parachute training in preparation for a secret mission behind the lines and had twisted his ankle after one jump; he had come to Rome for a couple of days' rest and got drunk – and he was a bad drunk.

Lieutenant-Colonel Bill Gilchrist, who was now in charge of Canadian Public Relations in the Mediterranean Theatre, was at the front when he received a message from Major Royd Beamish about the incident, which had occurred in August, and by that time Morton had returned to the training base for Special Operations. It was only after Paul had completed his mission behind enemy lines that the colonel confronted him. 'It could have been a

---

*The *Maple Leaf* began publishing in Naples in March 1944. As managing editor, Doug MacFarlane really ran the paper, although the nominal editor was the head of Canadian Public Relations in the theatre at the time. In the beginning, that was R.S. 'Dick' Malone; he was succeeded by C.W. 'Bill' Gilchrist. The *Maple Leaf* was moved to Rome in July and was printed on the same presses that the Germans had used for their forces' paper; that plant was later taken over by the Italian Communists to bring out *Avanti*. Towards the end of 1944 the *Maple Leaf* moved to Brussels, and its main edition was printed on the presses of the Belgian newspaper *Le Soir*. Its final move was to Amsterdam. Major MacFarlane continued to run the *Maple Leaf* until October 1945, when he wrote a long editorial, which he ran on the front page, criticizing the army's repatriation policy as favouring the 'zombies,' the conscripts who were forced to go overseas at the end of the war, over veterans. This upset the politicians and the brass, and General Guy Simonds had him dismissed.

nasty situation, a possible court martial,' Bill Gilchrist said, 'but I managed to defuse it.' The rule that a war correspondent could not bear arms was written into the Geneva Convention. At any rate, Paul Morton was told that he was being dis-accredited and would be shipped home as quickly as possible. Gilchrist recalled that this action resulted in 'a hell of an uproar from the *Toronto Star*,' which was curious, considering the newspaper's subsequent behaviour (see chapter 14).

I did not really get to know the full story of Paul Morton's daring adventure until I read an article by Douglas How in *Dateline: Canada 1962*, a publication of the National Press Club in Ottawa. (At twenty-five years old, How was one of the youngest war correspondents on the Italian front. From 1959 to 1969 he was managing editor in Canada of *Reader's Digest* and edited the *Digest*'s histories, *The Canadians at War*.) I did some further research and was able to piece together an account of what was the most extraordinary and dramatic assignment of any Canadian war correspondent.

Shortly after we entered Rome, Paul Morton learned from Major Beamish that the British were looking for a reporter to be dropped behind the enemy lines; he got in touch with them and volunteered for this cloak-and-dagger assignment, which, incidentally, several British war correspondents had turned down as being too dangerous. British Intelligence was not usually given to publicity but did want to know what was going on with the partisan forces that it was supplying. Morton was under the impression that he would be parachuted into Yugoslavia; he knew that his newspaper would be in favour of such a jump, and the *Toronto Star* did give its permission. Whether there was a misunderstanding over where he was to be dropped is not clear, although a letter from Special Operations (Mediterranean) to Kenneth Edey, editor of the *Toronto Star* seems to indicate a change in plans: 'the one [operation] that he was destined to take part in fell through suddenly and without warning.'

The letter spoke highly of Morton: 'we have nothing but praise for the way in which he has prepared himself for the type of operation on which he has now set his heart.' During the training with the Special Operations unit, Paul was issued with an automatic pistol: a war correspondent with guerrillas was not covered by the Geneva Convention and, if captured, would be executed as a spy. (This was how he came to have a pistol when he shot up the PR mess in Rome.) As the letter to Edey said, another operation would be set up, and after a couple of weeks' delay, Paul Morton and three other fellows, including a South African war artist, Geoff Long, were parachuted at midnight into the hills around the great enemy-held city of Turin.

The Italian partisans were divided between the Monarchists and the Communists, and, as might be expected, the British were supporting the Monarchists. Special Operations had worked out an elaborate systemn of bonfires so that their men would be dropped in the right place, among the right people. However, a nearby Communist guerrilla group, which was desperately in need of arms and had probably infiltrated the Monarchists, heard about this mission and duplicated the bonfires so convincingly that, as Morton said, 'we parachuted to them instead.' 'Our adventure,' he went on, 'started with a kidnapping, the Communists stealing us out of the sky in a manner that I shall never forget.'

During a rather bumpy landing, Morton twisted his ankle, probably the same ankle that he had twisted while training, and the South African artist finished up in a tree. There was a crazy, dream-like quality to the next few weeks: they toured around with the Communist guerrilla group and, according to Doug How, 'were escorted along open highways by a colorful powdered guerrilla leader with a machine gun mounted on the hood of his touring car.' They had brushes with German patrols and spent a week under fire in a partisan-held village. They met downed Allied airmen and helped them to find the established escape routes. Morton did not spend all his time in the countryside, which the guerrillas dominated, but was able to persuade his hosts to take him to the underground anti-fascist organizations in the cities.

He visited not only the Communists but also those he called 'Moderates,' whose leader was a schoolteacher, 'no more than five feet tall but possessed of an immense dignity.' Six of the small man's followers stood in a semicircle around his chair, and two of them, although dressed in civilian clothes, gave the Canadian military salute, 'which many Italians,' Morton said, 'seem to believe is our version of the now forbidden Fascist gesture.' The fact that he was conducted quite openly to the homes of these clandestine political leaders was a sign of how little control the Germans and Mussolini's Fascists had by the fall of 1944. Morton felt that he had seen the beginning of a 'party system' and wondered whether he had not been 'privileged to witness the rebirth of democracy in this unhappy land.' Finally, Morton and his three companions, according to Doug How, 'walked through the German artillery lines along the Franco-Italian border, walked past Nazi guards to the sea, and rowed by night into Allied territory in Southern France.'

What happened to Paul Morton and his great 'scoop' I did not find out till later (see chapter 14). I was on my way to London and to Canada, and, when travelling, I tended to concentrate on getting there to the exclusion of anything else. On 13 October, I left Rome for Naples by the afternoon plane: I went to the British Officers' Club (where I bumped into Sub-Lieutenant Scott Young) and the Royal Navy Club and took in a couple of ENSA shows, including the play, *George and Margaret*, but I was soon recording in my diary, 'Naples is a most depressing place. This is the second time that I have been stuck here – waiting is like suspended animation.' I was back in the Serena Hotel of ill memory, the senior British officers' hotel, but also a flop house. 'The people here (in Naples),' I noted, 'are small, shrivelled, obvious products of disease and malnutrition. I visited a market where I saw twisted old women picking up offal. The girls here have wonderful breasts but horrible sores on their legs or horrible blue varicose veins. A toothless man cleaned my shoes and jabbered away with a pregnant girl with a chinless bucktoothed face and thin stick like legs. The whole place and everyone in it seems unclean.'

I took the opportunity, while waiting for travel orders, to visit Pompeii, which had been cleaned of ash from the March eruption of Vesuvius. I wondered whether the pornographic paintings had been embellished, but I wrote in my diary: 'The flying penises and other signs of prosperity seemed to be genuine. Our guide, a bottle-nosed old reprobate, delighted in telling us about the debaucheries of the Romans.' In a letter home I said that the ruins of Pompeii were so much better than those in Rome, and I noted 'how little small Italian towns have changed in two thousand years.'

On 19 October, after six days in limbo in Naples, I got the order to go, and the next day we took off at 7:30 a.m. 'We flew via Marseilles to England,' I wrote in a letter to my parents, 'It was very interesting passing from one climate to another, and you could almost see the change of weather around the centre of France where it became cloudy and rainy. We passed over Paris and I got a glimpse of the Eiffel Tower ... the voyage across the Channel was quite rough and I was quite glad when we put down.' It took less than a day to reach London and the CBC Overseas Unit, compared with the roundabout trip of ten days just a year earlier.

14

Home for Christmas 1944

London, 20 October 1944:
Canadian forces are meeting fierce resistance in fighting along the sodden dykes and banks of the Scheldt. Latest attacks have failed to open the port of Antwerp to Allied shipping.

When I left Italy I expected to return to Canada after a week's stop-over in London. Matthew Halton had gone to the dominion for the Victory Loan campaign, however, and the CBC wanted me to stay in London until he returned in about four weeks' time. I assured my parents that I would be home for Christmas. Actually, I was quite glad to have a longer stay in London, since there were some loose ends to be tied up and some people I wanted to see.

The day after arriving, I got a glimpse of my first V-1, the buzz bomb or 'doodlebug,' as it was called: it was a pilotless jet plane with one ton of explosives in its nose, and it flew with a sputtering roar a short distance away past our window – I was staying in Bert Powley's rooftop flat on Harley Street – and disappeared over some buildings. It was obviously coming down, and I was told that the engine would cut off and there would be ten seconds of silence before it hit. Sure enough, the angry sputtering stopped, and there was a tense wait before an earth-shattering blast that shook our apartment. 'Somewhere near Marble Arch' was the guess. People seemed to think that the V-1s hitting London were coming from Antwerp and were outraged that the Allies had not been able to clear the Germans out of the Belgian port, but this idea was absurd, since the enemy held only the approaches on the Scheldt, denying the use of the port which was entirely in our hands; in fact, the Nazis were firing V-1s at Antwerp from bases in the Netherlands.

My book, *Journey into Victory*, had sold out very quickly; only 4,000 copies had been printed – that was all Harrap's could manage with its wartime paper quota. I had received the first copy of the book when I was in Rome, and I remember sitting in the lounge of the Albergo Citta, the British PR hotel, and opening it up. There can be no greater thrill for a writer than to see his first book. I was delighted with its appearance, but I was a bit concerned that on the dust jacket Harrap's had described me as being a news editor with the 'Columbia Broadcasting Company.' I wrote to Dan McArthur apologizing for this error, saying that I had had nothing to do with it and that he would see that the CBC was given full credit in the body of the book. However, it was a sign that the Canadian Broadcasting Corporation was not well known abroad.

The reviews were generally good, and the publisher had put together a collection of 'extracts from press cuttings' for me. Most of the critics noted the fact that the book contained the first account of the construction and opening of the Alcan Highway and that this distinguished it from the 'all too many accounts' of other war correspondents. As the *Times Literary Supplement*, which listed it in its 'books recommended' box, said: 'Mr Stursberg's book is different from the others in that his opening chapters are devoted to describing the Alaska Highway, that magnificent feat of military engineering of which we in this country know all too little ... From Alaska to Sicily is a far cry, but in describing the splendid bearing of Canadian regiments there and their later landing in Italy, Mr. Stursberg is equally informative.'

I was disappointed that there had been no Canadian edition and that so few copies had been sent to the dominion, and I told George Harrap so. George was always good for a bang-up lunch at a swank restaurant around the corner from his publishing house, where rationing seemed unheard of. When I suggested that I could update the book, however, in the hope of reprinting and in this way producing a Canadian edition, the publisher, who was a son of Harrap's founder, had the perfect put-down. 'War books,' he said, 'are out – escape is in.'

During the eight months or more that I had been in the Mediterranean Theatre, I had given some thought to my future. It was obvious that the war was drawing slowly and savagely to an end. There were some people who expected it to be over by Christmas, but in a letter to my parents dated 20 September, I said that 'at present I would say that it had a good chance of lasting till next spring.' A prescient remark, but I was depressed by the way the Allies were bogged down on the Italian front. At the beginning of 1944 everyone had expected the war to be over in a few months and certainly before the year was out. It would have been so, according to John Grigg, the British historian and political analyst, if it had not been for the fundamental mistakes made by the Americans and the British. In his book *1943 – The Victory That Never Was* Grigg claimed that the cross-channel assault should have been in 1943, and the fact that it had not occurred then, which was largely owing to British fears of another Dunkirk, allowed the Russians to overrun so much of central Europe.

For now, I was sure that I could continue as a war correspondent. Still, the war was going to end sometime in 1945; then what would happen to me? I wanted to cover the postwar period in Europe, but I knew that Halton's contract with the CBC stated that he would continue as a foreign correspondent based in London. The corporation would never have two men in Europe. Although it would have been a second choice, I would have agreed to cover national affairs, but any mention of a correspondent in Ottawa made the strongest CBC executive swoon.

The rule that the corporation should not be involved in reporting was carved in stone by Dan McArthur, and the tablet was not broken till long after he had retired as chief news editor: the exigencies of television forced the CBC to appoint Norman DePoe as its correspondent in Ottawa in the early sixties. The ruling applied not just to domestic reporting but to all reporting, although it was chipped away by the hiring of Matt Halton. By the fifties, when I had rejoined the CBC, the corporation had four foreign correspondents – Halton was in London, Doug Lachance was in Paris, I was at the United Nations in New York, and James M. 'Don' Minifie was in Washington – all under contract. At that, a minute of the CBC board of directors was needed in 1952 before Matt and I could say that we were 'of the CBC.' (Halton was the first newsman to be hired under contract; it was the only way to get around the civil service structure of the corporation and give him the salary that he expected.)

If I was to stay with the CBC after the war, I would most likely return to a newsroom as a news editor, rewriting agency copy. It was a fate that I would not wish on any radio reporter. Then there was the dead hand of the bureaucracy. After a year and a half as a war correspondent, and much of it at the front, I was given a higher grade (as a news editor) and a very small raise. 'I can only compare it [the raise] with the twenty-five dollars a week which a friend of mine among the correspondents here received because of his coverage of the [Italian] campaign,' I wrote to Dan McArthur from Rome and continued:

Effort and initiative mean nothing to the CBC evidently. I have no doubt that I would have risen to my present salary if I had stayed at home.

It's very discouraging. I know that you've been doing your best for me, but I wish that you would take this matter up to the highest quarter.

As I've said before, and I'll repeat it again, I like working for the CBC and I want to continue working for it. However, I'm not going to feel satisfied till I get the kind of substantial increase that my friend got.

I may as well lay my cards on the table and admit frankly that I want $4,000 a year. As a matter of fact, I don't think I'm asking for much.

Whenever I was in London, I kept in touch with friends I had made when I was an Empire Press Union exchange reporter on the *Daily Herald* just before the war. I used to meet them in the pubs around Endell Street, where the newspaper had its office, just across the road from the Covent Garden opera house. Now that I was uncertain about my future, I sought out the editor, Percy Cudlipp, and found him to be most accommodating. He had been impressed by my book, *Journey into Victory* – it brought me more prestige than money, since I think I received less than £200 in royalties. At any rate, Cudlipp said that if I decided to leave the CBC, the *Daily Herald* would welcome me on its staff 'first as a war correspondent and later as a special correspondent,' and he put this offer in writing.

It was a nice change, being back in London after so many months at the front, and I enjoyed doing a daily commentary on the war and engaging in the office routine of a nine to five job. Again I met with the regulars at The Cock tavern, including Hamish McGeachy and other friends from Canadian military establishments around town. Georgina Murray of the CBC in Vancouver had joined the WRENS and was in London with the Canadian navy's Public Relations. Aside from the buzz bombs, living conditions seemed to have improved, and restaurants had a greater variety of fresh food, probably coming from France; more West End theatres were open and they were playing to full houses, as were the movie palaces; but the blackout was still as rigorously enforced. 'No chink of light to guide the buzz bombs,' we muttered into our beers while surveying the scene from The Cock.

Halton returned towards the end of November. He had been in Canada during much of the 'conscription crisis,' about which we had heard very little. Matt said that it almost brought the Liberal government down: the defence minister, Colonel Ralston, insisted that overseas conscription was necessary because of the shortage of reinforcements at the front, but Prime Minister Mackenzie King, who was fearful of reaction in Quebec, would not agree; he forced Ralston's resignation and appointed General McNaughton in his place on the understanding that the former army commander could persuade enough men to volunteer. McNaughton failed, and on 22 November, within three weeks of the general's appointment, King had to accept overseas conscription. There was, however, one piece of news from North America that we followed closely till the early hours of the morning at a cheerful and celebratory party:

London, 7 November 1944:
President Franklin Roosevelt wins an unprecedented fourth term with a landslide victory over Governor Thomas Dewey. The electoral college vote comes to 432 to 99.

My movement orders came through at the beginning of December. I was to sail on the *Mauretania*. There were seven other Canadian war correspondents beside me in a cabin meant for two first-class passengers, and some 5,000 troops in the lower decks. Two meals a day – and no waiters to be seen in the great dining-saloon of the former luxury liner that had been turned into a self-serve cafeteria. The correspondents were put to work, and I did some talks on the intercom. The *Mauretania* drove alone through the Atlantic at a shuddering speed, which no U-boats could match; in any case, they were no longer a menace. The only remarkable feature of that voyage was that the ship was carrying the first war brides to Canada, and one of the former first-class public rooms had been turned into a nursery.

There were a half-dozen trains waiting by Halifax harbour to take the returning heroes and the first war brides plus the first war babies home for Christmas. It was a tremendous feat of logistics, and for once the military did themselves proud and there was no SNAFU. I spent a couple of days in Montreal and Toronto, and the way that I was fêted was a forewarning of what was to come. I was interviewed, I was dragged from one radio show to another, I was treated as a celebrity. I shall never forget seeing a van with my name emblazoned across its side slipping and sliding through the snow-covered streets.

I had a drawing-room for the train trip to Vancouver, which I took as a mark of appreciation for my work as a war correspondent. Perhaps the CBC could get no less; for it was the holiday rush, and the corporation had a reputation for treating the stars it created like Frankenstein monsters. Still, I had a drawing-room, and it was the most luxurious way of travelling across Canada; someone had given me a bottle of rye and I drank it looking out at the swirling snow, the great wilderness of the Soo, the unending prairies, the spectacle of the Rockies, and the little towns, as forlorn as the sound of a distant train whistle. The dining-car: white tablecloths, silver service, and uniformed waiters, a first-class restaurant as good as anywhere in Canada at the time, with the possible exception of Montreal.

During the four days on the transcontinental train, I thought about the impact radio had. Although it was so commonplace – almost everyone had a set by the forties – it was still a marvel to the average Canadian, making news out of thin air, bringing the sound of battle over an ocean and across a continent. At the same time, it was a much more personal medium: there was the reporter or his voice in the living-rooms and even the bedrooms of the nation. This was the reason why Matthew Halton and I had become so well known that we were household names, whereas fine correspondents such as Ralph Allen of the *Globe and Mail*, Toronto, and J.A.M. Cook of the *Winnipeg Free Press* were famous only to those who read those newspapers. In introducing me to the readers of *Maclean's* magazine, H. Napier Moore said in his column, 'In the Editor's Confidence':

In the history of the Mediterranean wars one of the first war correspondents we know of was Pheidippides. In 490 B.C. he ran 26 miles to Athens with news of the battle of Marathon, shouted 'Rejoice, we conquer,' and fell dead.

Today, voices bring us news of Mediterranean battles in which Canadian troops are fighting. They reach us over invisible spans thousands of miles long; carried by air waves. For instance, several times a week Canadians in every part of the Dominion listen to the voice of Peter Stursberg describing the progress of our troops in Sicily.

One of 15 men serving with the CBC overseas unit, he was the first
Canadian radio correspondent to land on the beaches on July 10 ...

After the four-day train trip and the midnight ferry from
Vancouver to Victoria, I was home for Christmas 1944: it was a
family Christmas with just my mother and father and my brother,
Richard, who was now out of the army after two frustrating years.
The Pacific coast was the lush, green edge of the cold, grey mass
of the continent, and though Victoria was as mild and beautiful as
I remembered, the city had changed. There was hardly anyone
whom I knew left in town. Most of my friends were in the armed
forces, and a few had been killed. Of course, it was five years ago,
but not one of the merry-makers who had been at the Saturday
night dance in the Empress Hotel and gone on to the private party
to listen to Chamberlain's declaration of war was around. I felt like
a stranger. It was just another sign that you cannot go back and
expect to resume the life that you left behind.

My brother's experience was a horrible example of the way that
Ottawa bungled its manpower resources. He was six feet, three
inches tall and in great physical shape, but he wore glasses; he
was short-sighted and had worn glasses since he was a schoolboy.
That did not prevent him from being able to shoot as well as
anyone with 20-20 vision or from taking part in the most exhausting exercises. However, his eyes prevented his going overseas: he
was rated E-5. When he joined up in October 1942 he was put in
the pay corps, and, since he had been a bank inspector, he was a
natural to check the books of the canteens where skullduggery was
suspected. He was made a canteen-audit acting-sergeant-without-
pay, but rank did not bother him, since the Royal Bank made up
the difference between the private's $1.30 a day and what they
were paying him as a young bank inspector – which was not a
great deal. Still it was enough when he was at Dundurn to spend
forty-eight-hour leaves at the Hotel Bessborough in Saskatoon.

In the spring of 1943 there was good news: Ottawa had decided
that men with E-5 eyes could go overseas if they were officers. So
Richard appplied to the Officer Selection and Appraisal Centre and

in June left the old Hotel Vancouver, which the army had taken
over as barracks, for the OSAC camp at Chilliwack. Then in August
he took basic training at Camrose, Alberta. Later, he volunteered
for the armoured corps and went to Dundurn, Saskatchewan; my
brother recalled that when he reported for duty at the base with
another officer cadet, they stamped and made sweeping salutes, as
was expected, but the major behind the desk said, 'Relax,
Stursberg, don't you remember me? I'm Henry and I was the
messenger at the Royal Bank in Victoria.' Just as he was complet-
ing his officer's training course, Ottawa changed the rules again:
no one with E-5 eyes could become an officer or go overseas.

Richard's disappointment was great, but since he was a good
skier, he was asked to take part in an experimental winter
operation. At the end of December 1943 my brother went to Prince
Albert, Saskatchewan; he was made a corporal and a ski instructor. The troops, who were mainly Zombies (conscripts), although
there were a couple of French Canadians who had been returned
from overseas because they were under age, were testing subarctic
equipment. They slept in tents at −35°F, and they engaged in
sham battles over the cold, snow-covered reaches above Prince
Albert. British and American officers watched these manoeuvres,
which were rumoured to be a rehearsal for the invasion of Norway.
Richard said, however, that you couldn't fight in the conditions
that prevailed during the test. You could fire only one shot from a
prone position, and the powder snow would cover the rifle and it
would freeze and jam.

The winter exercise ended in March 1944, and my brother
returned to Dundurn, where he was, ironically, made a battle drill
instructor. He could see that he was getting nowhere, however,
and he spoke to his commanding officer about applying for a
discharge. The CO said that all he could do was send him back to
his base, which was Military District 11, Vancouver. In July he
was back in the Little Mountain barracks; after the morning
parade and roll call at 8 a.m., there was usually nothing else to do.
So he spent the rest of the summer playing tennis at the
Vancouver Tennis Club, but he kept pressing the CO for a dis-

charge. 'Either send me overseas,' he said, 'or let me out of the army.' Finally persistence paid off, and in September he was granted a hearing by Mr Justice Alexander Manson, who agreed that Richard would be doing more for the war effort if he returned to the bank, and he gave him his discharge.

It was unprecedented that he should have been able to get out of the army so long before the war ended, whereas most of his fellow E-5s could not and continued to rot on the home front. There must have been many in Richard's condition, who wanted to go overseas but were rejected because of their eyes or some other minor disability. Paul Morton was turned down by the army because of ulcers. The change in the rules, and especially its reversion, was an example of the political infighting in Ottawa which amounted almost to a sabotage of the war effort.

(There were many in the top ranks of the military and of the civil service in Ottawa, including the so-called 'dollar-a-year men,' who believed that, as a matter of principle, there should be conscription for overseas service. They considered Mackenzie King's 'not necessarily conscription but conscription if necessary' to be political slime and an indictment of the prime minister as a wartime leader. As a result, they did nothing to help raise volunteers; in fact, they put obstacles in the way of those with minor disabilities going overseas, as in the case of my brother and others who wore glasses.)

As might be expected, the Victoria papers interviewed me: I said that the two subjects on the soldiers' minds were 'home leave' and the 'plans that the government was making for participation in the Pacific war.' The troops overseas were fed up with Ottawa's 'unending vacillation'; all they wanted to know is 'where they stand.' They were not greatly concerned with 'the "Zombie" question which so rocked Canada last month.'

That Christmas of 1944 was a lull before a storm of public appearances. There were insistent demands from the 'rubber chicken' or club circuit, and I made my first speech to the Men's Canadian Club in Victoria on 3 January 1945. A few days later I spoke to the Women's Canadian Club and, according to the report in the *Victoria Times*, I was introduced by my friend and fellow war correspondent Sholto Watt, who was in town at the time visiting his mother.

The CBC called it a 'speaking blitz.' I spoke to three other organizations in Victoria, and at least five times in Vancouver. The joint meeting of the lower mainland Rotary Clubs was the largest ever held in the Hotel Vancouver, and tables had to be set up in the hall and in other salons; my friend Jack Mahony and a couple of other VCs were at the head table. I also spoke to open meetings of the Canadian Club in Nanaimo and Chilliwack. In the Fraser Valley centre of Chilliwack, the CBC said, the interest was such that some stores and businesses closed for the afternoon meeting, where 600 turned up when 250 were expected.

While all this was going on, the hyperactive Pat Keatley, who ran the CBC's Press and Information Service in Vancouver, was making arrangements for me to go on a cross-country lecture tour for the Association of Canadian Clubs. (Pat was another who was turned down by the army because of a minor disability; after the war, he had a distinguished career in Britain on the *Guardian* newspaper.) Keatley put out a twelve-page *Press Book*, which, besides a detailed itinerary of a dozen or more cities that I was to visit, contained eye-catching snippets that Pat attributed to me such as: 'German pillboxes were built of solid concrete with sleeping quarters sixteen feet underground.' ' "So this is Rome' was all the Canadian soldiers could say – and their voices were filled with a form of ecstasy.' The tour arrangements were complicated because Pat had to fit in the Canadian Club lectures with my other commitments: a network radio show in Toronto, a film session in Ottawa at the National Film Board for the Victory Bond drive, and, most important of all, the annual convention of the Canadian Association of Broadcasters in Quebec City, where I was to be the featured speaker. All travel was by train. Since others took advantage of the tour, I could speak as many as four times at a stop, at a high school or a college in the morning, the Men's Canadian Club at luncheon, the Women's Canadian Club in the afternoon, and in the evening at a service club dinner.

I gave the same speech at every meeting until I knew it by heart. It was entitled 'The Capture of Rome' and it was as popular and patriotic as I could make it. The part that I remembered getting the greatest reaction was when I described visiting the Colosseum by moonlight:

We had an Italian as our guide, and, you know, the Colosseum is quite a stadium. At the height of the Roman Empire, in the days of the great and bloody circuses, the Colosseum held some fifty thousand spectators. Our Italian guide explained what it was like in those bad old days.

Just beneath us, he said, the Caesar would have sat, and, over on that side, the Senators, and, in that area there, the Vestal Virgins. Through those portals, the Italian guide said, the gladiators came – and, in the soft and hazy moonlight, you could almost imagine the Colosseum as it was with the Roman crowd in the tiers of seats and the mortal combat below.

We were lost in thought, but our purple reverie was disturbed by two American GIs who entered the Colosseum quite close to where we were. They stood for a moment in silence looking down on the moonlit arena, and I wondered if they too were overcome by the thoughts that possessed us. Then one turned to the other and said: 'We gotta bigger place than this in Philadelphia'.

In Ottawa, the Women's Canadian Club upstaged the Men's Club by having a luncheon meeting – I forget what kind of a meeting the men had. I felt somewhat conspicuous as the only male in a sea of women that filled the ballroom of the Château Laurier Hotel to overflowing; I was startled when madame president, introducing me, said, 'Ladies, I never realized that Mr Stursberg was so young.' There was a sort of sigh of agreement from the audience. That was the charm of radio, that one envisaged the person from the voice, and my harsh tones, which Dan McArthur told my parents were able to penetrate the static better than those of most broadcasters, must have sounded middle aged.

I suppose every war correspondent who returns home to a

lecture tour and a Victory Bond drive must be embarrassed by the acclaim he receives. Ernie Pyle certainly was: he hated it. Matthew Halton, when he returned to the front just before Christmas 1944, told A.E. Powley that his trip to Canada had been a 'tremendous success' but he did not like being treated like a hero. I felt, as he did, that the applause should have gone to the Canadian fighting men, but there was no way that it could. We were the messengers, but unlike Pheidippides, we lived!

In Toronto I ran into Paul Morton; I was on my way to address the meeting of the Women's Canadian Club in the Eaton Auditorium. Paul, who seemed to be at a loose end, announced that he would introduce me. When we arrived, the large auditorium in Eaton's College Street store was so full that women were sitting in the aisles, I said to madame president *sotto voce* that Paul Morton was with me and that she was getting two war correspondents for the price of one; although she appeared somewhat flustered, there was little she could do but accept the situation gracefully. Paul's introduction was hair raising. He had me dodging bullets to record the battle scene, crawling through ditches so close to the enemy that I could hear them speaking, driving pell-mell across a road under shell fire, and entering a village while the fighting was still going on.

Afterward, I wondered whether Paul Morton was really describing not what had happened to me but what had happened to him when he was dropped behind the enemy lines (see chapter 13). We had coffee, and Paul said that he was no longer with the *Toronto Star*. I gathered that he had been fired, but he made light of it and said that he would be getting a better-paying job on another newspaper. He said that he had not yet got his story of his adventures with the Italian partisans published, but he hoped to do so soon. I sensed that he was in trouble, but it was not till years later that I learned the full extent of his ordeal.

It was really the worst nightmare for a reporter to find that his greatest scoop, on which he had risked his life, was not believed. At first the *Toronto Star* had been supportive, and, as Bill Gilchrist said, had raised 'a hell of an uproar' when their correspondent was dis-accredited,* but then the newspaper had second thoughts and became suspicious and antagonistic. It was all because of a ghastly misunderstanding: the publisher, Harry Hindmarsh, had devised a crazy scheme whereby he wanted Victory Bonds purchased by Yugoslav readers of the *Star* to be delivered to Marshal Tito, and he thought that he had authorized Morton to do this when British Intelligence asked for permission to drop him behind the enemy lines.

Apparently Morton was able to send out a 'pool' dispatch while still with the partisans, or patriots, which was passed by the censors for all newspapers; it was published by the *Toronto Star* on 27 October 1944 and was an account of guerrilla action in northern Italy. Hindmarsh found this report incomprehensible, and, according to a column McKenzie Porter wrote in the *Toronto Telegram* of 6 March 1964, when Hindmarsh learned that Morton had never jumped into Yugoslavia, he fired him for 'faking' a story. Mckenzie Porter even asserted that Hindmarsh was so obsessed with this absurd Victory Bond mission that he rewrote a Morton story to give the impression that he was in Yugoslavia – but there is no evidence this was ever published.

Major Royd Beamish had another explanation of why the *Star*

*Paul Morton was the only Canadian correspondent to be disaccredited in the Second World War, but Bill Gilchrist recalled a *fake* Canadian war correspondent. Here are a couple of excerpts from Gilchrist's war diary:

'*September 1 1944*: Oddest story of the week has to do with an individual representing himself to be "Jack Martin" and claiming to be a CBC "newscaster." This worthy was reported to us by some suspicious war correspondents for whom he had been buying drinks in various local (Rome) bars. Investigation showed that he carried a fake war correspondent's pass ... He was promptly placed under arrest and subsequent investigation proved that he had been AWOL from the RCHA since last January during which time he had travelled freely on forged travel orders between Italy, Algiers, Casablanca and Gibraltar, and he boasted that he had made $20,000 smuggling black market goods!

'*September 7 1944*: Martin again - the CBC "newscaster." Reynolds Packard (UP correspondent) rang today that somebody looking suspiciously like the famous Martin was hanging about the bar at the Albergo Grande. Investigation proved that it was nobody else but. He had escaped from detention in Algiers and made his way back to Rome and straight to the Grande. Nothing but the best for Martin!'

believed that Morton was faking the account of his adventures with the Italian partisans. Beamish said that Paul had told him before he left to join the secret operation that he had a special job to do during the next few days. A new victory loan campaign was on in Canada, and the paper wanted him to do a story a day, interviewing soldiers and nurses, with the idea that what they said would make Canadians readier to buy the bonds. The PR major assured Paul that he would look after this assignment and would file the stories under his name to the *Star*. As a result, the paper had a dozen pieces sent from Rome with Morton's byline, and they only added to Hindmarsh's dark suspicions about his activities. (Incidentally, while Beamish did not excuse Paul for shooting up the mess, he pointed out that 'he had been tuned to a concert pitch, only to be frustrated at the last moment' by the postponement of the mission.)

The dispatch that Paul Morton filed from behind enemy lines, which appeared in the *Star*, was a progress report, and the full story of Morton's extraordinary adventures 'has never really been told, even yet,' according to Douglas How's article in *Dateline: Canada 1962*. Harry Hindmarsh was such a domineering figure in Toronto that local newspapermen believed him and regarded Morton as a phoney. The only official account of this incident was in Ross Harkness's book, *J.E. Atkinson of the Star*, published in 1963, which merely repeated the Hindmarsh claim: 'Paul Morton was sent to be dropped by parachute among the Yugoslav guerrillas, but never succeeded in making contact with them.' When Morton returned to Toronto, he found he could not get a job, or even work as a freelance. Wisecracks taunted him about his alleged mission.

For several years Paul Morton was reduced to working as a labourer in the bush. It was not till the early fifties that he began to recover his earning power as a public relations man. After he had become established in Toronto, he decided to write a full account of this, the most incredible and daring assignment of any correspondent of the Second World War; he submitted it to a number of Canadian publications, but all he got were rejection slips. He was downcast and he confided to a fellow in the Toronto Press Club that no one would publish his story. 'You'd almost think they doubted it was true,' he said, according to How. 'Of course they doubted it,' this fellow shouted, 'It simply isn't true ... You're a phoney.'

There could not have been a more damning accusation, and Paul Morton at last realized that he must do something to establish his bona fides. He tracked down the former Royal Navy officer, the head of the Special Operations unit, who had sent him behind the enemy lines: Commander G.A. Holdsworth, who was now a businessman in London, was only too glad to confirm that he had gone on this mission. 'Later,' Douglas How wrote, 'Morton got from the Parliamentary Under-Secretary of State for War [James Ramsden] in London a similar confirmation, an unusual confirmation because the War Office rarely confirms details of what are essentially intelligence operations.'

No further proof was required, but for those of us who had known Paul Morton in Italy, there had never been a need for confirmation. I never doubted that his story was true, and I know that the Canadian PR officers in Rome knew that he had been on this cloak-and-dagger operation, because we talked about it. Yet the cloud of suspicion remained. The proof came too late, his wife, Marjorie, said: 'Nobody cared.' Paul still could not get an account of his adventures with the Italian partisans or 'patriots' published in Canada – but he did in Italy. McKenzie Porter said in his *Telegram* column that the award-winning Italian documentary-film producer, Gian Luigi Polidoro, got in touch with Morton and commissioned him to write a series of TV scripts on Italian guerrilla activity in the final days of the war. These might have provided the material for the Italian booklet or paperback of which Paul Morton had a copy. It is entitled *Missione 'Inside': Fra i partigani del nord Italia*. Besides Paul's account of his adventures, the booklet is full of pictures by the South African artist Geoff Long, who dropped with him. It also reprints Douglas How's description of Morton's trials and tribulations in *Dateline: Canada 1962*, which shows that the Italian paperback was published in the mid-sixties.

To be called a phoney and a liar before his peers in the Toronto Press Club was a devastating blow. 'It really destroyed his life,' Mrs Morton said. He became morose and depressed and gave up his public relations business which had been doing well. For eight and a half years Paul Morton was in West Park Hospital in Toronto; previously he had spent three years in private nursing homes. He died in the hospital on 26 April 1992. It was a miracle, Marjorie Morton said, that he had lived to be nearly eighty.

When I was in Toronto on the lecture tour, I saw Dan McArthur, and, as I expected, he could not offer me a job as a reporter after the war ended. He said that I could continue as a war correspondent until the last shot was fired, but ..., and he shook his head sadly. It was best for the CBC to get its national news from the agencies, not to have its own reporters, not even an experienced reporter such as me. What about the BBC? I asked: it had its own reporters.

However, Dan's reply was that the CBC was the only public broadcasting system in North America, it was a sheep in the midst of a pack of private broadcasting wolves and had to be more careful. The rules that he had written for news were not about to be changed. (We parted on the best of terms, and some five years later Dan created the job for me as the CBC's UN correspondent.) It was agreed that I should continue to broadcast from the front for the CBC. I wired Percy Cudlipp that I would be returning to England at the end of February and joining the *Daily Herald*.

The last stop on the lecture tour, during which I estimate that I spoke more than thirty-five times, was Quebec City. This was where I was to address the convention of the Canadian Association of Broadcasters in the Château Frontenac Hotel, but I also had a Women's Canadian Club engagement. The ladies had their meeting in a nondescript hall, but afterwards we went around to an exquisite eighteenth-century house, part of a row of houses in the Old Town, where madame president served tea. When we came in out of the snow, it was to find ourselves in a very English setting, with chintz curtains, bright, flower-patterned covers on the furniture, and a maid serving tea and cucumber sandwiches.

Everyone who was anyone in radio was at the CAB, the Canadian Association of Broadcasters, convention. The Canadian Broadcasting Corporation, from the general manager down, was there in full force. This was in the days when the CBC was the regulatory body for private broadcasters, and it had an ambivalent attitude towards the CAB, which was the private broadcasters' association. The CAB for its part took the position that the CBC was both its regulator and its competitor; the private broadcasters had never felt that they were part of an overall Canadian broadcasting system under the leadership of the CBC, as the proponents and architects of public broadcasting had hoped.

All of which did not mean that the corporation did not regard the convention as important, and I was told that I could have any help that I wanted in the way of technical assistance; in fact, it was suggested that I should use some of the war recordings in the course of my presentation. I did just that. The whole great ballroom of the Château Frontenac was wired for sound. I used a couple of the battle reports as well as my broadcast of 'Lili Marlene' with a linking script. It was more than anything a show, and I think I was able to keep the attention of the rather rambunctious and drunken dinner crowd. Perhaps the dignified presence of the justice minister, Louis St Laurent, at the head table helped.

The next day I made for Halifax and the trip back to England and the war.

15

Victory Parades

On board ship, 7 March 1945:
American tanks reach the Rhine opposite the town of Remagen and find that the Nazis have not blown the bridge. U.S.
First Army troops are sent across and take up positions on the
other side.

There was a sleek, grey liner waiting for us when we reached Halifax, the *Pasteur*, which at 30,000 tons was smaller than the *Mauretania* but just as fast. I was delighted to find that I had a travelling companion, Sam Ross, my old mentor in the Canadian Press office in Vancouver, where I was sent, back in December 1940, to learn how to write newscasts. Roles were reversed, and Sam, who was now the news director of a Vancouver radio station, was taking advantage of an army-sponsored trip to the front; he asked me all kinds of questions about being a war correspondent and what conditions were like in London and with the Canadian forces in Europe, and so on.

It may have been because the *Pasteur* was quite new, but aboard it there was not the usual great difference in the treatment of officers and that of other ranks. There were a few first-class cabins, but most of them had been torn out to form dormitories with rows of bunks in tiers of three. Anyone fat would have had a difficult time fitting into these bunks, but the army was not sending anyone overweight overseas, although there were a number of civilians on board. I noted a couple of plump business-men, who eyed the bunks with some trepidation. They chose the lowest bunks. I took the topmost because we were bound to run into a storm at this time of the year in the North Atlantic, and I did not want anyone being sick on me. There were similar dormitories on the lower decks, perhaps a little more crowded, but there seemed to be no hammocks, or none that I saw. Just as on the *Mauretania*, we were given two meals a day.

We heard the news of the Remagen bridge on the ship's public address system. This was the first crossing of the Rhine, and others would soon follow. Once again I was worried that I might be too late for the big story: the last time it was the invasion of Europe and this time the collapse of Nazi Germany.

It was difficult to find hotel accommodation in London, but Sam Ross and I were able to get a large double room in the Waldorf, a comfortable hotel on the Strand, not far from the Savoy. The first night we were there, I remember listening to the radio and hearing Wynford Vaughan-Thomas describing in rapturous detail the 'huge American lorries, as big as railway boxcars' that were moving mountains of supplies up to the front. These must have been for Montgomery's long-heralded offensive across the Rhine.

The Waldorf was nicely situated between the offices of the *Daily Herald* and the CBC, and it was when I visited the CBC, that I experienced a V-2 or robobomb attack. There was no forewarning of the rocket's striking and I distinctly heard two shattering blasts – some people maintained that there was only one explosion and the second, if there was one, was an echo. The V-2 had hit a little more than half a mile from the CBC offices, and Andy Cowan and I went out to take a look. We walked up Oxford Street and soon came across shattered glass, so finely splintered as we got closer to the crater that it squealed underfoot like hard-packed snow in the Yukon. The crater, which was just across a side street from

Selfridge's department store, was big enough to bury a fair-sized building.

I had to get settled before going to the front, and I was fortunate enough to run into George Weidenfeld when I was visiting the CBC. He had just taken over the lease of 10 Park Village East, a charming Regency bungalow, and was looking for someone to occupy the basement, or garden floor. Peter Quennell, an author and a critic of nineteenth-century poetry, had the top floor, George had the main floor with its entertaining rooms, and I was only too happy to take the garden-floor room, which had been the dining-room because the kitchen was next door. There were French doors that opened onto a small, unkempt garden and the filled-in end of the Regent's Canal. The row of Nash houses in Park Village East had been badly shaken by the bombing of the nearby Camden Street railway station and would have to be rebuilt, but they were a haven in the overcrowded London of 1945.

Then by army transport to the Canadian press camp, which was in a monastery on the outskirts of Nijmegen. The first thing I did was visit the front, or, in army parlance, 'make a recce.' We drove through the Reichswald, a gloomy wooded area encrusted with snow, past convoys of the great trucks that Wynford Vaughan-Thomas had described in such glowing terms. Monty's slow build-up meant that I had not missed his storming of the Rhine, which was to be the main Allied thrust into Germany. The dark woods parted, and there was the Siegried Line, the serried rows of concrete dragon's teeth that ran through forest and farmland, across hill and dale, along the western frontier of the Reich. The Nazis called it the West Wall; it was built as a counter to the Maginot Line in France and proved to be as ineffective. Some British wag had strung up a wire and pegged a couple of heavy duty army-issue socks on it to show that, as the song said, they had hung 'their washing on the Siegried Line.'

We came to a forward element of the First Canadian Army (although it was actually a British unit) where there was a lookout from which we got a good view of the Rhine. There it was, the historic river, dark and muddy, flowing swiftly and silently past, and on the opposite bank the historic town of Cleve. This was the home of Anne of Cleves, the fourth wife of Henry VIII, and the one who lasted the shortest time because Henry did not like her *hausfrau* appearance. I could not tell what Cleve looked like, since all I could see of the town was a pile of rubble. There was sporadic artillery fire; otherwise all was quiet on the Rhine.

It had been a bitter winter of frustration, and the mood of the troops was sombre. The Canadians had spent so much of the time on the wet, cold banks of the Scheldt, up to their knees in mud and able only to inch their way forward. It had left the Canadian Army, and in particular its three Canadian divisions, according to A.E. Powley, 'thoroughly exhausted.' After they had cleared Walcheren in November 1944, the advance came to a halt, and for three months the Canadians stood guard on the northern flank of the Allied armies, along the so-called Nijmegen Salient and the banks of the Maas River. It was not exactly a rest, because constant patrolling and all the other horrors of static warfare in chill winter conditions continued. During the past month or so they had taken part in the grim struggle to clear the Germans from the west bank of the Rhine. That task had been accomplished and now they were preparing for 'Monty's big show,' the final assault on the Reich.

I found that the worst effect on morale was not the hard fighting in frightful weather but the disappointment over the failure of the British airborne division at Arnhem and the shock of the German drive over the snow-covered Ardennes towards Antwerp which ended in the Battle of the Bulge. Everyone thought that the Nazis were beaten, and no one believed they could mount such an offensive. 'How do they do it?' a Canadian sergeant asked, expressing the view of so many. 'Why do they fight the way they do when they know they're finished?' Others just shook their heads and said, 'They must be crazy.'

Max Hastings, the British historian, put it differently: 'The great enigma of this phase of the war was not Hitler's readiness to drag Germany down into catastrophe amid the fall of his empire, but the willingness of his people to endure, and to fight so hard until the bitter end.' But why was there this fanatical resistance? What was the answer to the questions the Canadian soldiers asked about the furious way the Germans fought when all was lost? Was it because of the area bombing which had destroyed their homes and killed so many of their loved ones?

The Canadian historians J.L. Granatstein and Desmond Morton noted, in *A Nation Forged in Fire*, that the German armies 'continued to fight with great skill and savagery until May 1945,' but they wondered 'whether that savagery increased because of the bombing of civilians.' It was 'a moot point.' Granatstein and Morton did say, however, that the bombing did not stop German war production. In fact, it continued to increase almost to the end of the war. 'More tanks, for example, were produced in 1944 than in any previous year.' The area bombing did not bring Germany to its knees. There were repeated raids on Berlin and other cities, but the results could be described only as a failure. Tens of thousands were killed and 1.5 million made homeless in Berlin, but a survivor of the bombing said that 'many primary targets such as the armament plants (now mostly dispersed or underground) and the railway lines (repaired within hours) functioned virtually to the end. As for the population's morale, though dulled by grief, physical exhaustion, and malnutrition, it was never broken.' (The survivor of the bombing of Berlin, who is quoted as to its effect, was the Russian Prince George Vassiltchikov; he edited his sister Princess Marie Vassiltchikov's *Berlin Diaries, 1940–1945*. The *New York Times* called this book 'the best eyewitness account we possess of the bombing of Berlin:' Others described it as 'a vivid insider's view of Nazi Germany:' and 'one of the most extraordinary war diaries ever written.')

German air defences were such and British losses (in planes and air crew) so heavy, that Max Hastings was to call the Battle of Berlin a defeat: 'Berlin won.'

Another British historian, John Grigg, wondered whether area bombing was not a war crime with which, as victors, the Allies were never charged. 'Area bombing, like unconditional surrender,' he said in *1943 – The Victory That Never Was*, 'was a gift to Nazi propaganda. It made the Western Allies seem scarcely less brutal and implacable than the Russians, and so made nearly all Germans feel resigned to a desperate, forlorn-hope struggle against all their enemies.' Yet it must be said that, despite the awful devastation of area bombing, which the Nazis called 'terror bombing,' the Germans preferred to surrender to the western Allies rather than to the Red Army.

Was the ultimatum of 'unconditional surrender' another factor in the enemy's fighting with such ferocity to the very end? The U.S. historian William B. Breuer in his book *Storming Hitler's Rhine* quoted the flamboyant and formidable American general George S. Patton, as saying: 'Look at this goddam fool unconditional surrender shit. If the Hun ever needed anything to put a burr under his saddle, that's it. Now he'll fight like the devil. It will take much longer, cost us more lives and let the Russians take more territory.' I liked that quote. I had met General Patton once, and that was the way he talked. I used to think that General Chris Vokes, who commanded the 1st Canadian Division in the Battle for Rome, was like General Patton, perhaps a poor man's General Patton; they were both down-to-earth, 'blood and guts' leaders, and equally foul mouthed.

Did area bombing and the terms of 'unconditional surrender' lengthen the war and cost hundreds of thousands of lives on both sides? It was a question that was often asked but could never be satisfactorily answered. Certainly, some historians and generals, such as Patton, felt that if it had not been for Roosevelt's declaration that the Allies would accept nothing less than 'unconditional surrender,' the war might have been over sooner – perhaps by November 1944, when the German armies had been pushed back to the borders of the Reich. Their assumption was that Hitler would have been overthrown, and there would have been negotiations for an armistice. An officers' revolt did occur on 20 July 1944, when Count von Stauffenberg tried to kill Hitler; it was probably premature, but it was brutally and ruthlessly suppressed. And what about the Russians? Would they have agreed to an armistice? Still, the war should have been over sooner. Most would agree to that.

254 The Sound of War

Finally, Montgomery was ready to launch his assault on the Rhine, which was to be the beginning of the last offensive against the crumbling bastion of the Reich. It began on 22 March 1945 with a thunderous, earth-shaking barrage for which Monty, the master of the set-piece battle, was famous; this was the biggest ever – thousands of guns along a fifty-mile front, and it served to pulverize the rubble that so many air raids had left on the east bank. In fact, the British and American air forces had dropped almost 50,000 tons of bombs two days before the attack. Nothing was left to chance, and the assault was preceded by the largest airborne operation of the war, in which the First Canadian Parachute Battalion took part. The barrage stopped to allow the air armada to pass, and for three hours, long streams of troop-carrying planes and gliders being towed by bombers flew quite low over our heads. It was an awe-inspiring sight.

The main assault across the river had the First Canadian Army on the left, with the II Canadian Corps attacking Cleve and Emmerich in the north, the British Second Army in the centre, and the American Ninth Army on the right, all of which meant the operation called 'Plunder' reached as far south as Duisburg and the edge of the Ruhr. Montgomery had three armies under his command, seventeen infantry divisions, eight armoured divisions, and two airborne divisions, as well as a number of independent brigades.

It would seem to have been a case of overkill, considering the wretched state of the German defences. However, while the Allies had crossed the Rhine with what was described as 'surprisingly moderate opposition,' Canadian and British troops ran into fierce resistance by German SS and paratroopers who were dug into the rubble. Furthermore, the airborne operation had a rough time, and many of the planes and gliders were shot down. From our vantage point on the west bank we saw a number of aircraft burst into flame. The Canadian Parachute Battalion met severe machine-gun and sniper fire in its dropping zone, and a medical orderly, Corporal F.G. Topham, won the Victoria Cross for repeatedly risking his life to rescue many wounded. (His heroism went virtually unnoticed, since we heard about it only at the end of the war.)

While the II Canadian Corps continued its drive along the Dutch border towards Oldenburg and Emden, the rest of the Canadian army wheeled around and began the final offensive to liberate the Netherlands. By the beginning of April the I Canadian Corps had rejoined the army after a well-executed move by land and sea from northern Italy that began at the end of February. For a little more than a month the First Canadian Army fought as a truly Canadian army instead of a mixed Allied force under Canadian command. On 6 April I reported to the CBC that the Canadian advance towards the Zuider Zee had forced the Germans to withdraw their V weapons from Holland. We had undoubtedly overrun some areas where the mobile launchers had been sited, I said, but there was not much to see. However, I met Frits, a Dutch student who had escaped from The Hague (which was why he did not want his surname to be used) and who had seen the robobombs being fired:

... Frits says that the Nazis launched most of their rockets against southern England from the northern suburbs of The Hague. Later when the RAF drove them from their fixed sites they used mobile platforms which they set up almost anywhere, sometimes even in the main squares in the centre of the Dutch capital. Frits describes these mobile launchers as huge trucks, something like our tank transporter, only much bigger, and with a much longer trailer. On this trailer was a giant mortar about three feet in diameter and at least thirty feet high. Near the mobile platform was a car which was always closely guarded, and Frits thinks that it contained the highly technical equipment for ranging the V-2s. When the rocket was fired, there was a heavy, dull explosion. The long projectile was hurled one hundred and fifty to two hundred feet into the air by the giant mortar; there it hung suspended for a moment before its engines began to work, and then with a roaring rushing sound it disappeared like a flash.

'However, not all the rockets worked after the initial propulsion from the mortar. Many of them, in fact, Frits estimates that fully a third of them, fell back on The Hague causing a great deal of damage to the city and killing more than two hundred civilians. And so our advance, which is reported to have forced the Germans to withdraw their V weapons, must have brought relief not only to the people of southern England but to the citizens of the Dutch capital as well ...

The monastery at Nijmegen that served as our press camp was a large, ugly, brick building. It was cold and draughty, and the public rooms on the main floor were tiled and had all the creature comforts of a public lavatory. Yet I have pleasant memories of this unsightly abbey, largely because I shared a monk's cell with Tim Matson, the publisher of the *Victoria Colonist*. I knew Tim, more by reputation than by anything else, as a wealthy playboy whose escapades had been the subject of much gossip; he had had some journalistic experience, having worked as a reporter on the *Toronto Star* and inherited the *Colonist*, which his family owned. He had taken to me perhaps because I was the only person whom he knew in the press camp; also, publishers who came over on junkets for a visit to the front, as Matson had done, were not welcomed by the regular war correspondents.

Although we had never gone on parties together in Victoria, we had shared some girlfriends, one of whom had become his third wife (he regaled me with some humorous accounts of that marriage, which had failed). Tim was an entertaining fellow and an amusing raconteur; he was older than I and the sort of club man whom I had never really known. At any rate, we had a great time, after lights out, lampooning the social life in Victoria. It was really scandalous gossip, but therapeutic after a tense day at the front, and we laughed so hard that we almost fell out of our camp-beds. Fortunately, the walls of our cell were so thick that nobody overheard us.

Since I was now on my own as the correspondent of the *Daily Herald*, I was not, of course, entitled to use CBC transportation. (In fact, Matthew Halton and Marcel Ouimet were both at the camp, and they had the heavy utility van and the portable recording equipment; as might be expected, they covered Monty's assault on the Rhine for the CBC.) There had to be two correspondents to a jeep, and I found this to be a very good system, since the army PR was careful not to put together competitors (in my case, another

British reporter), and two heads were always better than one in digging up stories. So I had as my first driving companion the Associated Press correspondent, Ned Nordness.

Ned, a lean, intense fellow, had a very good contact in the American liaison group at Canadian army headquarters, and he was to tip us off on the first-ever conference between the Germans and the Allies, the so-called food conference. Meanwhile, we tried to keep up with the Canadian advance; the infantry was moving forward through the wet countryside, but the tanks were of limited use because of the flooding. The Germans had opened the sluice gates and had even breached the great dykes holding back the Zuider Zee. It soon became apparent to us that the real story was that the Dutch people were being starved to death, particularly in what was known as the Fortress Holland area, which included the great cities of Amsterdam, Rotterdam, and The Hague.

At Apeldoorn, a city in the middle of the country, I got some inkling of the shortages in the prices that had to be paid for staple commodities: $4 a loaf for black bread, $15 a pound for sugar, $85 a pound for coffee (if you could get it), and $600 a ton for coal. Apparently, the prices were two to three times higher in Amsterdam, or so I was told by a woman who had been evacuated from that city. She had a servant and was quite well off, but, as I reported to the CBC, all she could give her three children for supper was a not very appetizing but very expensive stew of beans and potatoes. In order to survive, the Dutch had to go into the country on buying expeditions, and, as I said, the new wealthy class in the Netherlands were the farmers: 'they had most of the clothes and their wives most of the jewels in the land.'

I quoted a Canadian corporal as saying that it was terrible to see the hunger of the people here (in Apeldoorn), and that he had never seen anything like it anywhere. He spoke of grown-up men and women trampling on children and fighting over a box of hardtack. It was obvious that something had to be done quickly if the Dutch people were not to suffer a major disaster. As it was, thousands died of starvation, and when I visited Amsterdam, I saw the effects of malnutrition in the walking skeletons and, in the morgues, 'sights as horrible as any in the death camps of Belsen and Buchenwald.' The poor suffered the most, since they could not afford the prices on the black market.

The American liaison officer who was Ned Nordness's main contact kept telling us that something big was going to happen, and on a sunny day at the end of April he was more explicit, advising us to be at Nijmegen airport at around ten in the morning when a Very Important Person would be arriving. We stood by our jeep on the edge of the muddy field and watched General Bedell Smith, Eisenhower's chief of staff, step out of a Dakota, followed by a number of high-ranking officers, including a Russian general. They got into a row of staff cars and drove off the field in convoy, preceded by a jeep full of security guards and a couple of motor- cycle police. We tagged along behind the two motorcycles bringing up the rear, but when we stopped in a traffic tie-up on the Nijmegen bridge, the MPs signalled us to move forward and took up positions behind us. They had included us with the VIPs, for which we were grateful, because, once we were across the bridge, the convoy took off at great speed, sometimes driving on the wrong side of the road, and we would have had difficulty keeping up.

We drove along the flooded banks of the Grebbe River, the so- called 'Grebbe Line' that divided the Fortress Holland area from the rest of the Netherlands, and came to a halt at a one-storey schoolhouse on the outskirts of the village of Achterveld. Ned and I followed the brass into the building; the classroom where the meeting was held had glass doors, so we could watch the proceed- ings. On one side of the main table were the Allied representatives, including Lieutenant-General Charles Foulkes, the commander of the I Canadian Corps, General Bedell Smith, representing the supreme commander, and Prince Bernhard of the Netherlands. On the other side were the Nazis, headed by the Gauleiter, Seyiss- Inquart, and among them were a tough-looking parachute general and some Dutch civil servants. I could not believe our luck; no one had checked our credentials, but after we had been there some time, a Canadian brigadier spotted our war correspondent flashes and kicked us out.

Still, we had been eyewitnesses to the first conference between the Allies and the Nazis; it was a remarkable scoop, but by the time the censors released my report, Hitler had committed suicide; instead of being on the front page of the *Daily Herald*, it was on page four, which was the back page in those days. The report I did for the CBC sounded so much better; at least there was not the ignominy of being on the back page:

... Now that the news black-out has been lifted I can tell you the full story on the extraordinary conference that resulted in the agreement on feeding the starving Dutch. I was at this dramatic meeting – you know, it was the first full-dress meeting between the Allies and the Nazis in this war. As a matter of fact, Ned Nordness of the Associated Press and myself were the only correspondents to enter the schoolhouse in a little Dutch village on the Grebbe Line and see friend and foe sitting around some rough wooden tables talking instead of fighting. We were in the hallway of the schoolhouse but through glass doors we could see the Gauleiter of Holland, Seyiss-Inquart, General Eisenhower's chief of staff, General Bedell Smith, and other delegates. We were so close that I almost bumped into Seyiss-Inquart when he came into the hallway during the luncheon break. He limped past me to the room where the Germans were to eat. A heavy, almost gross man, wearing thick glasses, the Gauleiter looked baffled and beaten, and I couldn't help wondering if this were the same Nazi who had turned Austria over to Hitler and had run Holland like a feudal province ...

The delegates from the enemy side included several Dutch representatives, mostly civil servants from the former Netherlands government, who had stayed in office because, as they explained to me, someone had to run the country. The Dutch were no collaborators and refused to ride in the same cars as the Germans to the conference ...

There were no armistice negotiations at this meeting, and the parachute general made it clear that the Germans would continue to hold out. All that was done was to establish safe corridors for the food trucks and dropping zones for the cargo planes, but this concession meant a great deal to the 3.5 million starving Dutch in the Fortress Holland area – in many cases the difference between life and death.

Some days later, on 5 May, there was a conference on the

surrender of the German forces in Holland, and this time the war correspondents were invited to watch the proceedings. Once again, General Foulkes was the chief Canadian delegate and Prince Bernhard was at the table; opposite were Wehrmacht officers headed by General Johannes Blaskowitz, the commander-in-chief of all the German forces in the Netherlands. General Blaskowitz was a hard-looking professional soldier who showed little emotion, although we heard some time later that he had committed suicide. We wondered whether he was humiliated by the fact that he had to surrender to General Foulkes, a mere corps commander when he, General Blaskowitz, was an army commander. (It is more likely that Blaskowitz killed himself because of remorse over his failure as a commanding officer and the humiliating surrender of his troops. Such was the zeal and the commitment of the German general staff that, according to the British war historian Max Hastings, more than 100 German generals committed suicide towards the end of the Second World War. At least one of them, Field Marshal Erwin Rommel, was forced to kill himself.)

After that conference we moved into the Fortress Holland area, and the Canadian press camp was set up in a small hotel at Utrecht. The war was over, and the next few days were a jumble of victory parades, wildly cheering crowds, and even the odd skirmish between Dutch Resistance forces and German ss troops. The celebration began before we reached Utrecht, when a joyous mob descended on us and almost took over our jeep. I was pushed to one side, and the next thing I knew a pretty blonde girl had squeezed next to me and was stuffing golden tulips into my raincoat, and a boy was sitting on my knee. There must have been thirty or forty people on our jeep and trailer, and more were trying to get on as we entered Utrecht. I cannot remember the exact day-to-day sequence of events, but I know that I visited Amsterdam, Rotterdam, and The Hague.

It was in Amsterdam that we ran into some nasty street fighting. I should mention that Ned Nordness had left on another assignment, and I now had Bill Boni, also with Associated Press, as my driving companion. We drove around the Royal Museum, the German police headquarters, where Nazis stood sullenly on guard.

Everywhere there had been huge crowds, but they faded away when we reached the centre of town where there was the sound of rifle fire. The Germans were shooting from buildings around the Royal Palace, and I could see bodies lying at the end of the road. We turned down a side street, where a squad of men wearing blue overalls and steel helmets stood outside a Dutch Resistance headquarters: the commanding officer blamed the German SS troops for opening fire. In retrospect, however, it was more likely that some glory-seeking Resistance men had attacked the Germans, who had the right to defend themselves. Under the terms of the agreement, the enemy was to surrender to the Allies, not to guerrillas.

The crowds seemed to grow larger everywhere we went, and since it was tulip time, the Dutch threw tulips at our troops; a well-aimed bunch of tulips could hit with quite a smack. Johnny Canuck, the ordinary Canadian soldier, was treated like a hero or a film star; he was mobbed by an adoring public, hugged and kissed by pretty girls, and he even had to sign autographs. War correspondents like me shared in his glory, quite undeservingly, and the only excuse I could make was that we were surrogates for all the troops who could not take part in the liberation. Of course, it was fun. But it could be trying. I remember the stupefied smiles on the faces of a couple of Canadian soldiers who were being carried shoulder high by several jubilant Dutchmen. I suppose I looked equally ridiculous when I was carried up the steps of the city hall in Rotterdam. It was the most undignified and embarrassing experience, and I got down as quickly as I could.

Utrecht, Holland, 8 May 1945, 8 a.m.:
The fighting ends with the unconditional surrender of Germany. The Allies celebrate the victory in Europe, VE Day.

I remember standing with other correspondents in the front yard of the hotel that was the Canadian press camp, listening to the news on the radio of the CBC recording van. No one said much. After all, we had been celebrating victory here in Holland for the last two or three days. Bill Boni and I got into our jeep, which was already occupied by several Dutch civilians, including the blonde girl who had stuffed tulips into my raincoat. We headed for the capital, The Hague. On the outskirts we were slowed down by a dense crowd, and a young Dutchman leaped onto the hood of the jeep and announced from this perch that he was going to be our guide. If my memory is right, he was a journalist; at any rate, he was a stickler for protocol, and he took us to the Royal Palace first and insisted that we sign the visitor's book. I have always claimed that my name was the second in the book.

Then, he showed us the way to the city hall. I should have twigged that something was up by the orderly crowd and the serried ranks of the children, all freshly scrubbed and in their Sunday best. Our guide led Bill and me up the steps and through the hall, past smartly saluting resistance men, to the council chamber. There, in the richly panelled room, were all the city fathers standing in a half circle behind the burgomaster, who was resplendent in his chain of office. It was like a painting by Rembrandt. The burgomaster stepped forward, a smile of welcome on his face and his hand out, but our Dutch conductor whispered: 'Correspondents.' The smile left the burgomaster's face, I cannot remember whether he shook my hand. It was obvious that I had been mistaken for Lieutenant-General Guy Simonds. I told the burgomaster that I was sure that the general would arrive soon.

We left the council chamber and walked through the hall past the saluting Resistance men. The wheels of the official welcome had started and nothing could stop them now. When we reached the city hall's steps, I had a moment of panic when I realized that the well-behaved children whom we had seen when we arrived were massed school choirs. We had to stand stiffly to attention while they sang not only the Dutch national anthem but the anthems of all the western Allies. I felt such a fool, standing there accepting these heartfelt tributes when I had no right to them. We did not give our Dutch guide a chance to explain that we were impostors, since we shoved him back onto the hood of the jeep and took off as quickly and as gracefully as possible, waving to the cheering children.

Shortly after this episode I returned to London, because the *Daily Herald* wanted me to cover the liberation of Norway. Our Dakota, packed with correspondents and a couple of British PR types, was landed at Oslo airport by the Luftwaffe. In fact, we were driven downtown by the Wehrmacht in one of their buses. The British had taken the surrender of the German forces in Norway, but there were not enough of them on the ground to look after details such as transportation or traffic control at the airport. Except for the driver of our bus, however, there were no Germans to be seen on the streets; they were already mostly in POW holding camps.

We were in Oslo for the Norwegian national day, 17 May, and there was an Allied victory parade up the Karl Johans Gate to the royal palace. In connection with this celebration, I should mention that the press office was across the street from the Grand Hotel and in the same building that the Nazis had used for the press. One day I was leafing through some old periodicals, leftovers from the previous regime, when I came upon an illustrated magazine that had pictures of a German parade up the Karl Johans Gate, and the crowd on the street seemed to be just the same size as the crowd that cheered the Allied victory parade. Were they the same people? Perhaps they had had to turn out, but there seemed to be an ambivalance in attitude towards the Nazis. The Norwegians were certainly better off than the Dutch, and the Nazi puppet premier, Vidkund Quisling, took full credit, claiming that he had had to fight hard against the Germans to preserve the national welfare. There was no starvation, or none that I saw; the people had had an adequate diet, if a fishy one, and almost every place stank of fish, including the Grand Hotel. The Nazis had not been as harsh with Norway as they had been with other occupied countries; they had let the famous septuagenarian artist Gustav Vigeland continue his work in the small park devoted to his sculpture until his death in 1943, but the extraordinary columns of writhing human figures were the sort of art that Hitler would have approved of.

However, Quisling could protest as much as he liked that everyone had fled and there was no one but himself to deal with the Nazis, but that assertion would not ultimately save him. I found that the Norwegian government, which had been brought back to Norway by the British, was not highly regarded at the time of liberation; it had spent most of the war in Britain and suffered in comparison with the Danish government, which had remained in Copenhagen during the whole of the occupation. Quite clearly, the returning government had to restore its popularity and legitimacy, and Quisling was the best means to that end. He was arrested, charged with high treason, and brought to trial at the end of August. I covered the Quisling trial, which was the first of the so-called war-crimes trials. It was the end of the war, and public sentiment at the time was to hang all collaborators. War-crimes trials were strictly for losers and had as much justice as the inquisition's *auto-da-fé*. There was never any doubt of the outcome: Quisling was executed in October 1945.

Quisling was indeed guilty of high treason. Yet he was not as bad as his name, which, perhaps because of its sound to Anglo-Saxon ears, had become an eponym for a member of any enemy-sponsored government. He was no ordinary collaborator, because he had been prominent politically before the war: Quisling had been a protégé of Nansen, had had a brilliant military career, and was Norwegian defence minister in the 1930s before forming his own National Unity or Nazi party. There was always an escape route for Quisling, but when the Belgian Rexist leader, Léon Degrelle,* flew to Oslo the day before the end and begged him to accompany him to Spain, Quisling angrily turned him down. He would not desert his people, he said. He was convinced that he was a patriot.

---

*Léon Degrelle was condemned to death in absentia. When Belgium applied to Spain for his extradition, Franco refused. The Spanish dictator asserted that Degrelle was a colonel in the German army, while the extradition treaty was only for criminals. Actually DeGrelle was a Waffen SS General. He was in the news again in 1991 as a proponent of the neo-Nazi movement in Spain.

16

Hitler's Spoon and Fork

Berlin, 11 July 1945:
The Soviets today turned over to the British and Americans the sectors of the city allocated to them at Yalta – then the British and Americans assigned part of their sectors to the French.

That victory parade on Norway's national day, 17 May 1945, was one of the last. The enormous crowds that had celebrated liberation in Holland had gone home; the tumult and the cheering had ended. There had been the odd skirmish after VE Day, but by 11 May the last shots had been fired – except in the Balkans, where there was undefined guerrilla warfare. An eerie and portentous silence settled over the ravaged reaches of Europe; nobody knew what peace would bring. There were grim forebodings of Nazi werewolves skulking in the ruins, but they turned out to be the sort of bogeymen with which one frightened the gullible.

There was one loose end, however, and that was Berlin. The western Allies were due to enter Berlin and take over the sectors of the city that had been allocated to them at the Yalta Conference; but there were delays as they sought permission from the Russians, who had completed the investment of the city on 2 May.

The *Daily Herald* wanted me to cover our entry into Berlin, which was to be the last great story of the Second World War in Europe. Although I had expected this assignment, I was none the less pleased, because it would be a fitting end to my work as a war correspondent: to be able to add the German capital, the real power base of the Axis, to Rome, that other and secondary Axis capital. Little did I realize how long I would have to wait.

After a too-short stay in London, I was back with the troops, who were now reluctantly acting as occupation forces in Germany. There was already a clamour among the Canadians to get home, and the authorities, remembering the repatriation riots of the First World War, were doing their best to round up the necessary shipping. It was a tough job because they had to compete with the Americans, who had a lot more clout. The British press camp was in a building that looked like a large barn on the outskirts of a town on the North German plain called Herford, near Hamelin, of Pied Piper fame, not far from Hanover. The building had been some kind of hostel – 'probably for slave labour' was the sour view of the correspondents.

I was there for almost five weeks, and I had never been so bored. There was really nothing to do but wait for the Russians, who were notorious for procrastinating, to give us the green light. Non-fraternization was the order of the day, and while it was never really enforced, it was not officially lifted until months later, in October, and even then marriage or living with Germans was still *verboten*. All that non-fraternization – one of the more stupid policies of the victorious Allies – accomplished was to increase the venereal disease rate among the troops by almost 50 per cent: the private soldiers were afraid to ask for prophylactics. In any case, Herford was hardly the place for much in the way of fun and games. Nearby was a broken-down spa, Bad Oeynhausen, where we could go for a swim in a muddy outdoor pool.

There was one false alarm, and we rushed some eighty miles to Brunswick, the British assembly area for Berlin. After a couple of days there, listening to the men grumbling about the Russians keeping them out, we returned to Herford. The correspondents blamed the SNAFU on the 'bloody public relations,' which was hardly fair but was a sign of our frustration.

During our stay in the hostel at Herford, British Intelligence brought us eyewitnesses to the death of Hitler; this would be one of the stories that we would be after when we got to Berlin. One was Herman Karnau, the bunker guard, who had been surprised by the delivery of five jerricans of gasoline in the morning of one of the last days, a day in which, he recalled, there was more security than usual. The gasoline, he was told, was for the air ventilation plant, which he knew was 'nonsense.' Although Karnau had been told to stay away, he decided to go down into the bunker, but when he tried the main entrance, which was in the Chancellory, he found the door locked. He made his way out into the garden in order to enter by the emergency exit. What prompted him to brave the Russian shell fire, he did not say. It may have been a premonition. At any rate, he crept along the concrete side of the bunker and took cover in a 'dog shelter' near the emergency exit. It was then that he was astonished to see two bodies lying on the ground a few feet away from him. Suddenly, they burst into flames. Karnau could not explain this spontaneous combustion, but guessed rightly that someone had thrown a burning torch from the emergency exit onto the gas-soaked corpses. They were easily recognizable, Eva Braun, and Hitler, whose head was smashed, and was, according to Karnau, a repulsive sight.

Another witness was Eric Kempka, Hitler's chauffeur. He had carried Eva Braun's body part of the way from the bunker to the cremation site. (Eva Braun, who had married the Führer on the day before, took poison, while Hitler shot himself through the mouth.) Kempka had been with the small group of mourners who had stood in the shelter of the emergency exit and watched the five jerricans of gasoline poured over the Führer and his bride; he was able to confirm Karnau's guess that someone had started the blaze by throwing a torch, actually a gas-soaked rag that had been set alight, onto the corpses.

I was at both these briefings, and I remember that I and the other correspondents were suspicious of the testimony of Karnau and Kempka. After all, they were both in the SS: the lean, blond Karnau looked the part of an Aryan superman, and Kempka was an officer, a Sturmbannführer. Field Marshal Montgomery had characterized the SS as 'war criminals' and asserted that they should be left to rot in concentration camps. It was at a postwar press conference that Monty made this remark, and he was in a righteous and prophetic mood. He had moved his headquarters into one of the many German castles that had survived unscathed, and I remember driving, in a downpour of rain, up a winding gravel road to this dark, medieval fortress and thinking how Wagnerian everything looked. Monty declared that the German general staff should be incarcerated for an indefinite period, and he felt that the Allies would have to maintain occupation forces in Germany for twenty-five years. It was only the latter that we found hard to accept. Twenty-five years! Monty must be off his rocker.

At last, the signal came to enter Berlin. The plans had been changed, however, and we were to go in with the United States forces, not the British. This meant driving most of the night over the twisting Hartz Mountain roads to the American transit camp near Halle. (Actually Halle, which was near Leipzig, was in the Soviet Zone and would be ceded to the Russians later when the boundaries were fixed.) We arrived early in the morning, only to find that the main convoy was moving off before dawn. Another SNAFU. We cursed the army Public Relations while looking in the whitewashed cubicles of this former German barracks for a cot on which to have a few minutes' rest.

The convoy moved jerkily, the vehicle ahead of ours suddenly looming up, its red light blazing, or just as suddenly drawing away. A jeep came alongside, and by its headlights we could see for a moment the long column of vehicles before it disappeared into the darkness. My eyes were stinging from lack of sleep, as I wrote at the time, and my mouth burned with the metal and chlorine taste of army coffee. Our driver was wobbling from fatigue, and I spelled him at the wheel of the heavy utility personnel carrier while he slept. Midsummer's early light found us on the Autobahn to Berlin; we passed high-axled Soviet trucks moving singly or in pairs down the opposite lane. We were held up at a wooden bridge that the Russians had built across the Elbe, and, just beyond, we ran into a mass of Red Army troops on foot or in horse-drawn wagons. It seemed like a Tartar horde.

We started on this final journey of the war on 1 July, and I thought that this would have been an appropriate day for the Canadians to enter the enemy capital. (The Canadians were to have been part of the occupation force in Berlin, and a brigade group was formed for this purpose; however, it was disbanded in mid-June. The British had decided, after protracted negotiations with the Russians, that the condition of the city was such that there would be no room for other nations' troops. At any rate, they were not too keen to have any 'dominion' or 'colonial' troops sharing this prize. So a composite battalion was formed from elements of the Loyal Edmonton Regiment, Les Fusiliers Mont-Royal, and the Argyll and Sutherland Highlanders of Canada, including the pipe band of the last-named, but this token detachment did not enter Berlin until 4 July. After taking part in a couple of victory parades, it left on 27 July.)

Our first sight of Berlin made us gasp: I had seen a lot of destruction in my time as a war correspondent but not on this horrifying scale. Along the great boulevards like the Kurfustendamm there were pyramid-shaped piles of rubble, and walls, where they were still standing, were broken ramparts, supporting no roofs and without windows. The reason that the Russians gave for not letting us into Berlin until two months after they had taken the city was that it had to be cleaned up, and the sight of these monstrous ruins made us think they were right. After the Battle of Berlin the streets had been impassable, and there was no water, no electricity. Yet the delay served the Communists well, because it gave them time to remove industrial machinery without any prying westerners around. The greyness of the blasted cityscape was enlivened by red flags and rows of white notice-boards with red lettering:

Die Erfahrungen der Geschichte sagte
Das die Hitler kommen und gehen
Aber das Deutsche Volk, der Deutsche Stadt, Bleiben.

(The experience of history shows
that Hitlers come and go
But the German people and the German state remain.)

'*Die Erfahrungen der Geschichte*' every two hundred yards up the
Kurfustendamm and on other boulevards so that none could fail to
read. There were other notices about the Red Army's being race
free, but the one that remained with me all these years was '*Die
Erfahrungen der Geschichte...*'

A thunderstorm rumbled like a distant salvo of heavy guns as
we drove down the broad east-west axis through the shell-torn
Tiergarten to Unter den Linden. Even nature conspired to make
this conquered capital seem sinister. The streets were so wide that
people looked like ants crawling around the wreckage. Then a
pasty-faced boy came round a corner, whistling and kicking at a
piece of rubble.

The first place we made for was Hitler's Chancellory and the
bunker. The shell holes and broken trees made the Chancellory
garden look like a battlefield, and there, on the gravel outside the
emergency exit to the bunker, amid the uncleared litter of war,
were the rusty and bullet-riddled remains of five jerricans – so
Karnau was right! Nearby was a shallow depression that must
have been where Hitler's and Eva Braun's bodies were burned.
Our Russian guide, Major Platonov, asserted, however, that what
they had found there was Hitler's double, and a 'very poor double,'
he said. Major Feodor Platonov, a tough, squat Red Army officer
whose chest was covered with medals, commanded the shock
troops who had taken the Chancellory.

We went down into the bunker by the emergency exit; I counted
thirty-six steps to a wide main hall that divided the underground
shelter and was used for meetings. Everything was dirty and
greasy, and, just before it was evacuated, there had been a hasty

and half-hearted attempt to fire the bunker. Hitler and Eva Braun had had a suite of rooms, but they were not spacious, and I noted that Hitler's bedroom measured twelve by ten feet. The furnishings were of an ordinary utility type, the sort found in a boarding-house. The Führer's suite was beside the emergency exit, and towards the end of the main hall or conference passage were the cramped quarters of Dr Goebbels and his family; not only Frau Goebbels but his six children were with him; there were two tiered, wooden bunk-beds for them. The Goebbelses had committed suicide on the day after Hitler and Eva Braun had died, and the children were found in their bunk-beds dead from cyanide poisoning. It was all very sordid and squalid, this 'lair of the Nazi beast,' as Churchill called it.

The tour of the Chancellory made me think how Chaplinesque it all looked. Here was the final scene for *The Great Dictator*, just as Chaplin would have wished it: the gaping hole in the magnificent rotunda where a huge bomb had been dropped, Hitler's enormous marble desk thrown over on one side, the walls covered with the Cyrillic signatures of Russian soldiers, the foreign characters of the conquerors from the east, the great chandeliers on the floor of the banqueting hall. But most of all, the little touches: a Hitler bust pitched on its nose, a globe crumpled in the rubble outside, the globe that must have come from Hitler's study, the globe that the 'Great Dictator' had played with, tossing it lightly in the air, and catching it on his back, and the medals cascading down the steps into a small courtyard and covering that courtyard.

I found out that this crazy carpet of medals was the work of SMERSH, Soviet Counter-Intelligence: while searching the building for papers, SMERSH agents had come upon a room stacked with boxes of medals; they picked them up and emptied their contents down the steps and into the courtyard. I collected an assortment of these medals, and they now hang in a frame above my desk; they consist of service medals, including the grim one for the first winter campaign on the Eastern Front, a couple of iron crosses and a bar to the iron cross, SS and SA (brown shirt) decorations, a 1936

Olympic medal, and even a mother's medal! They had been lying on the ground and on the steps for weeks, and the Red Army soldiers had avoided them like the plague, although I found that after we had been in Berlin for a few days one of the Russian guards had picked up some of these medals to exchange them for western cigarettes or chocolates.

But was Hitler really dead? The Russians were tight-lipped about this: as far as they were concerned, it was a political issue; it was certainly a way of keeping the western Allies off balance, and, at the time, the Soviets were afraid that the Anglo-Saxons might gang up with the Nazis against them. There were many Americans from General Patton down who made no secret of their animosity towards the Soviets. Colonel-General Alexander Gorbatov, the head of the Inter-Allied Kommandatura, the man in charge of Berlin, declared at a press conference that the Nazis might be saying that Hitler was dead to put us off the search, or they might say that he was alive to keep up the myth of the Führer. It was the first press conference that any Soviet official had given, and the Red Army general, who had the round face of a Russian peasant, handled it with consummate ease. 'If Hitler were alive,' he assured sixty western correspondents who filled a carpeted hall at the Russian headquarters on the Luisenstrasse, 'He is not in the Soviet Zone.'

Yet it was reported that the Russians had hinted at dental evidence of Hitler's death, and that these allegations had been broadcast over the Soviet-controlled German radio station, the Deutschland Sender. As soon as we heard this report – and I should explain that for part of the time in Berlin I was fortunate enough to share a jeep with Henry Brandon of the *Sunday Times*, who spoke several languages and had some excellent contacts – we set out to find the office of Dr Hugo Blaschke, Hitler's dentist: It was on the Kurfustendamm and had somehow survived the Allied saturation raids and concentrated Russian shelling. A sumptuous place amid the ruins. The reception room looked like a fashionable drawing-room, with period furniture and tapestries hanging on the panelled walls. There we met Dr Fedor Bruck, a Jewish dentist who had succeeded Dr Blaschke – it seemed incredible, but there were cases of Jews being protected by leading Nazis as a kind of insurance in the event of defeat.

I remember Dr Bruck as a soberly dressed, little man, standing speaking to us while we sat on an Empire couch and scribbled down his every word. As he talked, Dr Bruck kept consulting a black notebook. A week after Berlin fell, he said, a Red Army officer and a woman interpreter came around to the clinic and wanted to see anyone who had worked on Hitler's teeth. Dr Blaschke had fled to the west, but his assistant, Frau Kathe Heusermann, and a dental technician named Fritz Echtmann, were located without any difficulty. The Russians wanted to know whether they could identify Hitler's teeth. Frau Heusermann said she could, and the technician Echtmann said that he had made for the Führer's mouth a bridge that was unique. So they were taken to Soviet headquarters in East Berlin and a couple of days later returned home.

After the visit to Soviet headquarters, Frau Heusermann came round to see him, Dr Bruck said, glancing at his notebook, and he described her as being in a highly nervous state. She confessed that she had been shown Hitler's teeth and she was convinced that he was dead. However, what alarmed her most was being told by a Russian colonel that she was the only person who could prove that Hitler was dead. A few days later, according to Dr Bruck, the Soviet officers returned and ordered Frau Heusermann and the technician Echtmann to pack their bags, since they were required for further interrogation. That was almost two months ago and they had not returned. I should point out that both Frau Heusermann and Echtmann were members of the SS – all of those close to Hitler or on his staff had to be members of the SS – and therefore could be held as prisoners of war.

(It was not till more than twenty years later that the Russians were to admit that they had incontrovertible proof of Hitler's death. The dental evidence that they hinted at in a Berlin broadcast back in May 1945 and the actual autopsy report made by a Red Army commission are in Lev Bezymenski's *The Death of Adolf Hitler*, together with some gruesome pictures of Hitler's and Eva Braun's teeth and their remains, and the corpses of Dr

Goebbels and his children. The slim volume was published in 1968 – was the American edition expurgated? Lev Bezymenski, a journalist and German scholar on Marshal Zhukov's staff, served as interpreter at the interrogation of Field Marshal Paulus, who surrendered the German Sixth Army to the Russians after the Battle of Stalingrad. Bezymenski mentions Dr Bruck in his book and writes at length about the dental evidence of Frau Heusermann and the technician Echtmann. He does not say anything about their fate.)

The Americans had set up a combined western press camp in the outer and hardly damaged suburb of Zehlendorf. The correspondents were quartered in requisitioned apartment buildings around the main square, and I was assigned a dark flat up two flights of stairs. My room had so many heavy pieces of furniture, chests of drawers and wardrobes, that I could get into the bed only by crawling over the end. Horsehair oozed out of the broken leather chairs in the living-room, and there was no way of stopping the dining table from tipping. The flush toilet was primitive, but at least it worked; the iron bathtub, red with rust, was never used, since there was no hot water. The only thing to be said for this dreary accommodation was that it was directly opposite the restaurant that had been taken over by the U.S. army as a communal dining hall.

It was definitely 'chow' that was served at this American establishment: flapjacks for breakfast and cocoa and peanut butter with almost any meal. The British correspondents did not appreciate this fare. Furthermore, they regarded the six o'clock time for dinner as being 'positively barbaric.' As soon as they could, they set up their own press quarters in the small Hotel Amzoo on the Kurfustendamm, one of the few hotels that was still standing in the city. The British major who was the manager – a mild-mannered man known as 'The Slasher,' the generic pseudonym of any major in the army service corps – saw to it that there was a well-stocked bar and waiters in 'tails' who served dinner at eight. The different times at which the Allies ate made a friend of mine on the Control Commission in Berlin remark: 'How can we ever get

together when the Americans have dinner at six o'clock, the
British at eight, the French at ten and the Russians at midnight?'

One advantage of having dinner at six was that it left time for
the night-life, and we were intrigued to find that nightclubs and
bars were flourishing amid the ruins. We found nothing like them
in the British Zone, and in fact the Germans there clung stubborn-
ly to Hitler's post-Stalingrad order not to dance. There was something appealing and yet sinister about these places of gaiety when
all around them were death and destruction. As I reported: 'A
common street scene is of a black coffin on a hand cart being
dragged to a cemetery. On the road side an obelisk with a red star
marks a Russian grave. Everywhere is the sickly sweet smell of
death rising from the ruins or from clogged and poisonous canals.'
Most of the nightclubs were in the vicinity of the Kurfustendamm;
they were not makeshift dives but famous pre-war places, such as
the Kabaret der Komikar and the Femina, which had come through
the bombing with minimum damage. The night-clubs opened early
and closed at ten o'clock to allow civilians to get home before the
eleven o'clock curfew. Prices were not exorbitant: for a glass of
watered red wine I paid 4.50 marks, which at the official rate of
exchange would have been a little more than $2; at the black
market rate it would have been 20 cents.

At the Femina there was a mistress of ceremonies who announced the cabaret turns in Russian, English, French, and
German, and in that order. A portrait of Stalin had hung behind
the bandstand, but that had been removed because the Femina
was now in the British sector. Eventually, Red Army soldiers were
to stay away and the quadra-lingual MC was to go, but when we
visited the Femina, a good number of Russians were there, as well
as British and American soldiers and German girls. Non-fraternization had become the subject of jokes, which the mistress of
ceremonies made only in English because the Soviet soldiers would
have found them completely incomprehensible. I noted that the
Berlin ladies were well dressed, although mostly in black; some of
them had on wide-brimmed hats, also black, while many had old-
fashioned page-boy bobs.

Non-fraternization, which was meant to express the chins-up, nose-in-the-air superiority of the Allied forces, served a puritanical purpose – when it was suggested that the troops should be allowed to say 'Good morning' to German girls, Field Marshal Montgomery turned the proposal down, saying that it would probably not stop there but lead to liaisons. This ridiculous attempt to impose morality could not survive the nightclubs and bars in Berlin; the British and American soldiers were soon dancing with German girls and dating them, and no one, not even the formidable Monty, could put a stop to this wholesale abuse of non-fraternization.

The German women came on their own to the nightclub. As the girl who spoke English at our table said, they had no work and were bored and looking for a good time. In any case, there were virtually no male escorts in Berlin, no husbands to be ignored, as the Italian husbands were in Rome. Most of the German men I encountered were too old to serve in the final and hopeless Nazi defence of the city, and that meant they were very old indeed. The women of Berlin appeared to be even more available than the women of Rome. They almost threw themselves into the arms of the British, Americans, and Canadians (even though the latter were in Berlin for a short time) as if they were seeking protection from the barbaric Slavic hordes – and, in fact, they said they were. It was almost impossible to talk to one of the women without being told about some person, not usually herself, who had been raped many times by Russian soldiers. Some of the stories were undoubtedly true, but others were exaggerated, if not fabricated, so that they seemed part of a deliberate campaign to divide the Allies.

It was true that, as conquerors, the Russians behaved more like Tartars or Mongols, and yet, when all was said and done, they had treated the Germans harshly but humanely compared with the brutal manner in which those civilized Europeans, the Germans, had treated the Russians when the roles were reversed and the Germans were the conquerors. But the fact was that the ladies had been going to the Femina before the British arrived and removed Stalin's portrait from behind the bandstand; they had been going there for one purpose: to meet the Red Army men. Still the stories of rape did have an effect on people like my British army driver: they increased his antipathy towards the 'goddamned Russkies.' And that was what they were meant to do. The only apparent difference between the women of Rome and the women of Berlin was that the former seemed to me to be more elegant and better off, and that was because Rome was an 'Open City,' while Berlin was not and was destroyed.

The Kabaret der Komikar and the Femina were where Lale Andersen and Iwa Wanje, the wife of Norbert Schultze the composer, sang 'Lili Marlene' when it was at the height of its popularity and fame. Now the Germans did not want to hear the song, and only the Allied soldiers hummed and sang it. When we entered Berlin, however, there was another song being sung in the cabarets that was said to have as great an appeal and just as catchy a tune as 'Lili Marlene.' It was called 'Berlin kommt wieder:'

Berlin will rise again,
To be sure not over night.
But as after the dark night
The sun comes up again;
So will the lindens bloom
In Unter den Linden.
Berlin is still Berlin!'

Even the English translation had an emotional impact, and when Brigette Mira, the curly-haired little chanteuse, sang 'Berlin kommt wieder,' the German girls at the little round tables in the Femina broke down and wept. Within a few days, we heard that the British military government had banned the song and had kicked Brigette Mira plus band out of the nightclub. We reporters tracked down the composer, Heino Gaze, and when he asked why 'Berlin kommt wieder' should be suppressed, we said that the British felt that it was a bit arrogant to have a song about Berlin rising again so shortly after the surrender. The composer looked bemused. 'Well, gentlemen,' Heino Gaze said, 'the Russians asked me to write it.' In the aftermath of taking the city, the Soviets had ordered all artists to open theatres, write songs, and raise the spirits of the people.

The banning of 'Berlin kommt wieder' was an example of the obduracy and pigheadedness of the British military government. These same officials, many of whom were veterans of the Indian civil service, had ordered the dissolution of the pre-Hitler German Labour Congress, which had been revived by anti-Nazi trade union leaders just released from concentration camps. The reason given for this action was that there was too much politics in the Gewerkschaft and politics could not be tolerated in Germany at the present time. In contrast, the Russians allowed the restoration of not only the Communists and Socialists but the Christian Democrats and all parties as long as they were anti-Fascist. In fact, a Christian Democrat, Andreas Hermes, was named the food administrator for Berlin, but when this gentleman became too friendly with the Americans, he was denounced by General Gorbatov as an undercover Nazi. We did not at first know whom the Red Army commander was accusing, since he called him 'Germes'; then we realized that in Russian the 'H' was pronounced as 'G.' Thus, in the demonology of the Soviets, the letter 'G' was a predominant factor because, for them, there were Gitler, Goebbels, Goering, Gimmler, Gess, and now Germes.

It was the first time that the British and American military had to work with the Red Army, and the western officers did not know quite how to behave. On one occasion they were patronizing and demanding, and on another, they were cooperative to the point of obsequiousness. They had been so anxious to get into Berlin that, as one correspondent said, they had come 'barging in without any agreement on the most important civic issues.' The British troops arrived in Berlin to find that there were no orders or plans for billeting them. But more serious was the fact that no arrangements whatsoever had been made for feeding the 1.65 million people in the western sectors (900,000 in the British sector, 750,000 in the U.S. sector, and 1.1 million in the Soviet sector).

Added to the population of Berlin were the DPs (displaced persons) and refugees. Some 25–30,000 arrived every day in the city; they were put up at camps for the night, given a meal, and then ordered to move on. The ragged, hungry refugees, most of whom were women and children, were among the millions of Germans (the estimate I was given was 6 million) who had been driven out of East Prussia and Danzig and the part of Silesia turned over to Poland. It was said at the time to be the greatest march or migration in history, and vast numbers who had been fleeing the Red Army had been on the move for months.

The British and Americans had blithely taken it for granted that the Russians would continue to provision the whole city, including their sectors. When they found out that the Soviets intended to do no such thing, an American officer and former Chicago advertising agent, Brigadier-General Howley, cried out, 'We may as well go home. There's no point in our staying.' The 'Howler,' as he was known, was reprimanded for this outburst.

As long as there was no agreement on food and fuel, the Russians continued to run Berlin, and the ultimate authority was Colonel-General Gorbatov. The city had always lived off the surrounding countryside, and the rations provided by the Russians, which were considered adequate, came mostly from the Soviet Zone, although some of it was from Red Army supplies. The British and Americans complained that if they had to feed and fuel their sectors from their zones, it would mean a haul of more than 100 miles on the Autobahn. But that was what they had to do. It was not until ten days after we entered Berlin that an agreement was reached and the British and Americans could take over full military control of their sectors. (Then they were able to allocate a part of their sectors to the French.) A high-level meeting of the Control Commission, with Marshal George Zhukov present, decided that until the British and Americans could organize the movement of supplies from their zones, the Russians would continue to feed the whole population of Berlin (estimated at that time to be 2.75 million compared with pre-war 4.25 million). Afterward, I quoted the British commander, Major-

General L.O. Lyne, as saying, 'We reached complete unanimity on everything we discussed.'

In retrospect, it seems incredible that the British and Americans had entered Berlin, as stipulated by the Big Three at Yalta, without any understanding, let alone agreement, on who was to feed and fuel their sectors. The confusion that this oversight caused, despite the sweet words about pleasant and friendly meetings, only increased the already deeply felt antagonism of the westerners towards the Soviets, and this resentment was one of the major factors that led to the beginning of the Cold War.

The Allied confrontation occurred at a time of general moral breakdown. For Berliners, their excuse was the terrible, cataclysmic end of the war; yet the enormous extent of the ruins, the mountainous piles of rubble being cleared at a snail's pace by bucket brigades of women, had an effect on the conquerors as well as the conquered.

A black market flourished at the Alexanderplatz, in the centre of the city, and beside the monumental ruins of the Gedechneskirche, and at almost any street corner. British and American soldiers were actively involved in exchanging pounds and dollars for marks; a week after we entered Berlin I reported that the black-market rate for the pound sterling was 500 marks or for the dollar at least 120 marks, and rising. The mark would soon become valueless and the main currency would be cigarettes. Above a dance hall on the Kurfustendamm was a signboard that read 'Alles für zehn Cigaretten' ('Everything for ten cigarettes'). While the slogan did not say so, the implication was that that was the price for sex. The German girls did it for cigarettes, for chocolates, for the small creature comforts that the victors could provide, and also for their own pleasure.

Anything of intrinsic value, such as watches or jewellery or cameras, fetched many more cigarettes. At a black market on the broken steps of the blasted Reichstag, I was offered a gold ring for 100 cigarettes. One could pay 500 cigarettes or more for a Rolleiflex or Leica camera. It was all a question of supply and demand, and cameras were in great demand. The black market grew exponentially with the arrival of the British and Americans in Berlin; in a short time the conquered city crawled with black marketeers, like a rotting carcase with maggots; they could be easily identified by their briefcases, those former badges of respectability, now the instruments of illicit barter. As might be expected, it was condemned by the palatines of the military government as reprehensible and sinful. Yet, at the same time, the black market could be said to be the first stirring of commercial activity in the devastation of Berlin.

Some of the cigarettes that were used as currency were actually smoked, but I found out that most were not when I visited a black-market centre. I climbed up the cement steps of a large apartment block just off the Kurfustendamm to a sparsely furnished room on the second floor whose windows and part of the wall had been blown out. There I met three well-dressed young men; they might have been Germans who had somehow escaped capture, although they said they were Bulgarians. One of them spoke English, and he assured me that business was good; as proof, he opened a couple of trunks which were full of cigarettes, cartons of Camels and Lucky Strike, packages of Players and Sweet Caporals, and loose cigarettes in shoe boxes. The trunks were the equivalent of bank vaults, and with their contents these black marketeers could get anything, including the flashy clothes they wore. Quite obviously, the cigarette had a certain value, whereas the mark was nothing but a dirty piece of paper; it was a substitute for currency when there was chaos and the economy had collapsed. The cigarette had become the wampum for the losers in the Second World War.

It was with cigarettes that the soldiers could get souvenirs, although most were looted or 'liberated,' and souvenirs meant a great deal to the Canadian, the British, the American, and even the Russian soldiers; souvenirs were a benefit, perhaps the only benefit, that they got out of having fought in the Second World War. I doubt if the cameraman who shared the apartment where I was billeted in Zehlendorf had spent any cigarettes on the pile of junk that he had accumulated. War photographers, or cameramen as they preferred to be called, were among the most dedicated looters. When they had shot their pictures and sent them off to their agencies, they were free to scour the ruins; whereas we reporters, after we had got our stories, had to write them.

This cameraman, who went by the name of George, stacked his collection against the wall by his kitbag. Among the souvenirs he had obtained were a dirty, rumpled SS officer's jacket, a doorknob from Hitler's Chancellory, a large Nazi standard of faded rose colour with some gold insignia embroidered on it, a German water bottle, assorted Nazi badges and medals, some German government papers that he could not read but that he was convinced were of great historical value, and his latest addition, a large piece of twisted metal that he said came off Hitler's car. I thought of the souvenirs that I had collected: the Luger pistol that had been given me by the officer in charge of the prisoner-of-war dump in Holland and the Zeiss binoculars and Austrian compass obtained in the same way. (The Luger pistol was a prize possession, but I left it behind in my room in London and it was stolen – I hate to think what was done with it.) When George left our gloomy quarters in Zehlendorf, he took home with him a quarter-hundredweight of souvenirs.

That was well after our expedition to Hitler's bunker. One evening, when I had finished my work and had eaten the tasteless hamburgers covered with glutinous gravy dished up at the U.S. army's communal dining-hall, George broached the subject of going to Hitler's bunker and seeing what we could find. It would be a waste of time, I said; the visiting brass and the military government boys would have picked it clean. But George was sure that there would be lots left, and I thought, what the hell, it would be something to do, and I would like to see the bunker again before it was destroyed. (It was blown up, but not until some time later.) So we set out in the jeep past the miles of awesome ruins, which that had become so familiar now that we did not notice them, to the last 'lair of the Nazi beast.'

When we reached the Chancellory garden, we found some British and American soldiers walking around with their heads down, like bloodhounds searching for a scent; every now and then they would stop to pick up a piece of film-strip or paper or other refuse that littered the shell-torn grounds; these were sought after as souvenirs. A couple of Red Army soldiers, who were no more than pimply-faced youths, lounged against the rough, unfinished sides of the bunker. We entered by the emergency exit; it was dark, and although we had a flashlight, I remembered there were thirty-six steps and carefully counted them. A dank odour of decay greeted us as we neared the bottom. We found a crowd of British, American, and Russian officers and other ranks rummaging around in the narrow confines of the bunker; the dim light of a single, naked bulb was augmented by burning torches of rolled paper. I looked around Hitler's rooms, and, as I expected, there was nothing left – the most prized souvenirs were silver ashtrays with the Führer's signature engraved on them (which was ironic, because Hitler did not smoke and did not allow smoking in his presence), and of course they had long been taken.

The atmosphere was fetid and becoming so smoky from the burning torches that my eyes began to sting. We pushed our way through the soldiers along the wide passage that had served as a conference hall to the rooms where Dr Goebbels and his family had lived and died. George wanted a piece of the bunk-beds where the children had been poisoned and made known his wish in sign language to a Red Army man who had a crowbar, and he quickly broke off a post for him. I was becoming desperate because I could see nothing that I wanted, and I had to have something to show that I had been in the bunker. At the end of the passage where there were dining-tables we found a butler's pantry, and there on a greasy sideboard was a box full of dirty, almost black spoons, forks, and knives, kitchenware, or so it seemed. I figured that they were the only souvenirs that I was likely to find, so I took a spoon and fork; the cameraman grabbed a handful. Later when I cleaned off the grime and soot, I found that my spoon and fork were silverware: one had the German eagle embossed on it and belonged to the old Chancellory set, while the other had 'A.H.' engraved on it and was part of the new set struck for Adolf Hitler.

We made our way back through the mob to the steps leading up to the emergency exit, since there was nothing more to see and nothing more that we wanted to 'liberate.' Just as Hitler's huge marble desk in the wrecked Chancellory above had been broken into fragments to provide souvenirs, so the furnishings in the underground bunker were being demolished for the same purpose. This was a scene that I would never forget: the camaraderie of British, American, Russian soldiers as they jimmied open desks and broke up the chairs and other things in the smoky light cast by the flaming paper torches, a macabre masque in the sinister setting of the cellar that had been the last headquarters and the mortuary chamber of Adolf Hitler. The effect was Wagnerian: a Götterdammerung, the looting and burning of Valhalla, the final destruction of the Nazis.

Epilogue

I was in Berlin from the beginning of July till 10 August 1945, for nearly six weeks, which was not as long as the more than two months that I spent in Rome, but long enough to give me some perception of the conquered capital. The Big Three met at Potsdam just outside Berlin from 17 July to 2 August, and I covered this last great wartime conference. It was a frustrating experience, since the whole area was sealed off during the conference and we correspondents had to be content with briefings in Berlin by Allied press officers who had no information for us but social notes: 'President Truman played the piano after his dinner party last night for Marshal Stalin and Prime Minister Churchill. The menu was ...'

A whole division of Russian frontier guards surrounded Potsdam when Stalin arrived in an armoured train; Truman and Churchill did some sight-seeing of Berlin, Stalin did not. The Big Three met at the Cicilienhof, one of the former kaiser's palaces. After they had gone, we were shown around the rambling, ivy-covered mansion and the high-ceilinged conference room with its round table and three separate entrances.

The biggest news at the Potsdam conference was not the final communiqué that was released in London, Washington, and Moscow even before it was issued in Berlin, but the change in the British leadership. On 27 July Winston Churchill left; on the following day the new British prime minister, Clement Attlee, took over. This was because of the general election of 5 July 1945. Since the count was delayed for three weeks, the astonishing results were not made known till 26 July: Labour had won by a landslide, 388 seats out of 640 in the British House of Commons; Churchill's Tories had been demolished.

I talked to several 'Tommies,' and the Labour victory might have been even greater if they had been able to vote; many British soldiers had been disenfranchised because of the army's ignorance and disdain of the ballot. The class divisions in Britain were never more evident than in the way that the election results were received: the officers and military government officials were horrified, while the other ranks were elated; 'it was,' as I reported, 'like another VE night among the British garrison troops in Berlin.'

This was a watershed election, and coming as it did within a few weeks of VE Day, it was a demonstration of what effect the conflict had had on the population as a whole. By voting to oust Churchill, the ultimate war hero, the British were making it clear that they were no longer entranced by tunes of glory. They had seen that their forces, which had been bolstered by large contingents from the empire, including a Canadian army, played a much lesser role in the victory campaign than either the Americans or the Russians. They were tired and fed up with a war effort that had gone on too long. There was no advantage to being a secondary Great Power, and they wanted the comfort and security of a welfare state. That should be their reward. I remember the arguments in The Cock and other London pubs at the end of the war that Britain's future was to become a Holland or even a Denmark. The 5 July 1945 election set the stage for the dissolution of the empire.

Once it accepted its new responsibilities as a result of this political upheaval, the *Daily Herald*, which had become the 'government newspaper,' began to take notice of the British colonies and possessions, many of which were in turmoil. As a result, I was sent to India, Africa, and the West Indies. The trouble was that, aside from the land mass of India, most of the empire consisted of

widely scattered bits and pieces of territory, a jungle here, a desert
there, not to mention islands divided by hundreds of miles of sea.

The Labour party felt that the best way to guide these colonies
to self-government and eventual nationhood was to link up as
many as possible in federations. This was in keeping with the
ideals at the war's end of popular groups such as the World Feder-
alists, who saw in the formation of the United Nations the beginning of 'a Federal Government of the World and the Parliament of
Man.' It was also part of a widely held liberal and social democratic belief that disparate people of different races would work
together and cooperate for the common good. A cooperative commonwealth federation.

So, there were to be: an East African Federation of Kenya,
Uganda, and Tanganyika; a Federation of North and South
Rhodesia and Nyasaland; a West African Federation of Gambia,
Sierra Leone, Gold Coast, and Nigeria; a Federation of Malaya,
including the Malay states, Singapore, Brunei, Sarawak, and
North Borneo; a West Indies Federation, which would have as
members not only Jamaica, Trinidad, Barbados, and other islands,
but also the mainland colonies of British Guiana and British
Honduras. Those were the federations I heard about; there were
others. I covered the 1946 attempt by Sir Stafford Cripps and a
cabinet mission to leave India as a whole union; it failed dismally
and the country was hastily and bloodily divided. The West African
Federation never got off the drawing board, and the other federations collapsed under the hammer blows of tribalism, nationalism,
and anti-European racism. Most of the successor states that
emerged from the dissolution of the British Empire clung to the old
colonial borders.

As for the Canadian Broadcasting Corporation, one of its recording vans and a couple of its correspondents accompanied the token
Canadian detachment into Berlin. They stayed for only a few days,
but in that time, Marcel Ouimet was delighted to find his dossier
in the ruins of the Gestapo headquarters; he was a bit disappointed that it was only three lines long.

The CBC Overseas Unit was packing up like the rest of the

Canadian armed forces. Most of the portable recording units, those cumbersome black boxes with which we were able to broadcast the actual sound of battle, were to be shipped home. Only one of the recording vans, the army vehicles that had been fitted out as mobile studios, was to be returned to Canada. Altogether, there were three of them, one for the Italian campaign, the other in France and northwest Europe, and one held in reserve in the United Kingdom; four, if one counted 'Big Betsy' in London, which was too large to use at the front.

The recording van in Italy was the first in action; it saw service in Sicily, at Potenza and Campobasso, the Sangro and Moro rivers, Ortona, Cassino, the Hitler Line, Rome, the Gothic Line, Rimini, and finally the Liberation of Holland, but it was the worse for wear. Art Holmes decided on the second van and had its honour roll painted on its side: 'Normandy Beachhead – Cäen – Falaise – Scheldt Estuary – Reichwald – Hochwald – The Rhine – Berlin.' The others were stripped of their turntables and the rest of their electronic gear and returned to the Canadian army.

When the recording van reached Toronto, Holmes recalled that it was welcomed by no less a person than the premier of Ontario, George Drew. It was destined for the far east and the war there, but the Japanese surrendered before the preparations for its departure had been made. The van ended up at the CBC's Toronto studios, where the bureaucrats running the corporation did not know what to do with it. They were anxious to get back to normal operations, and they could think of no use for this old army vehicle which was occupying one of the limited parking spaces at the CBC building. During the winter of 1945–6 the van was fitted with a bulldozer blade and used as a snow plough; after that, according to Holmes, it was sold as junk.

The portable recording units suffered a similar fate; they were not needed and most were cannibalized and then scrapped. When Art Holmes noted the CBC's lack of enthusiasm for the equipment that its Overseas Unit had used in reporting the war, he decided to keep a few items – after all, he had designed and built them – and thus preserve at least some of them for posterity. In this connection, it should be said that the CBC had no storage facilities; its archives, if they could be called that, occupied a single room, where there were piles of mostly uncatalogued discs. Holmes maintained that the Canadian War Museum would have taken the van and one of the portable recording units, and the museum even asked for them but got no reply.

At the CBC's new 'Broadcast Centre' in downtown Toronto, where all its widely scattered radio, television, and other operations were to be concentrated, the plans called for displays in the public halls surrounding the studio core; these showcases were to feature the CBC's past, its present, and its future. As might be expected, one of them was to be about the war reporting, and a search was made for the old recording equipment.

It was known that Art Holmes had some of these vacuum tube relics in his workshop at his Port Credit home; in fact, they had been borrowed on at least one occasion for an exhibition and returned to him. However, on 4 January 1991 Holmes died suddenly at the age of eighty-seven; the surviving members of his family sold his ham radio equipment, but they thought the rest was junk and threw it out. They would have been happy to give it to the CBC if they had only been approached in time. As a result, all that could be found were one of the wartime microphones and bits and pieces of an old amplifier which had been on show in the Ottawa science museum; the display would have to rely on photographs.

The CBC did preserve the war reports, although it was a wonder, considering the corporation's attitude and the primitive state of what passed for its archives in 1945. Every one of our broadcasts, with the exception of my 'live' report on the capture of Rome, was recorded twice and even three times, once at the source and then when it was received and put on the network (those that were recorded three times were routed through Britain and then to Canada). Thus there was a vast accumulation of aluminum-backed discs. In the months after VE Day thousands of these twelve-inch platters were shipped to the Toronto studios from the BBC in London and the Britannia receiving station just outside Ottawa. The managers and directors of the corporation who had seen no value in the recording van and other equipment realized that the war reports were the stuff of history, but they were overwhelmed by this avalanche of discs.

Something had to be done quickly. Not all of the recordings could be or should be kept. So when Norman DePoe, who had just been demobbed as an infantry officer, joined the CBC, he was put to work sorting through the great stacks of discs. In making his selection, DePoe said: 'The emphasis is on eyewitness reports, interviews in which the men who did the fighting tell their own stories, and descriptive reports which give a picture of the everyday life of the soldier, sailor and airman, both in and out of action. The selection attempts only incidentally to answer the question "What happened?" It is more concerned with the questions "What was the war like?" "How did Canadians fight it?"'

Some 500 war reports were selected; the catalogue listing them runs to thirty-one foolscap pages. In the late fifties the aluminum-backed discs with their soft wax impressions were transferred to tape for more permanent preservation. Later, the war reports were moved to the National Archives in Ottawa, where they have greater security. Some of them have been put on show in small mobile displays, but the purpose of these travelling exhibits was more or less promotional. There was never any attempt to put all of them in a museum or on exhibition.

No other country has such a collection of descriptive actualities of the fighting that were recorded at the time and in the heat of action. Neither the U.S. networks nor the BBC broadcast the sound of battle. NBC, CBS, and the other American companies had a binding rule that forbade recording the news, and there was no other way of covering the troops in action, if only because of censorship. The British had no such prohibition, but chose not to do actualities of the fighting, perhaps because they did not have the facilities. Only the CBC had the necessary high-fidelity equipment, the recording vans, and the portable units that could be used at the front, as well as the engineers to run them. It was an extraordinary achievement, and the war reports, safely stored in the National Archives in Ottawa, are a vivid oral and sound history of the Canadian fighting men in the Second World War.

Bibliography

Bezymenski, Lev. *The Death of Adolf Hitler*. New York: Harcourt Brace & World 1968

Breuer, William B. *Storming Hitler's Rhine*. New York: St Martin's Press 1985

Broadfoot, Barry. *Six War Years, 1939–1945*. Toronto: Doubleday 1974

Bullock, Alan. *Hitler*. New York: Harper & Brothers 1952

Burns, Lieutenant-General E.L.M. *General Mud*. Toronto: Clarke, Irwin 1970

Butcher, Harry C. *My Three Years with Eisenhower*. New York: Simon & Schuster 1946

Christy, Jim. *Rough Road to the North*. Toronto: Doubleday 1980

Churchill, Winston S. *The Second World War*. Vols. 4, 5 and 6. London: Cassell & Co. 1951, 1952, 1954

Comfort, Charles. *Artist at War*. Toronto: Ryerson Press 1956

Cooper, Duff. *Operation Heartbreak*. London: Rupert Hart-Davis 1950

Creighton, Donald. *Canada's First Century*. Toronto: Macmillan 1970

Dancocks, Daniel G. *In Enemy Hands* [Canadian prisoners of war]. Edmonton: Hurtig 1983

– *The D-Day Dodgers* [The Canadians in Italy]. Toronto: McClelland & Stewart 1991

Donoghue, Jack. *The Edge of War*. Calgary: Detselig Enterprises Ltd 1988

Downton, Eric. *Wars without End*. Toronto: Stoddart 1987

Eksteins, Modris. *Rites of Spring*. Toronto: Lester & Orpen Dennys 1989

Ellis, John. *Cassino – The Hollow Victory*. London: André Deutsch 1984
Ferguson, Ted. *Desperate Siege: The Battle of Hongkong*. Toronto:
  Doubleday 1980
Ferrell, Robert H., ed. *The Twentieth Century, An Almanac*. New York:
  Bison Books 1985
Galloway, Strome. *55 Axis with the Royal Canadian Regiment*.
  Montreal: Provincial Publishing Co. 1946
– *The General Who Never Was*. Belleville, Ontario: Mika 1981
Granatstein, J.L., and Desmond Morton. *A Nation Forged in Fire*.
  Toronto: Lester & Orpen Dennys 1989
Grigg, John. *1943 – The Victory That Never Was*. London: Eyre
  Methuen 1980
Halton, Matthew. *Ten Years to Alamein*. Toronto: Saunders 1944
Hapgood, David, and David Richardson. *Monte Cassino*. New York:
  Congdon Weed, St Martin's Press 1984
Hastings, Max. *Victory in Europe*. Boston: Little, Brown 1985
Hillary, Richard. *The Last Enemy*. London: Macmillan 1942
Hoar, Victor, with Mac Reynolds. *The Mackenzie-Papineau Battalion*.
  Toronto: Copp Clark 1969
How, Douglas. 'The Cloud of Disbelief.' *Dateline: Canada 1962*
– ed. *The Canadians at War*. 2 volumes. Montreal: Reader's Digest
  1969
Howe, Quincy. *The World between the Wars*. New York: Simon &
  Schuster 1953
Hutchison, Bruce. *The Incredible Canadian* [Mackenzie King]. Toronto:
  Longmans, Green & Co. 1952
Kennedy, Paul. *The Rise and Fall of the Great Powers*. London: Unwin
  Hyman 1988
Kiriakopoulos, G.C. *Ten Days to Destiny*. New York: Avon Books 1985
Knightley, Phillip. *The First Casualty*. New York: Harcourt Brace
  Jovanovich 1976
Lukacs, John. *The Last European War*. New York: Anchor Press,
  Doubleday 1976
McDougall, Colin. *Execution*. Toronto: Macmillan 1958
Malone, Richard S. *A Portrait of War, 1939–1943*. Toronto: Collins 1983
– *A World in Flames, 1944–1945*. Toronto: Collins 1984
Munro, Ross. *Gauntlet to Overlord*. Toronto: Macmillan 1946
Natkiel, Richard. *Atlas of World War II*. London: Bison Books 1985
Nichols, M.E. *The Story of the Canadian Press*. Toronto: Ryerson 1948

Nicholson, Lieutenant-Colonel G.W.L. *The Canadians in Italy*. Ottawa: Queen's Printer 1956

Nolan, Brian. *Hero: The Buzz Beurling Story*. Toronto: Lester & Orpen Dennys 1981

– *King's War*. Toronto: Random House 1988

Peers, Frank W. *The Politics of Canadian Broadcasting*. Toronto: University of Toronto Press 1969

Powley, A.E. *Broadcast from the Front*. Toronto: Hakkert 1975

Pyle, Ernie. *Brave Men*. New York: Henry Holt 1944

Reyburn, Wallace. *Rehearsal for Invasion*. London: George G. Harrap 1943

– *Some of It Was Fun*. Toronto: Thomas Nelson 1949

Rolf, David. *Prisoners of the Reich*. London: Leo Cooper 1988

Shapiro, Lionel. *They Left the Back Door Open*. Toronto: Ryerson 1944

– *The Sixth of June*. New York: Doubleday 1955

Shirer, William. *The Rise and Fall of the Third Reich*. New York: Simon & Schuster 1960

Smith, Philip. *It Seems Like Only Yesterday* [History of Air Canada]. Toronto: McClelland & Stewart 1986

Stacey, Colonel C.P. *The Canadian Army, 1939–45*. Ottawa: King's Printer 1948

– *Six Years of War*. Ottawa: Queen's Printer 1955

– *The Victory Campaign*. Ottawa: Queen's Printer 1960

– *Arms, Men, and Governments*. Ottawa: Queen's Printer 1970

– *A Very Double Life* [Mackenzie King]. Toronto: Macmillan 1976

– *A Date with History*. Ottawa: Deneau 1982

Stewart, Sandy. *A Pictorial History of Radio in Canada*. Toronto: Gage 1975

Stursberg, Peter. *Journey into Victory*. London: George G. Harrap 1944

– *Those Were the Days* [Memoirs of the thirties]. Toronto: Peter Martin 1969

– *Mister Broadcasting: The Ernie Bushnell Story*. Toronto: Peter Martin 1971

– 'Assignment in Sicily.' *Maclean's*, 1 September 1943

– 'Front Line Hospital.' *Maclean's*, 15 September 1943

– 'What Soldiers Think.' *Maclean's*, 15 June 1944

– 'So This is Rome.' *Maclean's*, 15 July 1944

– 'Woe to the Victor.' *Maclean's*, 15 February 1945

– 'It Happened in Norway.' *Maclean's*, 1 August 1945
– 'Return to Cassino.' *Saturday Night*, 26 May 1962
– 'How to Publicize Canada despite the British.' *Dateline: Canada 1965*
– 'The Awful Story of Frau Heusermann and the Führer's Teeth.' *Dateline: Canada 1969*

Swettenham, John. *McNaughton*. Vols 1, 2, and 3. Toronto: Ryerson 1968, 1969

Thomas, Hugh. *Spanish Civil War*. New York: Harper and Row 1961

Trevor-Roper, H.R. *The Last Days of Hitler*. London: Macmillan 1947

Troyer, Warner. *The Sound and the Fury*. Toronto: John Wiley & Sons 1980

Vassiltchikov, Marie. *Berlin Diaries 1940–1945*. New York: Vintage Books, Random House 1988

Vaughan-Thomas, Wynford. *Anzio*. London: Longmans, Green & Co. 1961

Vokes, Major-General Chris, with John Maclean. *Vokes, My Story*. Ottawa: Gallery 1985

Weir, E. Austin. *The Struggle for National Broadcasting in Canada*. Toronto: McClelland & Stewart 1965

CBC War Recordings

U nless otherwise noted, the reports or interviews listed below are by
   Peter Stursberg: the old CBC identification numbers for the discs
are no longer relevant, since most of the recordings have been
transferred to the National Archives; however, the dates when broadcast, subject matter, and length are given.

Undated (Nov. 1942)	Opening of Alcan Highway. Interviews with men who built road recorded but not used in this program (15 min.).
Undated (June 1943)	'Eyes Front,' No. 5. Lead interview with H.G. Wells. *Of Things to Come* and need for world unity (4 min.).
26 July 1943	First broadcast on Sicily campaign. Description of Medi-terranean trip, storm before landing, etc. (15 min.).
27 July 1943	Canadians drive inland. Italians surrender. Dust and heat, etc. (15 min.).
27 July 1943	More on Sicilian campaign. Description of General Montgomery's visit to Canadian troops, his special inter-est in Canada (his brother lives in Vancouver). Battle in hills near Enna (15 min.).
1 Aug. 1943	First sound of liberation. Bells of Agira ring, Seaforth Highlanders of Canada band plays in town square (6 min.).
7 Aug. 1943	Aderno, Sicily. 'Dust, death and ashes.' Canadians come out of the line (4 min.).

8 Aug. 1943	Interview with General Guy Simonds, commanding 1st Canadian Division in Sicilian campaign (no time).
3 Sept. 1943	Preparations for crossing Strait of Messina. Canadians among assault troops. Spectacular barrage (15 min.).
4 Sept. 1943	Part played by Royal Canadian Navy in getting Canadians ashore on mainland of Italy (5 min.).
7 Sept. 1943	(Matthew Halton) Advance up toe of Italy. Germans in full retreat (no time).
8 Sept. 1943	Italy surrenders. Canadian soldiers join Sicilians in celebrations on slopes of Mount Etna (4 min.).
13 Sept. 1943	First broadcast of 'Lili Marlene.' Italian version rendered by Sicilian band. Story of how it became great song of Second World War (12 min.).
4 Oct. 1943	(Marcel Ouimet) First battle sound. Artillery barrage, planes roar overhead as Canadians attack hill town near Potenza (5 min.).
19 Oct. 1943	Bands play on return of first Allied POWs on Swedish liner. Emotional scenes (15 min.).
14 Dec. 1943	(Art Holmes) Eyewitness description of sinking of Allied troopship on way to Italy (12 min.).
28 Dec. 1943	(Matthew Halton) Street fighting in Ortona on Christmas Eve. Actuality of Canadian engineers building a Bailey bridge under fire (5 min.).
28 Dec. 1943	(Matthew Halton) Christmas dinner at Canadian field dressing station near Ortona (4 min.).
29 Mar. 1944	Static warfare along Arielli River. Patrolling in winter weather (4 min.).
20 Apr. 1944	Report with actuality of dedication of Canadian cemetery near Ortona (5 min.).
10 May 1944	Canadian engineers brought to Anzio to build underground headquarters (5 min.).
10 May 1944	Visit to American Canadian Special Service Force on Anzio perimeter. Interviews (5 min.).
16 May 1944	Heavy barrage that opened assault on Cassino and Gustav Line (5 min.).
16 May 1944	Canadian tanks in fighting around Cassino (5 min.).
22 May 1944	Fall of Cassino. Narrator tours battlefield, sees carnage, and climbs into ruins of monastery (9 min.).

26 May 1944	Canadians storm Hitler Line. Recorded at forward observation post. Gunfire so loud at times that narrator has to stop talking (5 min.).
28 May 1944	Hitler Line broken. Tour of battlefield. Chase up Liri Valley begins (9 min.).
29 May 1944	Running fight up Liri Valley observed from a spotter plane. Germans in full retreat (5 min.).
1 June 1944	With tank regiment that forced crossing of Melfa River. Action described by CO. Interviews with tank crews (8 min.).
4 June 1944	On outskirts of Rome. Description of surroundings and fighting still going on (8 min.).
4 June 1944	Entry into Rome. (Only live broadcast made from front) (no time).
26 June 1944	Canadians advance towards Florence in bad weather (4 min.).
4 July 1944	How Dominion Day was celebrated in Italy (5 min.).
9 July 1944	Introduction of pope's message (English) (3 min.).
13 July 1944	Interview with Major Jack Mahony on how he won VC (5 min.).
2 Aug. 1944	King George VI reviews Canadian troops in Italy. On-the-spot recording with actuality (9 min.).
17 Aug. 1944	Interviews with Canadian navy officers who landed troops in southern France (no time).
19 Aug. 1944	Eyewitness account of landing in southern France (no time).
24 Aug. 1944	Battle for Toulon (no time).
24 Aug. 1944	Visit to Marseilles while most of city captured but enemy still firing from port area (no time).
14 Sept. 1944	Canadians break into Gothic Line. Actuality of attack on Coriano (6 min.).
17 Sept. 1944	Coriano Ridge taken after several bloody assaults (5 min.).
19 Sept. 1944	Bitter battle for Fortunato feature near Rimini (5 min.).
21 Sept. 1944	Capture of San Martino, known as 'Little Cassino.' (5 min.).
Undated (Sept. 1944)	Description of Rimini just after it was captured (6 min.).

30 Sept. 1944	Canadians cross 'Rubicon.' Illusory nature of hope that tanks would be able to manoeuvre on Lombardy Plain (5 min.).
5 Oct. 1944	Ten Canadian gunners spend eight days behind German lines, sending information to advancing troops by radio (4 min.).
9 Oct. 1944	On banks of Fiumicino River. More fighting through mud and water (5 min.).
10 Oct. 1944	Gradara Castle of Francesca da Rimini fame: 'tourist attraction' for Canadian soldiers while rain held up advance (3 min.).
29 Oct. 1944	(Bill Herbert) Paul Morton describes his two months behind German lines with Italian partisans (5 min.).
25 Feb. 1945	(Matthew Halton) Canadian battalion suffers 50 per cent casualties in one battle (Rhineland). His impression as it returns (no time).
24 Mar. 1945	(Matthew Halton) Rhine crossing. Narrator describes ground operations (4.50 min.).
24 Mar. 1945	(A.E. Powley) Rhine crossing, as seen from air (14.30 min.).
6 Apr. 1945	Canadians' advance in Netherlands stops V-2 rocket attacks on England (4.50 min.).
22 Apr. 1945	Apeldoorn, first liberated town in Dutch 'famine' belt. Description of plight of people (4.30 min.).
2 May 1945	Eyewitness account of first meeting between Allies and Germans, to arrange food shipments for starving Dutch (no time).
7 May 1945	Liberation of Amsterdam. Vast crowds celebrating. Shooting in streets (4.30 min.).
8 May 1945	(Marcel Ouimet) VE Day in Holland (5 min.).
9 May 1945	Liberation of Rotterdam and The Hague. In latter, narrator gets reception meant for Canadian commander (4.37 min.).
5 July 1945	(Don Fairburn) Official entry into Berlin of Canadian composite battalion. Band plays. Victory parade (4 min.).
Undated (Nov. 1959)	PROJECT 59. 'The Battle for Ortona' Documentary. Narrator with Bruno Gerussi (60 min.).

Undated (1962)	Interview with D.C. McArthur, first chief news editor, on his life and war reporting; also rules he laid down for CBC news (60 min.).
Undated (Apr. 1963)	Interview with Field Marshal Viscount Alanbrooke on Sicilian campaign and his role in having General McNaughton removed as Canadian army commander (20 min.).
Undated	Interview with General A.G.L. McNaughton about his experiences in the First and Second World Wars (90 min.).
21 May 1990	Documentary. Art Holmes describes how he recorded Blitz and equipment he designed for broadcasting battles. With war reporting inserts (28 min.).

Index